TAGALOG & FILIPINO Made Easy

A Practical Guide to Language Mastery

Sven Biller

Imprint

ISBN: 978-3-949732-40-9 (Paperback)

1st Edition 2024

The author is represented by the publisher Sven Biller, Methfesselstraße 65, 20257 Hamburg, Germany.

Cover Design: Sven Biller

Content

Introduction

First, welcome to this course, your gateway to mastering the Tagalog and Filipino language, spoken throughout the Philippines. Knowing a language, even just the basics, allows access not only to the language itself but also to the culture and people of the country. Since I started learning Tagalog, Filipino and Cebuano, I not only understand Philippine culture better, but people are happier about it, they are more open towards me, and I get to know them better. The language also opens up access to the humor and positive attitude of the people, which now enriches my life as well.

Starting with small steps is okay; learning takes time. Set goals you can really achieve and break them into steps. Even if you're busy, a little practice every day helps. Make a plan that fits your life and stick to it. Most people overestimate what they can do in a short time and underestimate what they can achieve long term. Imagine in a year, you're chatting in Tagalog easily, enjoying the vibrant Philippine culture, and making new friends. Think about how proud you'll feel, speaking Tagalog without a hitch. Memorize the feeling from visualizing how great it will be to speak Tagalog well. Draw motivation out of this positive feeling. Let this motivate you, even when it's tough. With effort and a good plan, you'll be surprised at what you can achieve.

Learning a new language is not just about mastering words and grammar; it's about opening your mind to new possibilities and embracing the world in all its diversity. So, keep pushing forward, stay curious, and enjoy the journey! I wish you a lot of fun learning Tagalog and discovering this culture and its people.

This comprehensive course is **designed with simplicity and practicality in mind**, ensuring that learners of all levels can dive into Tagalog with confidence and ease. Here's what makes this course and language guide an invaluable resource for anyone keen to learn Tagalog:

Structured Learning Path: The course is meticulously organized into 100+ compact lessons, covering everything from the very basics of the language to more complex aspects like focus, sentence structure, and grammar. This structured approach ensures a smooth learning curve, making the language accessible even to complete beginners.

Versatile Content: While the lessons build on each other to provide a comprehensive understanding of Tagalog, they are also designed to serve as a handy reference. Whether you're starting from scratch or need to look up specific phrases for daily situations, this guide has you covered. It's both a step-by-step course and a quick reference tool in one.

Thematic Grouping for Practical Use: Vocabulary and phrases are grouped thematically, enabling you to focus on areas most relevant to your needs. Whether it's preparing for a particular social interaction or needing to communicate effectively in a pinch, you'll find the course organized to help you quickly find and learn what you need.

Effective Learning Strategies: To facilitate effective learning, the course recommends studying a section every few days, allowing information to be absorbed without overwhelming the learner. Regular repetition of vocabulary is emphasized to aid in transferring knowledge to long-term memory, a crucial step for language retention. Revisiting sections reinforces learning and ensures you're always building on a solid foundation.

Focus on Essential Vocabulary and Grammar: Key to this course is its emphasis on essential vocabulary and critical grammatical concepts. This focus ensures that learners are equipped with the tools needed for everyday conversations, travel, and navigating life in Tagalog-speaking regions.

Hands-on Learning Experience: Beyond just reading and memorization, this course encourages a hands-on approach. Practice exercises, real-life application of phrases, and interactive elements make learning dynamic and engaging, helping to cement your newfound language skills.

Verb Conjugation Made Easy: Often a challenging aspect of new languages, verb conjugation is demystified in this course. With clear explanations and practical examples, you'll grasp how to use verbs in different tenses and situations confidently.

This guide is designed to deeply understand the language in easy steps, which I believe is essential for mastering a new language with distinct grammatical structures. I recommend concentrating on topics that you can apply and practice in your everyday life. Learning should seamlessly blend into your daily routine, making it more engaging. For instance, when in the Philippines, you can practice by conversing with a taxi driver or ordering coffee in Tagalog. At home, consider placing post-its with Tagalog words on household items. For example, when I began learning, I placed a post-it on my kitchen door with the Tagalog word for "door.", then I added verbs like to open and to close and in a third steps I formed complete phrases. This method allows you to effortlessly repeat and remember words, eventually forming sentences for each post-it you see, like saying in Tagalog and English, "I am opening the door." This approach ensures regular, integrated practice within your daily life.

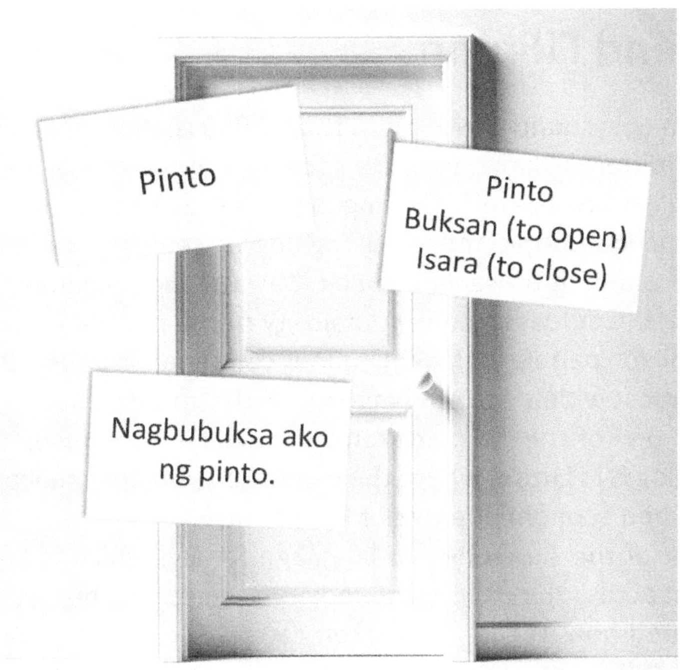

Personal experience plays a crucial role when learning a new language. From the moment you grasp your first phrases like "hello," "good morning," and "how are you?" it's beneficial to start using them in real-life situations right away, even if you're not yet able to form complete sentences. Staying within the confines of your room and studying behind closed doors won't suffice if your goal is to speak fluently and engage in conversations. By immersing yourself and applying new vocabulary in actual interactions, you enhance your learning significantly. This hands-on approach accelerates understanding and helps you become comfortable with the language faster, as real-world practice is invaluable for mastering a new language.

By the end of the Tagalog course, you'll not only have a strong grasp of the language but also the confidence to use it in your daily interactions. This course is your comprehensive guide to understanding and speaking Tagalog and Filipino, opening up a new world of opportunities for personal and professional growth.

Get ready to unlock the richness of the Tagalog language and culture!

Tagalog and Filipino

In the Philippines, a country with more than 7,000 islands and over 100 million people, many different languages are spoken. Among these, Tagalog (or Filipino) and English are the official languages. According to the 2020 census, around 24.4 million people reported Tagalog as their native language. However, when considering those who speak it as a second language, the number is much higher, encompassing a vast majority of the population. It's estimated that over 70 million people in the Philippines can speak Tagalog to some extent, making it the most widely spoken language in the country. So, it is not just any language—it's one of the most spoken languages in the Philippines. The core region of Tagalog is in Luzon, where the capital city, Manila, is located. This area is the political and economic center of the country.
Tagalog is part of the Austronesian language family, which is a group of languages spoken across the Pacific and Indian Oceans. The history of the Philippines has shaped how Tagalog is spoken today. The country was a colony of Spain for over 300 years, and then the United States took over in the late 19th century. These influences have left their mark on the language.

Tagalog and Filipino are very similar languages. Tagalog serves as the traditional language and lays the foundation for Filipino. As the modern, national language, Filipino is based on Tagalog but then adds words and elements from other Philippine languages, as well as from English and Spanish. This blend creates a language that everyone in the Philippines can share and understand, making Filipino a more inclusive version that aims to unite the diverse cultures of the country. Therefore, this Tagalog course, while focusing on practical aspects, acknowledges these influences from English, Spanish, and various Philippine expressions. It effectively serves as a guide not only to modern Tagalog but also to Filipino, helping learners grasp the nuances of both languages in today's context.

Lesson 1 - Alphabet & Abakada

The alphabet used in Tagalog is known as the "Abakada," which consists of 20 letters. The name, "Abakada," is derived from the first four letters of the alphabet.

Letter	Pronunciation	Example Word	English Meaning
A	Ah (Vowel)	ama	father
B	Ba (Consonant)	bata	child
K	Ka (Consonant)	kamay	hand
D	Da (Consonant)	daga	mouse
E	Eh (Vowel)	elepante	elephant
G	Ga (Consonant)	gabi	night
H	Ha (Consonant)	hapon	afternoon
I	Ee (Vowel)	isda	fish
L	La (Consonant)	langit	sky
M	Ma (Consonant)	mata	eye
N	Na (Consonant)	nayon	village
Ng	Ng (Consonant)	ngiti	smile
O	Oh (Vowel)	oras	time
U	Oo (Vowel)	ulo	head
P	Pa (Consonant)	paa	foot
R	Ra (Consonant)	rosas	rose
S	Sa (Consonant)	salamat	thank you
T	Ta (Consonant)	tala	star
W	Wa (Consonant)	watawat	flag
Y	Ya (Consonant)	yaman	wealth

The pronunciation of "ng" can be unusual since it's a single letter that represents a sound not commonly found at the beginning of English words. However, it's similar to the "ng" in English words like "singing," where it forms its own syllable.

Tagalog has been influenced by both English and Spanish, making Filipinos familiar with the alphabets of these languages. Many English words have been integrated into Tagalog. When these words are adopted, they are sometimes spelled according to Tagalog's phonetic rules:

Letter	Pronunciation Adaptation
C	"k" for hard sounds, "s" for soft sounds
F	becomes "p"
J	adapted to "dy"
Q	changes to "kw"

V	replaced with "b"
X	turns into "ks"
Z	pronounced as "s"

English to Tagalog Adaptations: For example, "color" in English becomes "ku-lay".

English	Tagalog
color/colour	kulay
computer	kompyuter
visitor	bisita
traffic	trapik
carpet	karpet

Spanish to Tagalog Adaptations: For example, "cuarto" in English becomes "ku-warto".

Spanish	Tagalog
cuarto (room)	kuwarto
bicicleta (bicycle)	bisikleta
guapo (handsome)	guwapo
carne (meat)	karne
coche (car)	kotse
fiesta (feast)	piyesta

Lesson 2 - Pronunciation

In Tagalog, the rule is straightforward: **How it's spelled is how it's pronounced, and how it's pronounced is how it's spelled.** This means every letter is pronounced, including when there are sequences of two or more vowels.

But, let's take a deeper look at pronunciation. In Tagalog, vowels play a crucial role in forming words. Every syllable in a word includes a vowel, and each syllable, along with its vowel, is pronounced distinctly. This structure is key to mastering pronunciation and reading. Here's how you can easily understand this concept:

Identify the vowels and syllables: Recognize that each syllable will contain a vowel, which means the number of vowels indicates the number of syllables. For example, the word "Merkado" (Market) has three vowels and is therefore broken down into three syllables: Mer-ka-do.

Tagalog	Pronunciation
Merkado	Mer-ka-do

Stress: In many Tagalog words, stress is usually placed on the penultimate (second-to-last) syllable of the root word, like "Mer-**ka**-do."

Let's examine another example. The phrase "Magandang umaga." means "good morning." Breaking it down into syllables looks like this:

Tagalog	Vowels	Syllables
Magandang umaga.	Magandang umaga.	Ma-gan-dang u-ma-ga.

The intonation can be quite similar to English, especially in how questions might end with a rising tone. For example, the question "Pupunta ba siya sa Cebu bukas?" can be broken down into:

Tagalog	Pronunciation
Pupunta ba siya sa Cebu bukas?	Pu-pun-ta ba si-ya sa Ce-bu bu-kas?

This question translates to "Will he/she go to Cebu tomorrow?" Here's a brief breakdown of each word's meaning in this context:

- Pupunta translates to "will go"
- Ba is a question marker used to turn statements into yes/no questions.
- Siya means "he" or "she," as Tagalog doesn't differentiate gender in third-person pronouns.
- Sa is a preposition meaning "to," or more general a marker for locations.
- Cebu is the name of the place.
- Bukas means "tomorrow."

Understanding how vowels and syllables work in Tagalog not only aids in pronunciation but also in reading. While these guidelines provide a good starting point, mastering the nuances of pronunciation comes with practice and active

listening.
Additionally, the emphasis on words can alter their meanings significantly. Here are a few instances where stress changes the meaning of words:

Babá vs. Baba

Tagalog	Stress	Meaning
Babá	First syllable	Chin
Baba	Second syllable	Down or to go down

Bukás vs. Bukas

Tagalog	Stress	Meaning
Bukás	First syllable	Open
Bukas	Second syllable	Tomorrow

Páto vs. Pato

Tagalog	Stress	Meaning
Páto	First syllable	Duck
Pato	Second syllable	Fraud or Scam (Slang)

Lábas vs. Labas

Tagalog	Stress	Meaning
Lábas	First syllable	Going out or to go out
Labas	Second syllable	Outside

Sákit vs. Sakit

Tagalog	Stress	Meaning
Sákit	First syllable	Pain
Sakit	Second syllable	Sickness or Disease

Don’t worry too much about perfect pronunciation. People appreciate it when you make an effort to speak their language, and they’ll usually understand you from the context of the conversation. Additionally, be aware that some words can have multiple meanings. For example “bukas” can mean both “tomorrow” and “open.” This was confusing when I first learned it, which is why I wanted to include this point in the lesson. Now, we’ve covered that as well.

Lesson 3 - Dialects

In Tagalog, like in many languages, dialects can vary greatly across different regions, reflecting diversity in pronunciation, vocabulary, and even syntax. Here's an overview of some of the dialectical variations within Tagalog that learners might encounter:

1. Variations in Pronunciation and Dialects
Pronunciation of "e" and "i": In some regions, particularly in rural areas, there's a tendency to interchange the pronunciation of "e" and "i".

- Standard Tagalog: "Meron" (There is)
  Variation: Some might pronounce it closer to "Miron".
- Pronunciation of "o" and "u": Similar to "e" and "i", the vowels "o" and "u" might be pronounced similarly in certain areas.
  Standard Tagalog: "Puno" (Tree)
  Variation: Pronounced closer to "Pono" in some dialects.
- "Laban" vs. "Lavan": The word "laban" (against) in some dialects might be pronounced with a softer "b," making it sound closer to "lavan."
- "Baboy" vs. "Babuy": The word for pig, "baboy," might be pronounced as "babuy" in some areas, reflecting a more indigenous or older form of Tagalog.

2. Vocabulary Differences
Different words for common items or concepts:

- Standard Tagalog: "Kumain" (To eat)
  Variation: "Mangan" in some Batangas dialects, influenced by neighboring languages.

Terms specific to certain regions:

- Standard Tagalog: "Aso" (Dog)
  Variation: "Iro" in some parts of Southern Luzon, borrowing from other Philippine languages like Cbuano.

3. Syntactical Variations
Tagalog sentences usually follow a verb-subject-object (VSO) structure, but they can vary in different dialects, especially in casual speech.

- Standard Tagalog: "Maganda ang bahay." (The house is beautiful.)
  Variation: In informal settings, some dialects may use different emphases or rearrange elements slightly. For instance, particles might be omitted or the order of subjects and predicates inverted for emphasis.
  Example: "Ang bahay, maganda." (The house is beautiful.)

While these examples aim to highlight some of the diversity, it's important to note that **the language remains largely uniform** across its speakers, and variations are generally understood by all.

Lesson 4 - Greeting

Greeting someone in Tagalog can leave a positive impression, as using the local language shows respect and builds connections. Here's a basic vocabulary list to help form greetings:

Tagalog	English
maganda	good
araw	day
umaga	morning
tanghali	noon
hapon	afternoon
gabi	evening
din, rin	also, too
ikaw, ka	you
Kumusta?	How is/are?

Now, let's look at some common greetings:

Tagalog	**English**
Magandang umaga.	Good morning.
Magandang araw.	Good day.
Magandang hapon.	Good afternoon.
Magandang gabi.	Good evening.
Magandang umaga rin.	Good morning, too.
Kumusta ka?	How are you?
Mabuti, ikaw?	Good, and you?
Saan ka pupunta?	Where are you going?
Saan ka patungo?	Where are you headed?
Saan ka galing?	Where are you from?
Dito lang.	Just around.
Pupunta ako sa hotel.	I am going to the hotel.

The word maganda (good) is often paired with different parts of the day to form greetings like "Magandang umaga." The "ng" at the end of "maganda" before "umaga" serves as a linker to smoothly connect the adjective (maganda) with the noun (umaga) - morning.

Note: Asking "Where are you going?" and "Where are you from?" is a common way to greet friends on the street. Since it's more of a greeting than a question, a non-specific answer like "Dito lang" (Just around) is perfectly acceptable.

Saan ka pupunta? - Let's break it down:

- Saan - "Where"
- ka - "you"
- pupunta - "going"; the future tense of the verb "punta" (to go)
- Meaning "Saan ka pupunta?" translates to "Where are you going?"

Saan ka galing? - Breaking it down:

- Saan - "Where"
- ka - "you"
- galing - "coming from"
- So, "Saan ka galing?" translates to "Where are you from?" or more directly, "Where are you coming from?"

Let's break down "Pupunta ako sa hotel." for a clearer understanding:

- Pupunta - This verb means "will go," derived from "punta" (to go) with a future tense indicator.
- Ako - The pronoun for "I"
- Sa - A preposition meaning "to," indicating direction.
- Hotel - Borrowed noun from English.
- So, "Pupunta ako sa hotel." translates to "I will go to the hotel."

Practice Tip: Always remember to use "magandang" and "kumusta ka?" These phrases are very useful.

Dialog:

Tagalog	**English**
Magandang umaga!	Good morning!
Kumusta ka?	How are you?
Mabuti naman, salamat. Ikaw?	I'm fine, thank you. And you?
Ayos lang ako.	I'm okay.

Exercise: Choose one greeting and one kumsta question. Write it down, learn and practice it.

Tagalog	**English**

Lesson 5 - Goodbye

Let's learn some simple words to say goodbye. Understanding and using these expressions can make partings feel warmer and more personal.

Tagalog	English
Paalam	Goodbye
Ingat	Take care
Sige	Okay
Kita	to see
Hanggang	next

Now, let's form some common phrases with these words.

Tagalog	English
Paalam, magkita tayo mamaya!	Goodbye, see you later!
Paalam, ingat!	Goodbye, take care!
Paalam, ingat ka sa biyahe!	Goodbye, take care on your trip!
Ingat ka lagi!	Take care always!
Salamat sa oras mo. Paalam. - Sige, walang anuman.	Thanks for your time. Goodbye. - Okay, you're welcome.
Magkita tayo ulit.	See you again or We'll see each other again.
Kitakits.	See you. (Informal and colloquial version of "see you again")
Hanggang sa muli.	Until next time

Let's break down the phrase "Magkita tayo ulit." as an exercise:

- Magkita - This word comes from "kita," meaning "to see" or "to meet" The prefix "mag-" indicates an action that will happen in the future, so "magkita" translates to "will see" or "will meet."
- tayo - This pronoun means "we" including both the speaker and the listener.
- ulit - This word means "again."
- Putting it all together, "Magkita tayo ulit." translates to "Let's meet again" or "We will meet again." It's a way of saying goodbye with the implication that you're looking forward to the next meeting.

Both "Magkita tayo ulit" and "Hanggang sa muli" are expressions used in Filipino to convey the idea of seeing someone again. Here's what they mean:

"Magkita tayo ulit."

- Magkita - to meet or to see each other
- tayo - we/us (inclusive, involving the speaker and the person spoken to)
- ulit - again
- Translation: "Let's meet again."

"Hanggang sa muli":

- Hanggang - until
- sa - in/to
- muli - again
- Translation: "Until next time."

Exercise: Choose a phrase from the lesson, write it down, learn and practice it.

Tagalog	English

Lesson 6 - I, You, He, She, ... (Personal Pronouns)

Personal pronouns are essential parts of speech that identify the subject in conversation. Let's explore the singular and plural personal pronouns and how they are used in sentences.

Tagalog	English	Notes
Ako	I	
Ikaw / Ka	You	"Ikaw" is typically used at the beginning of sentences, while "ka" can be found within or at the end of sentences.
Siya	He/She	"Siya" does not distinguish gender and can mean either "he" or "she", based on the

		context.
Kami	We (exclusive)	Refers to "we" excluding the listener.
Tayo / Kita	We (inclusive)	"Tayo" is used more commonly than "kita" in modern Tagalog, referring to "we" that includes the speaker, the listener(s), and possibly others.
Kayo	You (plural)	Used when addressing two or more people.
Sila	They	Refers to a group of people, not including the speaker or the listener.

Examples of Using Personal Pronouns:

Tagalog	**English**
Nagtrabaho ako ngayon.	I am working now.
Nagtrabaho ka ngayon.	You are working now.
Nagtrabaho siya ngayon.	He/She is working now.
Nagtrabaho kami ngayon.	We are working now (exclusive).
Nagtrabaho tayo ngayon.	We are working now (inclusive).
Nagtrabaho kayo ngayon.	You are working now (plural).
Nagtrabaho sila ngayon.	They are working now.

For future tense and using "tomorrow" instead of "now," the structure changes slightly to reflect the future action. Here are the adapted sentences:

agalog Phrase	**English Translation**
Magtatrabaho ako bukas.	I will work tomorrow.
Magtatrabaho ka bukas.	You will work tomorrow.
Magtatrabaho siya bukas.	He/She will work tomorrow.
Magtatrabaho kami bukas.	We will work tomorrow (exclusive).
Magtatrabaho tayo bukas.	We will work tomorrow (inclusive).
Magtatrabaho kayo bukas.	You will work tomorrow (plural).
Magtatrabaho sila bukas.	They will work tomorrow.

These sentences use "Magtatrabaho," which is the future tense form of the verb "to work," combined with "bukas," meaning "tomorrow," to indicate

future actions.
In Tagalog, unlike in English, the form of the verb typically does not change with the personal pronoun. However, the verb will change form based on aspects such as completed (past), ongoing (present), or contemplated (future) actions, which can be seen in more advanced lessons.
Exercise: Choose two pronouns, write them down, learn and practice them.

Tagalog	English

Lesson 7 - My, Your, His, Her... (Possessive Pronouns)

Possessive pronouns like "my," "your," "his," and so on, are crucial for showing ownership or belonging, such as "my house" or "my friends."

Here's how personal pronouns relate to possessive pronouns in English:

Personal Pronouns	Possessive Pronouns
I	My
You	Your
He	His
She	Her
We	Our
You (plural)	Your
They	Their

Tagalog employs a unique set of possessive markers that can be placed either before or after the noun, depending on the structure of the sentence. Here's a brief overview.

Before	After	English
Aking	Ko	My
Iyong	Mo	Your (singular)

Kanyang	Niya	His/Her
Aming	Namin	Our (exclusive)
Ating	Natin	Our (inclusive)
Inyong	Ninyo	Your (plural)
Kanilang	Nila	Their

The structure after the noun is commonly used in everyday conversation and is more straightforward in denoting possession.

Let's look at some examples:

Tagalog	**English**
Ito ang libro ko.	This is my book.
Iyan ang kotse niya.	That is her car. (or his)
Nawala ko ang susi.	I lost my key.
Pupunta kami sa bahay niya.	We are going to his house.
Kumusta ang tatay mo?	How is your father?
Ano ang pangalan mo?	What is your name?

Let’s break down some of these phrase word by word as an exercise and for better understanding:

1. Ito ang libro ko.
    - Ito - This
    - ang - (a marker indicating the subject)
    - libro - book
    - ko - my
    - Translation: This is my book.

2. Nawala ko ang susi.
    - Nawala - lost
    - ko - my
    - ang - (a marker indicating the subject)
    - susi - key
    - Translation: I lost my key.

3. Pupunta kami sa bahay niya.
    - Pupunta - will go
    - kami - we

- sa - to
- bahay - house
- niya - his/her
- Translation: We will go to his/her house.

4. Kumusta ang tatay mo?
    - Kumusta - How is
    - ang - (a marker indicating the subject)
    - tatay - father
    - mo - your
    - Translation: How is your father?

5. Ano ang pangalan mo?
    - Ano - What
    - ang - (a marker indicating the subject)
    - pangalan - name
    - mo - your
    - Translation: What is your name?

Exercise: Form phrases in the form "This is my ..." and "This is your ..." Use the dictionary to look for nouns. Write it down, learn and practice it.

Samples:

Tagalog	**English**
Ito ang telepono ko.	This is my phone.
to ang bag mo.	This is your bag.

Tagalog	**English**
Ito ang ________________ ko.	This is my ________________.
	This is your ________________.

Lesson 8 - Learning Pronouns

Learning Tip for the personal and possessive pronouns: First, lets recap them and then remember the patterns. Some of them have common letters, helping to remember them a bit easier.

Singular forms: Personal to Possessive

Ako (I) → **Ko** (My)

- Ako ay masaya. (I am happy.)
- Ito ang libro ko. (This is my book.)

Ikaw (You) → **Mo** (Your)

- Ikaw ay masaya. (You are happy.)
- Ito ang libro mo. (This is your book.)

Siya (He/She) → **Niya** (His/Her)

- Siya ay masaya. (He/She is happy.)
- Ito ang libro niya. (This is his/her book.)

Tip: Look for the Pattern. Notice the shift from personal pronouns (ako, ikaw, siya) to possessive (ko, mo, niya). The key to learning them is to recognize and practice this pattern in various contexts.

Personal Pronouns	Possessive Pronouns
Action + Personal Pronoun	Object + Possessive Pronoun
Nagluluto ako (I am cooking)	Ito ang kotse ko (This is my car).

Practice swapping between them in sentences to get comfortable.

Plural forms: Personal to Possessive

Kami (We, exclusive) → **Namin** (Our, exclusive)

- Kami ay masaya. (We are happy.)
- Ito ang libro namin. (This is our book.)

Tayo (We, inclusive) → **Natin** (Our, inclusive)

- Tayo ay masaya. (We are happy.)
- Ito ang libro natin. (This is our book.)

Kayo (You, plural) → **Ninyo** (Your, plural)
- Kayo ay masaya. (You [plural] are happy.)
- Ito ang libro ninyo. (This is your book.)

Sila (They) → **Nila** (Their)
- Sila ay masaya. (They are happy.)
- Ito ang libro nila. (This is their book.)

To memorize vocabulary effectively, the goal is to transfer words from your short-term memory to your long-term memory. There are various methods to achieve this, with repetition being the most common. Start with short intervals and gradually increase to longer gaps. Another method is linking new words with concepts already in your long-term memory, creating connections that are easier to recall.
Additionally, inventing imaginative stories, memorable phrases, or drawing little sketches that incorporate new vocabulary can be particularly effective. These should be as vivid and unique as possible to ensure they stick in your memory. For instance, when learning the Tagalog pronouns 'Ikaw' (You) → 'Mo' (Your), I crafted a quirky sentence: '**I**n the morning, the **caw** **mo**ves **you** around.' This sentence creatively combines the sounds and meanings of 'Ikaw', 'Mo', and the English meaning 'You' with a familiar scene, albeit in a silly way. The sillier the imagery or story, the quicker it's absorbed into long-term memory.
The key is personal creativity and inner visualization. By creating your own memorable and imaginative associations, you solidify the vocabulary in your memory. My silly phrase helped me remember these pronouns instantly, without the need for further study. Your brain's ability to link new information with creative or unusual images makes learning not just effective, but also fun.
For learning 'Siya' (He/She) → 'Niya' (His/Her), I used a personal memory. I know someone named Nina who once got yelled at by a friend. To remember these pronouns, I created the sentence: '**S**he **i**s **y**elling **a**gain at **Ni**n**a**.' This works for me because the first letters of the first four words are the word 'siya' and the 'N' from Nina hints me to 'Niya'. By connecting new words to a personal memory, you can connect something new to a scene that is already in your long-term memory, hence making the learning much faster. Just let your imagination and creativity flow when you learn something new.

Lesson 9 - I am... (Introducing Yourself)

Introducing yourself in Tagalog is straightforward and can be done using a simple structure. But first, let's learn some essential vocabulary that will help in crafting an introduction.

Tagalog	English
pangalan	name
taga	from/of
ko	my
nakatira	live/reside
edad	years
trabaho	work
taon	year
apelyido	surname

Now, here are examples of how you can introduce yourself:

Tagalog	English
Ako si Paul.	I am Paul.
Ang pangalan ko ay Lilly.	My name is Lilly.
Taga-America ako.	I am from America.
Nakatira ako sa America.	I live in America.
Ako ay dalawampu't anim na taong gulang.	I am 26 years old.
Nagtrabaho ako sa bangko.	I work at the bank.
Magtratrabaho ako dito ng dalawang taon.	I will work here for two years.
Ang apelyido ko ay...	My surname is...
Ito ang asawa ko.	This is my wife.

Note on Sentence Structure: In Tagalog sentence structure can differ from English. For example, "I work at the bank" in English begins with the subject "I". In Tagalog, it might start with the verb, thus "Nagtrabaho ako sa bangko".

Ako si Paul. - Here's the breakdown:

- Ako - "I"
- si - a marker used before proper names in Tagalog, indicating the following word is a name.
- Paul - a name; in this case, the speaker's name.
- Together, "Ako si Paul" translates directly to "I am Paul."

Ang pangalan ko ay Lilly. - Let's break it down:

- Ang - a marker indicating the subject or focus of the sentence.
- pangalan - "name"; the topic being discussed and marked as focus by the Ang-marker (more on this in a future lesson).
- ko - "my"
- ay - is; a verb linking the subject to its description.
- Lilly - a name
- So, "Ang pangalan ko ay Lilly." translates to "My name is Lilly."

Taga-America ako. - Breaking it down:

- Taga- - a prefix meaning "from" or pertaining to a place.
- America - a country.
- ako - "I"
- So, "Taga-America ako" translates to "I am from America."

Breaking down "Nakatira ako sa America":

- Nakatira - Verb for "living" or "residing," from the root word "tira" with the prefix "naka-" indicating an ongoing action.
- ako - Pronoun "I"
- sa - Preposition for location, "in" or "at," indicating where the action takes place.
- America remains the same in translation.
- So, "Nakatira ako sa America" translates to "I am living in America" or "I live in America."

Breaking down the sentence "Ako ay dalawampu't anim na taong gulang." word by word:

- Ako - I
- ay - (is/am/are; a verb linker or marker for predicate nominative)
- dalawampu't - twenty and (at - and - is shortend to ‘t)
- anim - six

- na - (a linker that connects adjectives to nouns or numbers to what they quantify)
- taong - years (from "tao" meaning person or year in this context, with "ng" linking it to "gulang")
- gulang - old
- Meaning: "I am twenty-six years old"

Breaking down "Magtratrabaho ako dito ng dalawang taon.":
- Magtratrabaho - Future tense of "to work," from the root "trabaho" with the prefix "mag-" and infix "-ra-" for future actions.
- ako - I
- dito - here
- ng - ng-linker to connect section of phrases
- dalawang - two
- taon - years
- Meaning: I will work here for two years.
- In Tagalog, the preposition "sa" is versatile, used for locations (indicating "in" or "at") and points in time (similar to "on," "at," or "in" in English), with its specific role clear from the sentence's context.

Dialogue:

Tagalog	**English**
Magandang araw! Ako si Juan.	Good day! I am Juan.
Kumusta ka? Ako naman ay si Maria.	How are you? I am Maria.
Ikinagagalak kong makilala ka, Maria.	I am pleased to meet you, Maria.
Ganun din naman ako, Juan. Tagasaan ka?	Same here, Juan. Where are you from?
Taga-Maynila ako. Ikaw, Maria?	I am from Manila. How about you, Maria?
Ako ay taga-Cebu. Anong trabaho mo?	I am from Cebu. What is your job?
Ako ay isang guro. Ikaw?	I am a teacher. How about you?
Nagtatrabaho ako bilang isang inhinyero.	I work as an engineer.
Napakaganda naman. Sana ay magkasundo tayo sa trabaho at iba	That's wonderful. I hope we get along well at work and beyond.

pa.	
Oo naman, Juan. Masaya akong na-kilala kita.	Certainly, Juan. I'm glad to have met you.

Exercise: Introduce yourself. Look at the lesson about numbers for your age and use the dictionary at the end of this book in case you need any additional words.

Introducing	**Tagalog**	**English**
Your name		
Where from		
Your age (use the lession for numbers).		
Why you are in the Philippines		
Asking „Who are you?" (Who is "Sino".)		

Solution:

Tagalog	**English**
Kamusta, ang pangalan ko ay ...	Hello, my name is ...
Ako ay mula sa ... / Taga-... ako.	I am from ...
Ako ay ... taong gulang.	I am ... years old.
Nandito ako sa Pilipinas para sa ba-kasyon.	I am in the Philippines for vacation.
Ikaw, sino ka?	Who are you?

Lesson 10 - Who Are You?

When you want to learn about someone's identity or gather basic information, you use "Sino" for "Who" and "Ano" for "What." These question words are placed at the start of the sentence.

Basic Questions:

Tagalog	English
Sino ka?	Who are you?
Ano ang pangalan mo?	What is your name?
Ano ang pangalan niya?	What is his/her name?
Ano ang mga pangalan ninyo?	What are your names?
Ilang taon ka na?	How old are you?
Taga-saan ka?	Where are you from?
Saan ka nakatira?	Where do you live?
Saan ka nakatira dito?	Where do you live here?
Ano ang trabaho mo?	What is your job?

Let's breakd down "Ano ang pangalan mo?" as an exercise and for better understanding:

- Ano - "What"
- ang - a marker that indicates the subject or focus of the sentence.
- pangalan - "name"
- mo - "your"
- So, when you put it all together, "Ano ang pangalan mo?" translates to "What is your name?"

Ano ang mga pangalan ninyo? - Breaking it down:

- Ano - "What"
- ang - a marker indicating the subject or focus of the sentence.
- mga - a plural marker, indicating that more than one name is being asked about.
- pangalan - "name" and "mga pangalan" means "names"
- ninyo - "your" (plural)
- Put together, "Ano ang mga pangalan ninyo?" asks "What are your names?"

Ilang taon ka na? - Here's the breakdown:

- Ilang - "How many"; used to ask about quantity or age.
- taon - "years"
- ka - "you";
- na - "already" (filler word)
- Together, "Ilang taon ka na?" means "How old are you (already)?"

Exercise: Choose a phrase from the lesson, write it down, learn and practice it.

Tagalog	English

Lesson 11 - Introducing Others

Introducing someone plays a crucial role in social interactions, similar to greetings. The verb for introducing is "ipakilala," which means "to introduce" or "to make known." Let's see how to use "ipakilala" in a sentence:

Tagalog	English
Gusto ko ipakilala sa iyo ang aking asawa.	I would like to introduce you to my wife.

Breaking down the phrase:

- Gusto: means "want" or "like," expressing a desire.
- ko: "I"
- ipakilala: "to introduce"
- sa iyo: "to you"
- ang: the marker for the subject or focus of the sentence.
- aking: "my"
- asawa: "spouse" or "wife."
- Combined, the phrase translates to "I want to introduce you to my wife."

Vocabulary for Introducing Others:

Tagalog	English
Asawa	Spouse or Wife
Bana	Husband (Though less commonly used in Tagalog, the term "asawa" is more prevalent for both husband and wife.)
Kaibigan	Friend
Ipakilala	To introduce

Common Phrases for Introductions:

Tagalog	English
Ito ang aking asawa na si Lilly.	This is my wife Lilly.
Gusto kong ipakilala sa iyo si Paul.	I would like to introduce Paul to you.
Ito ang aking anak na si Lisa.	This is my child Lisa.

Breaking Down a Profession Introduction: Siya ay guro.

- Siya: "He/She" a pronoun for the person being introduced.
- ay: "ay" functions as a linker or a copula that connects the subject "Siya" (he/she) with the predicate "guro" (teacher).
- guro: "Teacher"
- So, it translates to He/She is a teacher.

Let's take a look at a dialog with topics we have learned in the last three lessons:

Tagalog	English
Paul: Magandang araw! Ako si Paul mula sa America. Anong pangalan mo?	Paul: Good day! I'm Paul from America. What's your name?
Lisel: Ako si Lisel.	Lisel: I'm Lisel.
Paul: Masaya akong makilala ka, Lisel. Nasa Pilipinas ako para sa bakasyong dalawang linggo. Saan ka nakatira sa Pilipinas?	Paul: I'm happy to meet you, Lisel. I'm in the Philippines for a two-week vacation. Where do you live in the Philippines?
Lisel: Sa Manila ako nakatira. Sana mag-enjoy ka dito sa iyong bakasyon.	Lisel: I live in Manila. I hope you enjoy your vacation here.

Let's break down the vocabulary and structure of this dialogue:

Magandang araw! (Good day!)

- Maganda - beautiful or good
- Araw - day

Ako si Paul mula sa America. (I'm Paul from America.)

- Ako - I
- Si - a marker used before names
- Mula sa - from

Anong pangalan mo? (What's your name?)

- Anong (short for Ano ang) - What is
- Pangalan - name
- Mo - your

Ako si Lisel. (I'm Lisel.)

- Ako - I
- Si - a marker used before names

Masaya akong makilala ka, Lisel. (I'm happy to meet you, Lisel.)

- Masaya - happy
- Ako - I
- Makilala - to meet
- Ka - you

Nasa Pilipinas ako para sa bakasyong dalawang linggo. (I'm in the Philippines for a two-week vacation.)

- Nasa - in/at (indicating location)
- Pilipinas - Philippines
- Para sa - for
- Bakasyon - vacation
- Dalawang linggo - two weeks

Saan ka nakatira sa Pilipinas? (Where do you live in the Philippines?)

- Saan - where
- Ka - you
- Nakatira - live/reside

Sa Manila ako nakatira. (I live in Manila.)

- Sa - in
- Manila - Manila
- Ako - I
- Nakatira - live/reside

Sana mag-enjoy ka dito sa iyong bakasyon. (I hope you enjoy your vacation here.)

- Sana - hope/wish
- Mag-enjoy - enjoy
- Ka - you
- Dito - here
- Sa iyong - your
- bakasyon - vacation

Exercise: Choose a phrase from the lesson, write it down, learn and practice it.

Tagalog	English

Lesson 12 - Oneself (Reflexive Pronouns)

Expressing actions that relate to oneself or actions that reflect back on the doer involves reflexive pronouns. Reflexive actions are typically indicated by the use of "sarili," meaning "self" or "oneself."

Tagalog	English
Sarili	Oneself, own self (Reflexivity)

It is used with personal pronouns or set if pronouns introduced as possessive pronouns to show reflexivity.

Tagalog	English
Aking sarili	Myself
Iyong sarili	Yourself (singular)
Kanyang sarili	Himself/Herself
Aming sarili	Ourselves (exclusive)
Ating sarili	Ourselves (inclusive)
Inyong sarili	Yourselves (plural)
Kanilang sarili	Themselves

Common Expressions with "Sarili":

Tagalog	English
Naghuhugas siya ng kanyang sarili.	He/She is washing himself/herself.
Ang bata ay nag-aaral para sa kanyang sarili.	The child is studying for himself/herself.
Siya ay kumuha ng pagkain para sa kanyang sarili.	He/She got food for himself/herself.
Hindi niya gusto ang kanyang sarili.	He/She does not like himself/herself.

Naghuhugas siya ng kanyang sarili. - Here's the breakdown:

- Naghuhugas - "washing"
- siya - "he/she"
- ng - ng-linker, used before an object or in this case, to link the action to the person it's being done to.
- kanyang - "his/her"
- sarili - "himself/herself"
- Together, "Naghuhugas siya ng kanyang sarili" translates to "He/She is washing himself/herself."

Ang bata ay nag-aaral para sa kanyang sarili. - Let's break it down:

- Ang - a marker that indicates the subject of the sentence.
- bata - "child" (the subject who is performing the action).
- ay - This is a pivotal word in Tagalog that doesn’t have a direct English translation but serves as a grammatical tool to link the subject to the

predicate. It is used here to ensure that the sentence structure clearly indicates what the subject is doing or what is happening to the subject.

- nag-aaral - "studying"; the present progressive form of the verb "aral" (to study).
- para sa - "for"
- kanyang - "his/her"
- sarili - "self"; the object receiving the action, emphasizing that the studying is done for the child's own benefit.
- So, "Ang bata ay nag-aaral para sa kanyang sarili" translates to "The child is studying for himself/herself."

In Tagalog, when talking about performing actions without any help, two phrases are often used: 'by oneself' and 'alone.' Each phrase has its unique emphasis. 'By oneself' stresses personal agency and independence, indicating that the person chose to do the action without assistance, focusing on capability or preference. On the other hand, 'alone' highlights the physical state of being without others, which might not necessarily involve personal initiative. Here are the examples illustrating these differences:

Tagalog	**English**
Ginawa ko ito sa aking sarili.	I did it by myself.
Ginawa ko ito nang mag-isa.	I did it alone.

"Ginawa ko ito sa aking sarili" uses "sa aking sarili" to emphasize that the speaker independently completed the action, stressing personal effort and initiative.

"Ginawa ko ito nang mag-isa" uses "nang mag-isa" to convey that the speaker performed the action in a state of solitude, focusing more on the fact that there were no others involved rather than on independence.

Exercise: Translate the phrases. Here are some useful vocabularies:

Tagalog	**English**
pupunta	will go
sa tindahan	to the store

Tagalog	English
	I will go to the store alone.
	I will go to the store by myself.

Solution:

Tagalog	English
Pupunta ako sa tindahan nang mag-isa.	I will go to the store alone.
Pupunta ako sa tindahan sa aking sarili.	I will go to the store by myself.

Lesson 13 - Introduction to Verb Conjugation

In Tagalog, verbs are often conjugated to reflect the focus of the sentence, the verb group they belong to, and the tense or aspect of the action—whether it's completed, ongoing, or planned for the future. This brief guide introduces you to the basics of conjugating verbs in the active voice, specifically focusing on Actor-Focus (or active voice) verbs from the so called "Mag-" verb group.

Actor-Focus Verbs (Active Voice): In Tagalog, Actor-Focus verbs are used when the subject of the sentence is the doer of the action. These verbs are conjugated differently based on whether the action is completed, ongoing, or planned.

Mag-Verbs: The "Mag-" verb group is typically used for verbs that denote deliberate actions or ongoing activities. These verbs are particularly interesting because they explicitly indicate that the subject is actively engaging in the action. For example, "Magluto" (to cook), "Magbasa" (to read), and "Magtrabaho" (to work) all fall into this group.

Conjugation:

- **Completed Action:** To conjugate a "Mag-" verb for a completed action, you would typically use the prefix "Nag-", e.g., "Nagluto" (cooked), "Nagbasa" (read).

- **Ongoing Action:** For ongoing actions, the prefix 'Nag-' continues to be used, followed by the repetition of the first syllable of the root verb to indicate the ongoing nature, e.g., 'Nagluluto' (is cooking), 'Nagbabasa' (is reading).

- **Planned for the Future:** Future actions are usually indicated by modifying the prefix to "Mag-", followed by the repetition of the first syllable of the root verb e.g., "Magluluto" (will cook), "Magbabasa" (will read).

This simple framework of Actor-Focus conjugation in the Mag-Verb group provides a foundation for understanding how actions are expressed in Tagalog, depending on the role of the subject and the timing of the action.

Table Summary of Mag-Verb:

Tense/Aspect	**Root**	**Completed (Past)**	**Ongoing (Present)**	**Future**
Affixes	-	Nag-	Nag + first syllable	Mag + first syllable
Sample Verb	Luto	Nagluto	Nagluluto	Magluluto
Sample Phrase	-	Nagluto ako.	Nagluluto ako.	Magluluto ako.
English	-	I cooked.	I am cooking.	I will cook.

Exercise: Conjugate the verbs according to the given aspect / tense.

Root Verb	**English**	**Completed**	**Ongoing**	**Future**
luto	cook	Nagluto	Nagluluto	Magluluto
basa	read			
trabaho	work			
lakad	walk			
maneho	drive			

linis	clean			
biyahe	travel			
bili	buy			

Solution:

Root Verb	**English**	**Completed**	**Ongoing**	**Future**
luto	cook	Nagluto	Nagluluto	Magluluto
basa	read	Nagbasa	Nagbabasa	Magbabasa
trabaho	work	Nagtrabaho	Nagtat-rabaho	Magtat-rabaho
lakad	walk	Naglakad	Naglalakad	Maglalakad
maneho	drive	Nagmaneho	Nag-mamaneho	Mag-mamaneho
linis	clean	Naglinis	Naglilinis	Maglilinis
biyahe	travel	Nagbiyahe	Nagbibiyahe	Magbibiyahe
bili	buy	Nagbili	Nagbibili	Magbibili

Note about forming phrases: In Tagalog, sentences often begin with the verb, followed by the actor who performs the action. This structure, known as Verb-Subject-Object (VSO), emphasizes the action first.

Tagalog	**English**
Nagbili ako ng tubig.	I bought water.
Nagbibili ako ng tubig.	I am buying water.
Magbibili ako ng tubig.	I will buy water.

Exercise: Translate the phrases by considering the conjugation as per the table above.

Tagalog	**English**
lakad	walk
Naglakad ako sa palengke.	I walked to the market.
	I am walking to the market.
	I will walk to the market.

Solution:

Tagalog	English
Naglakad ako sa palengke.	I walked to the market.
Naglalakad ako sa palengke.	I am walking to the market.
Maglalakad ako sa palengke.	I will walk to the market.

The sentence "Maglalakad ako sa palengke." can be broken down word by word to understand its structure and meaning:

- Maglalakad - This is the verb, which is a future tense form of "lakad" (to walk). The prefix "Mag+la-" indicates a future action (will walk).
- ako - This is the pronoun for "I", indicating the doer of the action.
- sa - In Tagalog "sa" is a location marker. It can be considered as a preposition that means "to" in this case.
- palengke - This noun means "market"
- When combined, the sentence "Maglalakad ako sa palengke." translates to "I will walk to the market."

More about verb conjugation and forming of phrases in later lessons. This is meant as just a first introduction to start familiarizing you with specific Tagalog concepts.

Lesson 14 - Question Words

Let's dive into question words, which are essential for creating open-ended questions that solicit detailed responses, allowing your conversation partner to share more comprehensive thoughts, opinions, or information. Like in English, these question words are typically placed at the beginning of the sentence. Here's a quick guide to some of the most commonly used Tagalog question words:

Tagalog	English
Sino?	Who?

Ano?	What?
Saan?	Where?
Kailan?	When?
Ilan?	How many?
Magkano?	How much? (Referring to price)
Kanino?	Whose?
Paano?	How?
Kumusta?	How is it going? How is/are?
Bakit?	Why?
Gaano kadalas?	How often?
Para saan?	What for?

Examples of Usage in Sentences:

Tagalog	**English**
Sino ang kasama mo?	Who is with you?
Ano ang ginagawa mo?	What are you doing?
Saan ka pupunta?	Where are you going?
Ilan ang kapatid mo?	How many siblings do you have?
Kailan ang kaarawan mo?	When is your birthday?
Magkano ito?	How much is this?
Kanino ito?	Whose is this?
Paano mo ito ginawa?	How did you do this?
Kumusta ang araw mo?	How is your day?
Bakit ka malungkot?	Why are you sad?
Gaano kadalas ka mag-ehersisyo?	How often do you exercise?
Para saan ito?	What is this for?

Exercise: Sino ang kasama mo? - Let's break it down:

- Sino - "Who"
- ang - a marker indicating the subject of the question.
- kasama - "with" or "companion"
- mo - "your"
- So, "Sino ang kasama mo?" means "Who is with you?"

Ano ang ginagawa mo? - Here's the breakdown:

- Ano - "What"
- ang - a marker that indicates the subject or focus of the sentence.
- ginagawa - "doing"; the present progressive form of the verb "gawa" (to do or to make), indicating an ongoing action.
- mo - "your"
- Together, "Ano ang ginagawa mo?" translates to "What are you doing?"

Magkano ito? - Breaking it down:

- Magkano - "How much"; used to ask about the price or cost of something.
- ito - "this";
- So, "Magkano ito?" means "How much is this?" It's a question asking for the price of an item.

Exercise: Choose one question from the lesson, write it down, learn and practice it.

Tagalog	English

Lesson 15 - How Are You - Kumusta ka?

"Kumusta" is a fundamental greeting in Tagalog, derived from the Spanish "Cómo está", and is widely used to ask someone about their condition or how things are in their life. It is a versatile phrase that can initiate conversations, express concern, or simply serve as a way to catch up with someone. This lesson will guide you through various ways to use "Kumusta" in everyday conversations.

Tagalog	English
Kumusta ka?	How are you?

This is the most basic form of greeting someone with "Kumusta". It's a friendly way to ask someone about their well-being. You form this question with “Kumusta” followed by the personal pronoun.

Asking About Family and Friends:

Tagalog	English
Kumusta ang iyong asawa?	How is your wife?
Kumusta ang iyong tatay?	How is your father?
Kumusta ang iyong kaibigan?	How is your friend?

Asking About Individuals: When asking about specific individuals, simply use "Kumusta si [Name]?":

Tagalog	English
Kumusta si Lilly?	How is Lilly?
Kumusta si Paul?	How is Paul?

"Kumusta" in Tagalog can be used in a variety of contexts beyond just inquiring about a person's well-being. Here are some other ways "Kumusta" can be utilized:

Asking About General Well-being or Condition:

Tagalog	English
Kumusta ang pakiramdam mo?	How are you feeling?
Kumusta ang araw mo?	How was your day?

Inquiring About Events or Occasions:

Tagalog	English
Kumusta ang party/party?	How was the party?
Kumusta ang kasal?	How was the wedding?

Checking on Progress or Status:

Tagalog	English
Kumusta ang trabaho/proyekto?	How is the work/project?
Kumusta ang pag-aaral mo?	How is your study/studies going?

Asking About the State or Condition of Objects or Situations:

Tagalog	English
Kumusta ang panahon?	How is the weather?
Kumusta ang biyahe?	How was the trip/journey?
Kumusta ang iyong pagkain?	How is your food? How does your food taste?

Seeking Opinions or Thoughts:

Tagalog	English
Kumusta ang pelikula?	How was the movie?
Kumusta ang libro?	How is the book?

"Kumusta" is a versatile phrase that can start conversations in a variety of situations, not just limited to asking about someone's personal condition but also about their experiences, opinions, and the status of things around them.

Exercise: Choose a phrase from the lesson, write it down, learn and practice it.

Tagalog	English

Lesson 16 - What - Ano?

"Ano" is the equivalent word for "What". This lesson will focus on using "Ano" in various contexts to ask about actions, desires, and identification of objects.

Essential Vocabulary

Tagalog	English
bili	to buy
gusto	to want, to like
luto	to cook

Formulating **questions with "Ano":** To ask questions about ongoing actions or intentions, Tagalog often utilizes "Ano" followed by the marker "ang" and the appropriate form of the verb. Verbs are conjugated with affixes like 'nag-', 'mag-', or 'um-' for action verbs depending on the focus of the sentence. We will take care of verb conjugations later. Here we put the focus on asking questions. Let's dive into some standard expressions:

Tagalog	English
Ano ang binibili mo?	What are you buying?
Ano ang gusto mong bilhin?	What do you want to buy?
Ano ang binibili ni Lilly?	What is Lilly buying?
Ano ang niluluto mo para sa hapunan?	What are you cooking for dinner?
Ano ito?	What is this?

Let's break down the phrase "Ano ang binibili mo?"

- Ano - What
- ang - the; a marker indicating the focus of the sentence
- binibili - are buying (from "bili" meaning "buy", with the prefix "binibili" indicating an ongoing or habitual action)
- mo - you
- "Ano ang binibili mo?" translates to "What are you buying?"

Let's break down the phrase "Ano ang niluluto mo para sa hapunan?":

- Ano: "What"

- ang - the; a marker indicating the focus of the sentence
- niluluto: Niluluto involves a prefix and the repetition of the first syllable of the root word:
    - ni-: This is the prefix indicating the actor focus in the progressive aspect.
    - -luluto: Comes from repeating the first syllable of the root word "luto" (to cook) as part of the grammatical construction for the progressive aspect in Tagalog verbs, which shows that the action is currently happening.
    - So, niluluto means "is cooking" or "being cooked"
- mo: This is a personal pronoun, meaning "you" or "by you".
- para sa: This means "for", indicating purpose.
- hapunan: dinner (noun)
- The phrase "Ano ang niluluto mo para sa hapunan?" translates to "What are you cooking for dinner?"

Exercise: Choose a phrase from the lesson, write it down, learn and practice it.

Tagalog	English

Lesson 17 - Where - Saan?

"Saan" is used to ask "where". Let's start with learning some basic questions.

Tagalog	English
Saan ka?	Where are you?
Saan ka pupunta?	Where are you going?
Saan ang daan?	Where is the way?
Saan ka nagtatrabaho?	Where do you work?
Saan ang ospital?	Where is the hospital?
Saan ka tumira?	Where do you live? ("Tumira" means

	to live or reside.)

For past context, the word "saan" is often accompanied by a verb in the past tense to indicate that the action has already happened.

Tagalog	English
Saan ka nagpunta kahapon?	Where did you go yesterday?

Here's the breakdown of the sentence "Saan ka nagpunta kahapon?" word by word:

- Saan - Where
- ka - you (singular)
- nagpunta - went: Punta is "go". The prefix "nag-" is used to indicate actions in the past tense, ongoing actions, or habitual actions, depending on the context and verb form.
- kahapon - yesterday
- So, the sentence translates to "Where did you go yesterday?"

"Saan" in combination with "papuntang" and "daan" can be used to ask for directions. Let's break down this combination:

- "Saan" means "Where"
- "Papuntang" is a prepositional phrase that means "to the direction of" or "heading to." It is often used to specify the destination or direction of an action or movement. The term combines "pa-", indicating direction or destination, with "punta", meaning "to go" or "destination," and the linker "ng" which connects the phrase to the succeeding noun (the destination). So, "papuntang" effectively means "towards" or "going to" when talking about a place or direction.
- "Daan" in Tagalog means "way", "road" or "path".

So, the formular asking for a place is:

Tagalog	English
Saan ang daan papuntang ... (place)?	Where is the way to ... (place)?

Examples:

Tagalog	English
Saan ang daan papuntang palengke?	Where is the way to the market?
Saan ang daan patungo sa paaralan?	Where is the way to the school?
Saan ang daan papunta sa ospital?	Where is the way to the hospital?
Saan ang daan patungo sa simbahan?	Where is the way to the church?
Saan ang daan papuntang istasyon ng tren?	Where is the way to the train station?

Let's take a look an alternative way of asking the same question more formal and more polite:

- Saan po ba ang daan papuntang ... (place)?
  This structure is more polite and formal, due to the inclusion of "po" (a term of respect) and the question marker "ba" (a particle that can add emphasis or turn the sentence into a question). It's commonly used when asking for directions in a respectful manner, especially when speaking to someone you don't know well, someone older, or someone in a position of authority.

Examples:

Tagalog	English
Saan po ba ang daan papuntang palengke?	Where, may I ask, is the way to the market?
Saan po ba ang daan papuntang paaralan?	Where, may I ask, is the way to the school?

Breaking down the sentence "Saan po ba ang daan papuntang paaralan?" word by word:

- Saan - Where
- po - (a marker of politeness or respect, often used when speaking to someone older or in a more formal context)

- ba - ba-question marker (a particle used for emphasis or to indicate a question, somewhat equivalent to "may I ask" in this context)
- ang - the (a definite article used here as a marker for the noun that follows)
- daan - way or road
- papuntang - heading to or towards (pa- prefix indicates direction towards something, "punta" means go, and "-ng" connects it to the following noun)
- paaralan - school
- So, the sentence "Saan po ba ang daan papuntang paaralan?" translates to "Where, may I ask, is the way to the school?"

Practice Exercises: Try constructing your own sentences using "saan" based on the following situations:

- You're asking a friend where they bought their shoes.
- You're inquiring about where to find the nearest ATM.
- You're curious about where a friend lives in the city.

Useful Vocabulary for the Exercise:

Tagalog	**English**
binili	bought (the past tense of 'bumili', to buy, indicated by the prefix 'bi-')
sapatos	shoes
makikita	can be found (future or potential aspect of 'makita', meaning to see or to find)
pinakamalapit	nearest (from 'malapit', meaning close or near, with the prefix 'pinaka-' indicating the superlative degree)
na	that (a linker used to connect or modify adjectives with nouns)
nakatira	living/residing (the state of living or residing somewhere, from the root word 'tira' with the prefix 'naka-' indicating a state or condition)
sa	in/at (preposition indicating location)
siyudad	city

Tagalog	English

Solution:

Tagalog	English
Saan mo binili ang iyong sapatos?	Where did you buy your shoes?
Saan makikita ang pinakamalapit na ATM?	Where can I find the nearest ATM?
Saan ka nakatira sa siyudad?	Where do you live in the city?

Lesson 18 - Looking for Something

When looking for an item or a place, you can use 'saan' in combination with 'makikita'.

Tagalog	English
Saan ko makikita ang ... (item/place)?	Where can I find the ... (item/place)?

Sample phrases:

Tagalog	English
Saan ko makikita ang susi?	Where can I find the key?
Saan ko makikita ang banyo?	Where can I find the bathroom?
Saan ko makikita ang libro?	Where can I find the book?
Saan ko makikita ang istasyon ng bus?	Where can I find the bus station?
Saan ko makikita ang guro?	Where can I find the teacher?

The word "makikita" in Tagalog is a future tense verb form that means "will see" or "will be seen." It is derived from the root word "kita", which means "see" or "sight". The prefix "ma-" and the infix "-i-" are added to the root to indicate a potential or future action that involves seeing, finding, or encountering something or someone.
In sentences, "makikita" is commonly used to express the ability or possibility of seeing or finding something in the future. It can also imply where something can be found or located. Here are some nuances of "makikita":

- Future Action: Indicates that the action of seeing or finding will happen.
- Ability or Possibility: Suggests the capability or chance of seeing or finding something.
- Location or Presence: Used to ask about or describe where something can be found or seen.

For example:

Tagalog	**English**
Makikita mo ang susi sa lamesa.	You will find the key on the table.
Saang lugar makikita ang pinakamalapit na ATM?	Where can the nearest ATM be found?

In essence, "makikita" is about the future visibility or discovery of something, highlighting the anticipatory aspect of seeing or finding.

Exercise: Form your own phrases asking for the following items:

- Bathroom - Banyo
- Glass - Baso
- Milk - Gatas

Tagalog	**English**

Solutions:

Tagalog	English
Saan ko makikita ang banyo?	Where can I find the bathroom?
Saan ko makikita ang baso?	Where can I find a glass?
Saan ko makikita ang gatas?	Where can I find milk?

Lesson 19 - Where to & Where from?

Understanding how to express 'where to' and 'where from' involves the prepositions 'papunta' (to) and 'galing' (from).

Tagalog	English
Saan Papunta?	Where to?

Structure: Use "Saan papunta?" when you want to ask "Where to?" or "Where are you going?" This structure is useful for inquiring about someone's destination.

- Saan means "where"
- Papunta is a directional term that means "headed to" or "going to."

Examples:

Tagalog	English
Saan	where
Papunta	headed to or going to
Saan papunta?	Where are you going?
Saan papunta ang bus na ito?	Where is this bus headed to?

"Where from"

Tagalog	English
Saan Galing?	Where from?

Structure: Use "Saan galing?" to ask "Where from?" or "Where did you come from?"

- Saan still means "where"
- Galing indicates the origin or source of something or someone.

This is used to inquire about someone's point of origin.

Examples:

Tagalog	English
Saan galing?	Where did you come from?
Saan galing ang pera na ito?	Where did this money come from?

Exercise: Provide the translations.

Tagalog	English
Saan ka pupunta?	
Saan ka patungo?	
Saan ka nanggaling?	

Solution:

Tagalog	English
Saan ka pupunta?	Where are you going?
Saan ka patungo?	Where are you headed?
Saan ka nanggaling?	Where are you coming from?

Breaking down the sentence "Saan ka nanggaling?" word by word:

- Saan - Where

- ka - you (singular)
- nanggaling - coming from (derived from the root word "galing," meaning "to come from," with the prefix "nang-" indicating past or completed action)
- So, "Saan ka nanggaling?" translates to "Where are you coming from?"

Examples how to answer:

Tagalog	**English**
Sa malayo	From far away
Sa labas lang	Just outside
Mula sa trabaho	From work
Sa kaibigan ko	At a friend's place
Naglakad-lakad lang	Just went for a walk
Sa isang lugar	From a place
Galing ako sa hotel	I am coming from the hotel
Pupunta ako sa hotel	I am going to the hotel
Doon lang	From somewhere / Just there

"Doon lang" works as a general response to "Saan ka nanggaling?" It translates to "Just there" or "Over there" in English, implying a nearby or unspecified location without giving specific details. This reply is appropriately vague, making it suitable for situations where you prefer not to disclose your exact whereabouts.

"Taga-saan" is an expression used to ask someone **where they are from.** It combines "taga," which means "from," with "saan", which means "where". So, "Taga-saan ka?" translates to "Where are you from?". It's a common way to inquire about someone's place of origin or hometown.

Tagalog	**English**
Taga-saan ka?	Where are you from? (Origin)
Taga-saan siya?	Where is he/she from? (Origin)

Options to answer: Taga + location + ko: “Taga-America ako" directly translates to "I am from America".

- Taga: "Taga" is a prefix that indicates origin or location.
- America: "America"
- Ako: "I" or "me" (depending on the context)

You can also use "galing" (coming from): "Galing ako sa Amerika."

- Galing: coming from
- ako: I
- sa: from
- Amerika: America
- Meaning: I am coming from America / I am from America.

Exercises: Try forming your own questions using "Saan papunta?" and "Saan galing?" Here are a few situations to get you started. Choose two of them.

1. You want to know where your friend is going after school or work.
2. A friend arrives late to a meeting, and you're curious where he is coming from.
3. You're curious where a friend plans to eat lunch.
4. A friend just came back carrying shopping bags, and you wonder where he shopped.
5. You notice a friend is heading out dressed up, and you are curious where she is going.
6. Your friend mentions they need to leave early, and you are curious where he/she is going to that he/she needs to go early.
7. A friend shows up with gym equipment, and you are curious where he/she is coming from with this gym equipment.

Useful vocabulary for the exercise:

Tagalog	**English**
Saan	Where
papunta	going
pagkatapos	after
eskwela	school
galing	come from
bago	before
dumating	arriving

dito	here
kumain	eat
tanghalian	lunch
bitbit	carrying
shopping	shopping
bihis	dressed up
kailangan	you need
umalis	leave
maaga	early
dala	bring
gamit	equipment
pang-gym	for gym

Table for your phrases:

Tagalog	**English**

Solution: Below are potential solutions for the exercise to create sentences with "Saan papunta?" and "Saan galing?" along with their English translations and based on the given scenarios.

Tagalog	English
Saan papunta pagkatapos ng esk-wela?	Where are you going after school?
Saan galing bago dumating dito?	Where did you come from before ar-riving here?
Saan papunta para kumain ng tanghalian?	Where are you going to eat lunch?
Saan galing na may bitbit kang shop-ping bags?	Where did you come from with those shopping bags?
Saan papunta na bihis na bihis ka?	Where are you going all dressed up?
Saan papunta na kailangan mo nang umalis ng maaga?	Where are you headed that you need to leave early?
Saan galing na may dala kang gamit pang-gym?	Where did you come from with gym equipment?

Lesson 20 - Who - Sino?

Using "Who?" in Tagalog is quite straightforward. The word for "who" is "sino" Let's start with some examples using "sino" together with pronouns:

agalog	English
Sino 'yan?	Who is that?

Note on "'yan": This is a contraction of "iyan," which means "that" in English. In Tagalog,

Let' look at further useful phrases:

Tagalog	English
Sino ka?	Who are you?
Sino ang iyong asawa?	Who is your wife?
Sino ba siya?	Who is he/she?
Sino ito, pakiusap?	Who is this, please?
Sino ang kasama mo?	Who are you with?

Let's break down the question "Sino ang kasama mo?":

- Sino: "Who"
- ang: A marker indicating the subject of the question.
- kasama: "Companion" or "with"
- mo: "Your"
- So, "Sino ang kasama mo?" translates directly to "Who is your companion?" or simply "Who are you with?"

Tagalog	English
Sino 'yang mga tao?	Who are those people?
Sino, pasensya na?	Who, sorry?

Word by word breakdown of "Sino 'yang mga tao?":

- Sino: "Who"
- 'yang: Short for "iyang", indicating "that" (near the listener)
- mga: Plural marker
- tao: "People"
- Translation: "Who are those people?"

Now we are forming more complex questions. This can be done by the following formula:

- Sino + Verb + Object (SVO-Structure for questions)

Tagalog	English
Sino ang kumain ng manok?	Who ate the chicken?

Let's break down "Sino ang kumain ng manok?":

- Subject (S): "Sino" (Who) - Technically serves as the placeholder for the subject until identified.
- Verb (V): "kumain" (ate) - Indicates the action.
- Object (O): "ng manok" (chicken) - The thing that was eaten.

Further samples of forming questions like this:

Tagalog	English
Sino ang bumili ng tinapay?	Who bought the bread?
Sino ang nagluto ng hapunan?	Who cooked the dinner?
Sino ang sumira ng laruan?	Who broke the toy?
Sino ang nagsulat ng liham?	Who wrote the letter?
Sino ang nagbukas ng bintana?	Who opened the window?
Sino ang nagsara ng pinto?	Who closed the door?

When asking questions about future actions, the verb often gets the prefix "mag-" and the first syllable of the root verb is repeated.

Prefix	First syllable	root	Complete	English
mag-	-lu-	luto	magluluto	will cook

Here are some examples:

Tagalog	English
Sino ang maglilinis ng kwarto?	Who will clean the room?
Sino ang magluluto ng hapunan bukas?	Who will cook dinner tomorrow?
Sino ang magdadala ng pagkain sa piknik?	Who will bring food to the picnic?
Sino ang magpapatakbo ng proyekto?	Who will run the project?
Sino ang magsusulat ng ulat?	Who will write the report?
Sino ang magbabayad ng kuryente?	Who will pay for the electricity?
Sino ang mag-aalaga ng aso habang wala ako?	Who will take care of the dog while I'm away?
Sino ang magpaplano ng biyahe?	Who will plan the trip?
Sino ang magtuturo sa klase?	Who will teach the class?

Lesson 21 - Answering Who Questions

Answering "Who" or "Sino" questions about future actions in Tagalog often involves directly naming the person who will perform the action. Commonly, sentences start with "Ako" (I), "Siya" (He/She), "Sila" (They), or the person's name directly. This approach typically shifts the sentence structure away from the usual Tagalog VSO (verb-subject-object) form. Placing the person at the beginning emphasizes the focus on "who" is involved, clearly highlighting the requested information. Here are responses to the previous examples:

Tagalog	English
Sino ang maglilinis ng kwarto?	Who will clean the room?
Ako ang maglilinis ng kwarto.	I will clean the room.
Sino ang magluluto ng hapunan bukas?	Who will cook dinner tomorrow?
Si Lisa ang magluluto ng hapunan bukas.	Lisa will cook dinner tomorrow.
Sino ang magdadala ng pagkain sa piknik?	Who will bring food to the picnic?
Kami ang magdadala ng pagkain sa piknik.	We will bring food to the picnic.
Sino ang magpapatakbo ng proyekto?	Who will run the project?
Si Anna at si Luis ang magpapatakbo ng proyekto.	Anna and Luis will run the project.
Sino ang magsusulat ng ulat?	Who will write the report?
Ako na ang magsusulat ng ulat.	I will be the one to write the report.
Sino ang magbabayad ng kuryente?	Who will pay for the electricity?
Si Paul ang magbabayad ng kuryente.	Paul will pay for the electricity.
Sino ang mag-aalaga ng aso habang wala ako?	Who will take care of the dog while I'm away?
Siya ang mag-aalaga ng aso habang wala ako.	He/She will take care of the dog while I'm away.
Sino ang magpaplano ng biyahe?	Who will plan the trip?
Sila ang magpaplano ng biyahe.	They will plan the trip.
Sino ang magtuturo sa klase?	Who will teach the class?
Si Ginoong Malabago ang magtuturo	Mr. Malabago will teach the class.

sa klase.	

Lesson 22 - When - Kailan?

The primary word used for "When?" in Tagalog is "Kailan". Basic Use of "Kailan":

Tagalog	English
Kailan	When?
Kailan ka pupunta?	When are you going?

Past Events: To ask about when something happened in the past, "Kailan" is still used, but the verb will be in past tense.

Tagalog	English
Kailan ka dumating?	When did you arrive?
Dumating ako kahapon.	I arrived yesterday.

Asking About Specific Events: To inquire about the timing of specific events, you can use "Kailan" followed by the event.

Tagalog	English
Kailan ang kaarawan mo?	When is your birthday?
Ang kaarawan ko ay sa Hunyo.	My birthday is in June.
Kailan tayo magdiriwang ng iyong kaarawan?	When will we celebrate your birthday?
Magdiriwang tayo ng aking kaarawan sa Sabado.	We will celebrate my birthday on Saturday.
Kailan ka aalis para sa Maynila?	When are you leaving for Manila?
Aalis ako para sa Maynila sa Lunes.	I am leaving for Manila on Monday.

Further sample phrases to get familiar with Kanus-a questions:

Tagalog	English
Kailan ka kakain?	When will you eat?
Kailan ka babalik?	When are you coming back?
Kailan ka aalis?	When are you leaving?
Kailan ka darating dito?	When will you arrive here?
Kailan tayo pupunta doon?	When are we going there?

Regular Activities; Asking about the regularity or schedule of an activity also uses "Kailan."

Tagalog	English
Kailan ka nag-eensayo?	When do you practice?
Nag-eensayo ako tuwing Sabado.	I practice every Saturday.

Complex Questions: For more detailed inquiries, you can combine "Kailan" with additional words: like

Tagalog	English
Kailan dapat magpasa ng mga proyekto?	When should we submit the projects?
Dapat magpasa ng mga proyekto bago mag Biyernes.	We should submit the projects before Friday.
Kailan mo balak tapusin ang proyektong ito at ano ang susunod mong hakbang?	When do you plan to finish this project and what are your next steps?

For the beginning, just remember the basic structure: Kailan + Person + Event. For example, if you want to ask someone about their mealtime, you'd say: 'Kailan ka kakain?' which translates to 'When will you eat?

Starting your language learning journey with simple topics is a smart strategy. It ensures that you can remember and apply what you've learned in practical situations. By beginning with basic words and phrases in your daily life, you become familiar with the language, laying a strong foundation for tackling more complex sentences later on.

I recall my own experience when I first started learning Tagalog. One memorable moment was when I asked a taxi driver, "When will we arrive?" Despite already knowing the estimated arrival time from my taxi app, I seized the opportunity to practice speaking. It was a humorous situation that allowed me to use the first few words I had learned.

The friendly and humorous nature of the people of the Philippines made practicing Tagalog in real-life situations enjoyable and far from embarrassing. Embracing these opportunities to practice in everyday life is key to improving your language skills and making the learning process more enjoyable.

Exercise: Write down a “when” question and use it in a real-life situation.

Tagalog	English

Lesson 23 - How - Paano?

"Paano" is the Tagalog word for "how." Useful Vocabulary:

Tagalog	English
Paano	How
Gumawa	To do/make
Magluto	To cook
Mag-aral	To study
Sumayaw	To dance
Kumanta	To sing

Let's dive into useful questions. To inquire about doing something, start with "Paano" followed by the action verb.

Tagalog	English
Paano magluto ng adobo?	How to cook adobo?

Paano mag-aral nang mabisa?	How to study effectively?
Paano sumayaw ng tango?	How to dance the tango?
Paano kumanta nang may damdamin?	How to sing with feeling?

Exercise: Write down a "Paano" question and use it in a real-life situation.

Tagalog	English

Lesson 24 - Answering How Questions

Answering "How" questions: When answering, describe the process. You can start with "Para" (To) or just explain directly.

Tagalog	English	Tagalog	English
Paano magluto ng adobo?	How to cook adobo?	Para magluto ng adobo, kailangan mo ng manok, toyo, at suka.	To cook adobo, you need chicken, soy sauce, and vinegar.
Paano mag-aral nang mabisa?	How to study effectively?	Mag-aral ka nang may regular na iskedyul at gumawa ng mga nots.	Study with a regular schedule and make notes.
Paano sumayaw ng tango?	How to dance the tango?	Sumayaw ng tango sa pamamagitan ng pag-follow sa ritmo at hakbang.	Dance the tango by following the rhythm and steps.
Paano kumanta nang may damdamin?	How to sing with feeling?	Kumanta nang may damdamin sa pamamagitan ng pag-intindi sa lyrics ng kanta.	Sing with feeling by understanding the lyrics of the song.

Practice Dialogue:

Tagalog	English
A: Paano magluto ng adobo?	A: How to cook adobo?
B: Para magluto ng adobo, igisa mo muna ang bawang at sibuyas, tapos idag-dag mo ang manok, toyo, suka, at konting tubig. Pakuluan mo hang-gang sa lumambot ang manok.	B: To cook adobo, first sauté garlic and onions, then add chicken, soy sauce, vinegar, and a little water. Boil it until the chicken softens.

Lesson 25 - Why - Bakit?

"Bakit" is the Tagalog word for "why." It's used to ask about reasons or causes. Let's begin with practical words.

Tagalog	English
Bakit	Why
Dahil	Because
Gusto	Want/Like
Kailangan	Need
Ayaw	Dislike

Next up, let's study some standard expressions. Asking "Why" - To inquire about the reason behind something, start your question with "Bakit."

Tagalog	English
Bakit ka malungkot?	Why are you sad?
Bakit umuulan?	Why is it raining?
Bakit gusto mong matuto ng Taga-log?	Why do you want to learn Tagalog?
Bakit siya umalis?	Why did he/she leave?

Exercise: Write down a “bakit” question and use it in a real-life situation.

Tagalog	English

Lesson 26 - Answering Why Questions

Answering "Why": When responding to "why" questions, you can start your answer with "Dahil" (Because) followed by the reason.

Useful vocabulary:

Tagalog	English
Dahil	Because
Gusto	Want/Like
Kailangan	Need
Ayaw	Dislike

Sample phrases:

Tagalog	English
Dahil may problema ako.	Because I have a problem.
Dahil may bagyo.	Because there is a storm.
Dahil gusto kong bisitahin ang Pilipinas.	Because I want to visit the Philippines.
Dahil may emergency siya.	Because he/she had an emergency.

Sample Dialog I:

Tagalog	English
A: Bakit ka pumunta sa palengke?	A: Why did you go to the market?
B: Dahil gusto ko bumili ng gulay.	B: Because I want to buy vegetables.
A: Bakit ka nag-aaral ng Tagalog?	A: Why are you studying Tagalog?

B: Dahil kailangan ko ito sa trabaho.	B: Because I need it for work.
A: Bakit hindi ka kumain ng ampa-laya?	A: Why don't you eat bitter gourd?
B: Ayaw ko ng lasa nito.	B: I dislike its taste.
A: Bakit ka umalis ng maaga?	A: Why did you leave early?
B: Dahil kailangan ko pa maghanda para sa trabaho.	B: Because I need to prepare for work.

Sample Dialog II:

Tagalog	**English**
A: Bakit ka nag-aaral ng Tagalog?	A: Why are you studying Tagalog?
B: Dahil gusto kong makapag-com-municate nang maayos kapag bumi-sita ako sa Pilipinas.	B: Because I want to communicate effectively when I visit the Philip-pines.

Here is the word by word breakdown for the phrase "Dahil gusto kong makapag-communicate nang maayos kapag bumisita ako sa Pilipinas." for better understanding:

- Dahil - "Because"
- gusto - "want" or "like." It expresses a desire or preference.
- kong - This is a contraction of "ko" (I/me) and "ng" (a linking particle).
- makapag-communicate - "to be able to communicate." This is a loan-word from English, embedded into a Tagalog verbal affix that indicates a potential or ability to perform an action.
- nang - This is a particle used in many contexts in Tagalog. Here, it functions similar to "so" or "to," indicating a manner or condition.
- maayos - "properly" or "well."
- kapag - "when" or "whenever." It is a conjunction used to indicate a specific time or condition.
- bumisita - "visit." Derived from the Spanish word "visitar", it has been incorporated into Tagalog with the prefix "bumi-" indicating an action performed by the subject.
- ako - "I" or "me"
- sa - "in" or "to." It is a preposition indicating direction or location.
- Pilipinas - Philippines

- Putting it all together, the phrase "Dahil gusto kong makapag-communicate nang maayos kapag bumisita ako sa Pilipinas" translates to "Because I want to be able to communicate properly when I visit the Philippines."

Lesson 27 - How Much - Magkano?

"Magkano" is the Tagalog word used to ask about the price or cost of something. This lesson will guide you on how to use "magkano" in various contexts.

Useful Vocabulary

Tagalog	English
Magkano	How much
Ito	This
Iyan	That (close to the listener)
Iyon	That (far from both speaker and listener)
Pera	Money
Presyo	Price
Bili	Buy
Tinda	Sell

Asking "How Much": To inquire about the cost of items or services, you start your question with "Magkano."

Tagalog	English
Magkano ito?	"How much is this?"
Magkano ang presyo ng iyan?	"What is the price of that (close to you)?"
Magkano ang pera para sa iyon?	"How much money for that (far from both of us)?"
Gusto kong bili ito. Magkano?	"I want to buy this. How much?"
Magkano ang tinda mo?	"How much are you selling for?"

Magkano ang presyo ng libro?	"How much is the price of the book?"
Magkano ang tiket papuntang Cebu?	"How much is the ticket to Cebu?"
Magkano ang isang kilo ng mansanas?	"How much is a kilo of apples?"

Answering "How Much": Answers to "magkano" questions will typically involve stating the amount or price.

Tagalog	**English**
Ito ay Php 100.	This is Php 100.
Ang presyo ng libro ay Php 250.	The price of the book is Php 250.
Ang tiket papuntang Cebu ay Php 3,000.	The ticket to Cebu is Php 3,000.
Isang kilo ng mansanas ay Php 150.	A kilo of apples is Php 150.

Practice Dialogue

Tagalog	**English**
A: Magkano itong relo?	A: How much is this watch?
B: Php 500 ang relo.	B: The watch is Php 500.

Now, let's explore some further useful expressions.

Tagalog	**English**
Magkano ang bahay?	How much is the house?
Magkano ang halaga ng bahay?	How much does the house cost?
Magkano ang isda?	How much does the fish cost?
Magkano ang halaga ng isda?	How much does the fish cost?
Magkano ito?	How much is this?
Ilang aso ang meron ka?	How many dogs do you have?
Magkano ang pamasahe?	How much is the fare?

Exercise: Choose a phrase from the lesson, write it down, learn and practice it.

Tagalog	English

Lesson 28 - How Many - Ilang?

"Ilang" is the Tagalog word for "how many" and is used to ask about the quantity or number of items, people, or anything countable.

Useful Vocabulary

Tagalog	English
Ilang	How many
Mayroon (Meron)	Have
Kapatid	Sibling
Aso	Dog
Araw	Day
Libro	Book
Upuan	Chair
Mansanas	Apple

Asking "How Many": To ask about the quantity of something, start your question with "Ilang."

Tagalog	English
Ilang kapatid mayroon ka?	How many siblings do you have?
Ilang aso ang meron ka?	How many dogs do you have?
Ilang libro ang binasa mo ngayong taon?	How many books have you read this year?
Ilang araw ang bakasyon mo?	How many days is your vacation?

Exercise: Write down a “Ilang” question and use it in a real-life situation.

Tagalog	English

Lesson 29 - Answering “How Many” Questions

Answering "How Many": When responding to questions about quantities, simply state the number followed by the noun.

Tagalog	English
Mayroon akong dalawang kapatid.	I have two siblings.
Meron akong isang aso.	I have one dog.
Binasa ko ang limang libro ngayong taon.	I have read five books this year.
Ang bakasyon ko ay pitong araw.	My vacation is seven days long.

Practice Dialogue:

Tagalog	English
A: Ilang upuan ang kailangan natin bilhin?	A: How many chairs do we need to buy?
B: Kailangan natin ng apat na upuan.	B: We need four chairs.

Here's a breakdown of the phrase "Kailangan natin ng apat na upuan." word by word:

- Kailangan - Need
- natin - We (inclusive). Refers to the speaker and the listener together.
- ng - Ng-marker that often indicates the following noun is the object of the sentence or phrase.
- apat - Four
- na - A linker that connects modifiers to nouns or numbers to things they quantify.

- upuan - Chair
- So, "Kailangan natin ng apat na upuan." translates directly to "Need we four chairs." A smoother English translation would be "We need four chairs."

Lesson 30 - Yes & No Questions (Ba-Marker)

This lesson will cover how to form yes or no questions. Yes/No questions are closed questions that do not begin with a question word. They are formed with the question marker "ba", which is often inserted as the second word in a sentence.

In Tagalog, the question marker "ba" is used to turn statements into questions, but it has no direct translation in English. Unlike English, where yes/no questions often require changing the sentence structure or adding auxiliary verbs, Tagalog uses "ba" to indicate that a statement is a question.

How it works in English:
To ask a yes/no question in English, you typically rearrange the sentence by moving the verb or helping verb to the front. For example, the statement "You are happy" becomes the question "Are you happy?"

How it works in Tagalog:
In Tagalog, you simply insert "ba" after the topic or at a natural pause in the sentence. For example, the statement "Masaya ka" (You are happy) becomes "Masaya ka ba?" (Are you happy?). Here, "ba" doesn't change the meaning but signals that it's a question.

Useful Vocabulary

Tagalog	English
ba	Question marker
Oo	Yes
Hindi (Di)	No
Ka	You (singular informal)

Mayroon (Meron)	Have
Gusto	Want/Like
Kumain	Eat
Pumunta	Go
Nag-aral	Studied

Forming Yes & No Questions

To turn a statement into a yes or no question , you often just need to raise your intonation at the end of the sentence and adding "ba" after the verb or subject can help clarify it's a question. Let's study how to form yes/no questions:

Tagalog	**English**
Kumain ka na?	Did you eat already?
Gusto mo ba ito?	Do you like this?
Mayroon ka bang libro?	Do you have a book?
Nag-aral ka ba ng Tagalog?	Did you study Tagalog?

Here's a breakdown of the Tagalog phrase "Mayroon ka bang libro?":

- Mayroon - "There is" or "have" (used to express possession or existence)
- ka - "you" (singular)
- bang - The word "bang" is a combination of the question particle "ba" and the linker "ng". "Ba" is used to turn a statement into a question,. "Ng" is a linker that connects parts of a sentence,
- libro - "book"
- Put together, "Mayroon ka bang libro?" translates to "Do you have a book?"

Exercise: Translate the Tagalog phrases into Tagalog.

English	**Tagalog**
Are you Filipino?	
Is Charlie Filipino?	
Are you American?	
Is she Lilly?	
Is this vegetarian?	

Is Paul a student?	
Is he tall?	
Is this a good movie?	
Is this your book?	
Do you like wine?	
Is this delicious?	
Do you have any more questions?	
Is there a telephone here?	

Useful vocabulary for the exercises:

Tagalog	**English**
Pilipino	Filipino
Amerikano	American
si	a marker for a person
ba	question marker
ka	you (singular)
vegetarian	vegetarian
estudyante	student
matangkad	tall
maganda	beautiful/good
ang	the
pelikulang	movie
ito	this
iyong	your
libro	book
gusto	like/want
ng	object marker (unspecific)
alak	wine
masarap	delicious
mayroon	have
pa	still/more
bang	filler word - used for emphasis or to soften a question
ibang	other
tanong	question
si	a marker for a person
ba	question marker

Solution:

English	Tagalog
Are you Filipino?	Pilipino ka ba?
Is Charlie Filipino?	Pilipino ba si Charlie?
Are you American?	Amerikano ka ba?
Is she Lilly?	Siya ba si Lilly?
Is this vegetarian?	Vegetarian ba ito?
Is Paul a student?	Estudyante ba si Paul?
Is he tall?	Matangkad ba siya?
Is this a good movie?	Maganda ba ang pelikulang ito?
Is this your book?	Ito ba ang iyong libro?
Do you like wine?	Gusto mo ba ng alak?
Is this delicious?	Masarap ba ito?
Do you have any more questions?	Mayroon ka pa bang ibang tanong?
Is there a telephone here?	May telepono ba dito?

Note: In Tagalog, the question marker "ba" usually comes after the word being asked about, like the predicate, which is often the second word in the sentence. But when you're asking a question directly to someone using the word "ka" (you), "ba" comes right after "ka.", typically the third position in the phrase. For example:

English	Tagalog	Explanation
Are you Filipino?	Pilipino ka ba?	The question marker "ba" comes after the word "ka" (you), as it's directly addressing the person. (Third position)
Is Charlie Filipino?	Pilipino ba si Charlie?	The question marker "ba" comes after the subject "Charlie," as it's asking about Charlie's identity. (Second position)

Lesson 31 - Decision-Making Questions

The ba question marker is also used to ask for a decision between two possibilities or options. These are closed questions too, because they offer only two options to answer:

Tagalog	English
Gusto mo ba ng kape o tsaa?	Do you like coffee or tea?
Bibili ka ba ng puti o itim na sapatos?	Will you buy white or black shoes?
Kakain ka ba ng isda o karne mamaya?	Will you eat fish or meat tonight?

Exercise: Translate the phrases.

English	Tagalog
Do you want apples or bananas?	
Will you buy a book or a cellphone?	
Will you eat spaghetti or pizza for dinner?	

Vocabulary for the exercise:

English	Tagalog
do you want	gusto mo
apples	mansanas
or	o
bananas	saging
will you buy	bibili ka
a (object marker, unspecific)	ng
book	libro
cellphone	cellphone
will you eat	kakain ka
spaghetti	spaghetti
pizza	pizza
for dinner	sa hapunan

Solution:

English	Tagalog
Do you want apples or bananas?	Gusto mo mansanas o saging?
Will you buy a book or a cellphone?	Bibili ka ng libro o ng cellphone?
Will you eat spaghetti or pizza for dinner?	Kakain ka ng spaghetti o ng pizza sa hapunan?

Lesson 32 - Yes, No, Maybe Answers

This lesson covers how to use "Oo" (Yes), "Hindi" (No), and "Siguro" or "Baka" (Maybe) in various contexts.

Useful Vocabulary

Tagalog	English
Oo	Yes
Hindi	No
Hini po.	No (polite)
Siguro	Maybe (more certain)
Baka	Maybe (less certain)
Hindo ko alam.	I don't know.
Ewan ko.	I don't know.
Oo, pakiusap.	Yes, please.
Hindi, salamat.	No, thank you.
Hindi ako sigurado.	I'm not sure.
Eksakto	Exactly
Siguro	Surely
Hindi ko maintindihan.	I don't understand.
Sandali lang.	Wait a momnt.

"Hindi ko alam" and "Ewan ko" both mean "I don't know". "Hindi ko alam" is more formal and directly translates to "I do not know." "Ewan ko" is more informal or casual and also means "I don't know," but can carry a nuance of indifference or uncertainty about the answer.

Affirmative Responses: To affirmatively respond to a question, use "Oo."

Tagalog	English
Gusto mo ba ng kape?	Do you want coffee?
Oo, gusto ko.	Yes, I want.

Negative Responses: To negate a statement or answer a question in the negative, use "Hindi."

Tagalog	English
Pupunta ka ba sa party mamaya?	Are you going to the party later?
Hindi, hindi ako pupunta.	No, I'm not going.

Uncertain Responses: To express uncertainty or indecision, use "Siguro" if you're somewhat certain but still unsure, and "Baka" for less certainty.

Tagalog	English
Makakasama ka ba sa amin bukas?	Will you be able to join us tomorrow?
Siguro, kung wala akong gagawin.	Maybe, if I have nothing else to do.
Uulan ba mamaya?	Will it rain later?
Baka, mukhang madilim ang langit.	Maybe, the sky looks dark.

Practice Dialogue:

Tagalog	English
Gusto mo bang manood ng sine sa weekend?	Do you want to watch a movie this weekend?
Siguro, tignan ko muna schedule ko.	Maybe, I'll check my schedule first.
Kain tayo sa labas ngayon gabi, gusto mo?	Shall we eat out tonight, do you want to?
Hindi, mas gusto kong magluto na lang sa bahay.	No, I'd prefer to cook at home.
Marunong ka bang mag-drive?	Do you know how to drive?

Exercise: Translate the following English phrases into Tagalog.

Tagalog	**English**
	Are you hungry?
	Yes, I am hungry.
	Are you tired?
	Yes, I am tired.
	Have you eaten?
	Yes, I have eaten.
	Have you eaten?

Useful vocabulary:

Tagalog	**English**
Gutom	Hungry
Pagod	Tired
Kumain	Eaten
Oo	Yes
Hindi	No

Solution:

Tagalog	**English**
Gutom ka ba?	Are you hungry?
Oo, gutom ako.	Yes, I am hungry.
Pagod ka ba?	Are you tired?
Oo, pagod ako.	Yes, I am tired.
Kumain ka na ba?	Have you eaten?
Oo, kumain na ako.	Yes, I have eaten.
Kumain ka na ba?	Have you eaten?

Lesson 33 - Asking for Decisions

"Ba" is a question marker that can turn statements into yes/no questions. It's also used to ask for a decision between two possibilities or options, making these types of inquiries closed questions. This lesson will guide you on how to use "ba" for decision-making questions, offering only two options for the answer.

Understanding "Ba"

"Ba" is inserted after the subject or the first word of the sentence to signal a question, especially when you're asking someone to choose between two options.

Forming Decision Questions with "Ba"

To ask someone to decide between two options, you can structure your sentence by mentioning the options and including "ba" to indicate that it's a question. Here are some examples:

Tagalog	English
Kape ba o tsaa ang gusto mo?	Do you want coffee or tea?
Dito ba tayo kakain o sa labas?	Are we eating here or outside?
Ngayon ba o bukas ang alis natin?	Are we leaving today or tomorrow?
Pelikula ba o musika ang hilig mo?	Do you prefer movies or music?

Note: "Ba" decision questions often differ from the standard VSO (Verb-Subject-Object) format, especially when asking about decisions or choices. These questions typically structure the sentence to emphasize the options involved by placing them at the beginning. In the examples above, the choices are presented at the start, followed by "ba" and the predicate, focusing the question on the decision between the given options.

Exercise: Choose a phrase from the lesson, write it down, learn and practice it.

Tagalog	English

Lesson 34 - Making Decisions

This lesson will guide you on how to answer ba-decision questions. When responding to a question that uses "ba" for decisions, you simply state your choice among the given options.

State a choice:

Tagalog	English
Kape ang gusto ko.	I want coffee.
Sa labas tayo kakain.	We'll eat outside.
Bukas ang alis natin.	We are leaving tomorrow.
Pelikula ang hilig ko.	I prefer movies.

Exercise:

Tagalog	English
Ehersisyo: Paggawa ng Desisyon	Exercise: Making Decisions
Panuto: Sagutin ang mga tanong.	Instructions: Answer the questions.

Question	Answer
Scenario: You're at a coffee shop deciding what to drink. Question: Kape ba o tsaa ang gusto mo?	
Scenario: A friend asks if you want to eat out or cook at home. Question: Kakain ba tayo sa labas o magluluto sa bahay?	
Scenario: Deciding when to start a project. Question: Ngayon ba o bukas natin	

sisimulan ang proyekto?	
Scenario: Choosing between watching a movie or reading a book. Question: Manonood ba tayo ng pelikula o magbabasa ng libro?	

Solutions:

Question	**Answer**
Scenario: You're at a coffee shop deciding what to drink. Question: Kape ba o tsaa ang gusto mo?	a.) Kape ang gusto ko. (I want coffee.) b.) Tsaa ang gusto ko. (I want tea.)
Scenario: A friend asks if you want to eat out or cook at home. Question: Kakain ba tayo sa labas o magluluto sa bahay?	a.) Sa labas tayo kakain. (We will eat outside.) b.) Magluluto tayo sa bahay. (We will cook at home.)
Scenario: Deciding when to start a project. Question: Ngayon ba o bukas natin sisimulan ang proyekto?	a.) Ngayon natin sisimulan. (We will start today.) b.) Bukas natin sisimulan. (We will start tomorrow.)
Scenario: Choosing between watching a movie or reading a book. Question: Manonood ba tayo ng pelikula o magbabasa ng libro?	a.) Manonood tayo ng pelikula. (We will watch a movie.) b.) Magbabasa tayo ng libro. (We will read a book.)

Lesson 35 - Denying & Negation

Denying or negating statements and questions often involves the word "Hindi" (No), which is used to express disagreement, negation, or denial. This lesson will cover the basics of using "Hindi" in various contexts to negate statements and questions effectively.

Useful Vocabulary

Tagalog	English
Hindi	No/Not
Ayaw	Do not want
Wala	None/Nothing/No one
Hindi kailanman	Never
Hindi pa	Not yet

Basic Negation

To negate or deny something in Tagalog, "Hindi" is usually placed before the verb or adjective.

Tagalog	English
Hindi ako gutom.	I am not hungry.
Hindi siya malungkot.	He/She is not sad.
Hindi kami pupunta.	We are not going.

Denying a Question

When responding to a question, "Hindi" can directly precede your answer to negate.

Tagalog	English
Kumain ka na ba?	Have you eaten?
Hindi, hindi pa.	No, not yet.
Gusto mo ba ito?	Do you like this?
Hindi, ayaw ko.	No, I don't like it.

Using "Wala" for Absence

"Wala" indicates the absence of something or someone.

Tagalog	English
Wala akong pera.	I have no money.
Wala dito si Maria.	Maria is not here.

Expressing Complete Negation

For a stronger denial or negation, "Hindi kailanman" is used.

Tagalog	English
Hindi kailanman ako magiging tray-dor.	I will never be a traitor.

Here's a breakdown of the sentence "Hindi kailanman ako magiging traydor." word by word:

- Hindi - not
- kailanman - ever
- ako - I
- magiging - will be
- traydor - traitor
- Meaning: I will never be a traitor.

Practice Dialogue

Tagalog	English
Maglalaro ka ba sa amin mamaya?	Will you play with us later?
Hindi, may gagawin ako.	No, I have something to do.
Nagustuhan mo ba ang pelikula?	Did you like the movie?
Hindi, ayaw ko ng ganung tipo ng pe-likula.	No, I don't like that type of movie.

The Sentence Structure for Negation and Denial

Negation and denial revolve primarily around the use of "Hindi" (No/Not) and "Wala" (None/Nothing/No one/ Absence of something). Let's explore the structure for negating sentences.

Using "Hindi"

- Structure: Hindi + Subject + Verb.
- Example: Hindi ako kumakain. (I am not eating.)
- "Hindi" directly negates the action or state described by the verb or adjective following it. This structure is straightforward and similar to the placement of "not" in English sentences.

Using "Wala"

- Structure for Absence: Wala + [Possessive Pronoun] + [Noun]
- Example: Wala akong libro. (I don't have a book.)
- "Wala" is used to express the absence of something or someone. In sentences where "Wala" is used, the focus is on what is missing or not present.

Examples:

Tagalog	English
Hindi ako kumakain.	I am not eating.
Wala akong pera.	I have no money.
Hindi siya pumunta.	He/She did not go.
Wala dito ang susi.	The key is not here.
Hindi ko alam.	I don't know.
Wala akong kapatid.	I have no siblings.
Hindi kami nagkakasundo.	We do not get along.
Wala sa oras.	Out of time. / Not on time.
Hindi ito para sa akin.	This is not for me.
Wala nang pagkain.	There is no more food.

Denying Questions

To deny or negate a question, "Hindi" is often sufficient as a response. However, for clarity or emphasis, repeating the verb or key word negated by "Hindi" reinforces the denial.

Tagalog	English
Question: Kumain ka na ba?	Have you eaten?
Answer: Hindi, hindi pa.	No, not yet.
Question: Pupunta ka ba sa party mamaya?	Are you going to the party later?
Answer: Hindi, hindi ako pupunta.	No, I'm not going.
Question: Nag-aral ka na ba para sa pagsusulit?	Have you studied for the test?
Answer: Hindi, hindi pa ako nag-aaral.	No, I haven't studied yet.

Question: Gising ka pa ba kagabi nang hatinggabi?	Were you still awake at midnight last night?
Answer: Hindi, hindi na ako gising.	No, I was no longer awake.
Question: Gusto mo ba itong pelikula?	Do you like this movie?
Answer: Hindi, hindi ko ito gusto.	No, I don't like it.
Question: Nakapag-decide ka na ba kung saan tayo kakain?	Have you decided where we will eat?
Answer: Hindi, hindi pa ako nakapag-decide.	No, I haven't decided yet.

Exercise: Translate the following in Tagalog:

English	Tagalog
I don't like wine.	
Paul is not short.	
This is not good.	
I don't like that.	

Solution:

English	Tagalog
I don't like wine.	Hindi ko gusto ang alak.
Paul is not short.	Hindi maikli si Paul.
This is not good.	Hindi ito maganda.
I don't like that.	Hindi ko gusto iyan.

Lesson 36 - Filler Words & Emphasis

Filler words and phrases are used in spoken conversations to add emphasis or to think for a moment about what to say next. These words don't always translate directly into English with the same usage or meaning, but they play a significant role in making speech sound more natural and fluent. This lesson will introduce you to common filler words and how to use them for emphasis.

Tagalog	Function
Lang / Na lang	Used to convey a sense of limitation, simplicity, or preference for an option, often softening the statement or making it appear more casual or less demanding.
Talaga	Adds emphasis, expresses genuine surprise, or intensifies the meaning of a statement, making it more emotionally expressive.
pa	Indicates something is still ongoing, not yet completed, or adds a sense of continuity or expectancy to a statement. E.g. "May trabaho pa ako," meaning "I still have work".
hindi pa	not yet - Can imply that something hasn't happened yet but might in the future-
eh	Used similarly to "well," for explanation or transition in conversation. Eh can also add a tone of explanation or argumentation.

Using Filler Words for Emphasis

Tagalog	English
Talaga bang masarap ito?	Is this really delicious?
Dito lang ako.	I'm just here.
Gusto ko eh.	I want it, well, that's just what I want.

Exercise: Translate the dialog into Tagalog using "Eh," "Talaga," and "Sige":

English	Tagalog
A: Why haven't you eaten yet? **B**: Well, I'm still full.	
A: Really? Did you just eat? **B**: Yes, really. I ate before I came here.	
A: Alright, just eat later then. **B**: Okay, thank you.	

Solution:

English	Tagalog
A: Why haven't you eaten yet? **B**: Well, I'm still full.	**A:** Bakit hindi ka pa kumakain? **B:** Eh, busog pa ako.
A: Really? Did you just eat? **B**: Yes, really. I ate before I came here.	**A:** Talaga? Kakakain mo lang ba? **B:** Oo, talaga. Kumain ako bago ako pumunta dito.
A: Alright, just eat later then. **B**: Okay, thank you.	**A:** Sige, kain ka na lang mamaya. **B:** Sige, salamat.

Lesson 37 - Abbreviations & Contractions

Abbreviations and contractions are used to simplify and shorten common phrases or words, especially in informal conversations or text messages. Understanding these can help you communicate more efficiently and sound more natural in casual dialogues. Let's explore some commonly used abbreviations and contractions in Tagalog.

Common Abbreviations

Tagalog	English
'Di - Short for hindi	"no" or "not"
'Di ako sigurado.	I'm not sure.
Wa - Short for wala	no, nothing, absence of something
Wa akong tubig.	I have no water.
'Ko - Short for ako	"I" or "me"
Miss 'ko na kayo.	I miss you all.
'To - Short for ito	"this"
Ano 'to?	What is this?
G - Short for go	Used to express agreement or readiness
G ka na ba?	Are you ready?
KKB - Stands for kanya-kanyang bayad	Meaning everyone pays for themselves, used in group outings
KKB tayo sa dinner, ha?	Let's each pay for our dinner, okay?

Common Contractions

Tagalog	English
Meron	A contraction of mayroon, meaning "there is" or "there are."
Meron pa bang pagkain?	Is there still food?
Sa'kin	A contraction of sa akin, meaning "to me" or "mine."
Ibigay mo sa'kin.	Give it to me.
Sa'yo	A contraction of sa iyo, meaning "to you" or "yours."
Para sa'yo 'to.	This is for you.
Wala	A contraction of "Walang," often used to express the non-existence or absence of something.
Wala na akong pera.	I have no money anymore.
N'yo	A contraction of "ninyo," meaning "yours" or "you" (plural).
Kamusta n'yo?	How are you (all)?
Gusto'ng	A contraction used when "gusto" (like/want) is followed by a noun.
Gusto'ng kumain.	(Someone) wants to eat.
Kailan'g	A contraction used when "kailangan" (need) is followed by a noun.
Kailan'g umalis.	Need to leave.
Sa'n	A contraction of "saan," meaning "where."
Sa'n ka pupunta?	Where are you going?
Pa'no	A contraction of "paano," meaning "how."
Pa'no ito gagawin?	How is this done?

The combination of two steps, contraction and abbreviation, makes it particularly difficult for beginners, especially in a conversation. Deciphering the contractions becomes easier if you keep the abbreviations in mind. Therefore, let's look at typical abbreviations next, shorten and written out:

Contracted	Written-Out	Example	English
ako'na	ako + na	Ako'na ang maglilinis.	I'll be the one to clean.

'di na	hindi + na	'Di na ako maglalaro.	I won't play anymore.
'to	ito + ay	'To ang gusto ko.	This is what I like.
ikaw ba	ikaw + ba	Ikaw ba ang tuma-wag?	Was it you who called?
s'ya	siya + ay	S'ya ang nanalo.	He/She is the winner.
kami'y	kami + ay	Kami'y pupunta na.	We are going now.
wala'na	wala + na	Wala'na ang pagkain.	The food is gone/no more.
anong	ano + ang	Anong oras na?	What time is it?
s'akin	sa + akin	S'akin lang 'to.	This is just mine.
sa'yo	sa + iyo	Para sa'yo 'to.	This is for you.

Lesson 38 - Politeness

Politeness is an integral part of Filipino culture, and it extends deeply into the way Tagalog is spoken. Using polite forms of speech not only shows respect but also fosters good relationships. This lesson will cover basic expressions and structures in Tagalog that convey politeness.

Basic Polite Words and Phrases

Tagalog Term or Phrase	Meaning and Usage
Po and Opo	Used to show respect, especially to someone older or in a higher position. "Opo" is a polite "yes."
Example: Opo, naintindihan ko po.	Yes, I understand.
Salamat and Maraming Salamat	"Salamat" means "thank you," and "maraming salamat" means "thank you very much."
Example: Salamat po sa tulong ninyo.	Thank you for your help.
Paumanhin and Patawad	"Paumanhin" for "excuse me" or minor apologies, "patawad" for serious apologies.
Example: Paumanhin po, pwede po	Excuse me, may I ask a question?

bang magtanong?	
Pakiusap	Means "please," used to politely make requests.
Example: Pakiusap, pakiabot po ng asin.	Please, pass the salt.
Making Requests Politely	Use "pakiusap" or structure sentences to sound less demanding for polite requests.
Example: Pwede po bang makahingi ng tubig?	May I please have some water?

Addressing Others Respectfully: Using titles and honorifics when addressing others is a common way to show respect.

Tagalog	English
Kuya and Ate	Used for older men and women, whether related or not.
Example: Kuya, magkano po ito?	Brother, how much is this?
Sir and Ma'am	Used in educational or formal settings for teachers, superiors, or customers.
Example: Sir, pwede po ba akong pumasok?	Sir, may I enter?

Let's look at some further useful samples:

Tagalog	English
Walang anuman.	You're welcome.
Pwede po bang magtanong?	May I ask something?
Makaramdam ng pagsisisi.	To feel sorry.
Pasensya na.	Sorry.
Pasensya na, nagsisisi ako.	Sorry, I regret it.
Pakiusap, pahiram ng bolpen.	Please, lend me a pen.
Salamat sa tulong.	Thanks for the help.

Exercise: Break down "Pakiusap, patawarin mo ako, nagkamali ako." word by word as exercise and for understanding and decode the meaning:

- Pakiusap:
- patawarin:
- mo:
- ako:
- nagkamali:
- ako:
- Meaning:

Solution:

- Pakiusap - "Please"
- patawarin - "forgive"
- mo - "you" (object marker)
- ako - "mc/I"
- nagkamali - "made a mistake"
- ako - "I/me"
- Meaning: "Please, forgive me, I made a mistake."

Lesson 39 - Like & Dislike

Understanding how to express preferences and dislikes is key to everyday conversations. These expressions can convey your feelings towards food, activities, people, and more. Let's dive into how to express liking, preferring, and disliking.

Expressing Like

Tagalog	**English**
Gusto	Like
Gusto ko ito.	I like this.
Nais ko.	I wish.

Expressing Prefer

Tagalog	English
Mas gusto	Prefer
Mas gusto ko ito.	I prefer this.

Expressing Prefer Over: To specify a preference between two things, use "kaysa" to mean "over" or "than."

Tagalog	English
kaysa	over / than
Mas gusto ko ang A kaysa B.	I prefer A over B.
Mas gusto ko ang tsokolate kaysa kendi.	I prefer chocolate over candy.
Mas gusto ko ang pagsasayaw kaysa pagkanta.	I prefer dancing over singing.

Expressing Dislike

Tagalog	English
Ayaw	"Dislike"
Ayaw ko ito.	I dislike this.

You can also use "hindi gusto" to mean "do not like."

Tagalog	English
Hindi ko gusto ang malamig na panahon.	I do not like cold weather.

Examples in Use

Tagalog	English
Gusto ko ng manga.	I like mangoes.
Mas gusto ko magbasa kaysa manood ng TV.	I prefer to read rather than watch TV.

Mas gusto ko ang kape kaysa sa tsaa sa umaga.	I prefer coffee over tea in the morning.
Ayaw ko sa ampalaya.	I dislike bitter gourd.
Hindi ko gusto ang magulo na lugar.	I do not like noisy places.

Exercise: Write down one or two Items that you like and dislike. You can use the dictionary at the end of this book to find useful words.

Like	**Dislike**

Sample Solution:

Like	**Dislike**
Gusto ko ang tubig. - I like water.	Ayaw ko ang tuyong isda. - I dislike dried fish.
Gusto ko ang musika. - I like music.	Ayaw ko ang bagyo. - I dislike the storm.

Lesson 40 - Asking for Clarification & Understanding

In this lesson, we take a look at how to ask for clarification or confirm understanding, especially when you're learning. There are simple phrases that you can use to ensure you've understood something correctly or to ask someone to repeat or explain something more clearly. Let's explore some of these expressions.

Tagalog	**English**
Ano?	What?

Ano po?	What? (Polite)
Ano ito?	What is this?
Naiintindihan ko.	I understand.
Ah, okay. Salamat po.	Ah, okay. Thank you.
Maliwanag po.	Clear.
Ano ang sabi mo?	What did you just say?
Pwede po bang ulitin?	Can you please repeat that?
Anong ibig sabihin ng [word]?	What does [word] mean?
Pwede po bang ulitin ang tanong?	Can you please repeat the question?
Pakiulit, po.	Please repeat.
Hindi ko po naiintindihan.	I didn't understand.
Hindi ko po naiintindihan.	I don't understand.
Nagsasalita ka ba ng Ingles?	Do you speak English?
Marunong ka bang mag-Ingles?	Can you speak English?
Dahan-dahan lang, po.	Slow down, please.
Ano sa Tagalog ang "market"?	What is "market" in Tagalog?
Ano sa Tagalog ang "brother"?	What is "brother" in Tagalog?
Ano sa Ingles ang "libro"?	What is "libro" in English?
Ipaliwanag	To explain
Ipaliwanag mo sa akin.	Explain it to me.

Here is a word by word breakdown of "Pwede po bang ulitin ang tanong?" as exercise and for better understanding:

- Pwede: Can
- po: please (polite particle)
- bang: ba + ng: particle used to form yes-no questions
- ulitin: to repeat
- ang: the
- tanong: question
- So, when put together, it means "Can you please repeat the question?"

Here's a breakdown of the Tagalog phrase "Nagsasalita ka ba ng Ingles?:

- "Nagsasalita" means "speak" or "speaking."
- "ka" is the pronoun for "you."
- "ba" is a question marker that turns the statement into a yes-or-no question.
- "ng" serves as a marker for nouns and objects (more on noun markers in a later lesson.

- “Ingles" means "English.

Examples in Use

Tagalog	English
A: At kaya mo bang gawin ito sa Lunes?	A: And can you do this on Monday?
B: Ano po? Pwede po bang ulitin?	B: What? Can you please repeat that?
A: Siguraduhin mong dalhin ang lahat ng kailangan mo.	A: Make sure to bring everything you need.
B: Naiintindihan ko. Salamat.	B: I understand. Thank you.

Exercise: Asking for Clarification & Understanding. Choose the correct Tagalog phrase for each English statement or question below. Match the number with the letter that corresponds to the correct answer.

English Statements/Questions:

#	English	Match/Letter
1.	What did you just say?	
2.	Slow down, please.	
3.	What is "market" in Tagalog?	
4.	I don’t understand.	
5.	Can you speak English?	
6.	What is this?	
7.	What is “brother” in Tagalog?	
8.	Please repeat.	

Tagalog Phrases:

Letter	Tagalog
A.	Ano sa Tagalog ang “market”?
B.	Ano ito?
C.	Hindi ko po naiintindihan.
D.	Pwede po bang ulitin ang tanong?
E.	Marunong ka bang mag-Ingles?

F.	Dahan-dahan lang, po.
G.	Ano ang sabi mo?
I.	Ano sa Tagalog ang "brother"?

Solution: Here are the solutions for the exercise.

#	Letter	English	Tagalog
1.	G.	What did you just say?	Ano ang sabi mo?
2.	F.	Slow down, please.	Dahan-dahan lang, po.
3.	A.	What is "market" in Tagalog?	Ano sa Tagalog ang "market"?
4.	C.	I don't understand.	Hindi ko po naiintindihan.
5.	E.	Can you speak English?	Marunong ka bang mag-Ingles?
6.	B.	What is this?	Ano ito?
7.	I.	What is "brother" in Tagalog?	Ano sa Tagalog ang "brother"?
8.	H.	Please repeat.	Pakiulit, po.

Lesson 41 - Singular & Plural

The plural is formed with the plural marker mga. Pronounced as ma-nga, mga is placed directly before the word to form the plural.

Here are some examples:

Tagalog (Singular)	English (Singular)	Tagalog (Plural)	English (Plural)
Tao	Person	Mga tao	People
Bahay	House	Mga bahay	Houses
Kotse	Car	Mga kotse	Cars
Libro	Book	Mga libro	Books

Plural samples:

Tagalog	English
Mga bata sa eskwelahan.	Children at school.
Mga prutas sa mesa.	Fruits on the table.
Mga saging sa basket.	Bananas in the basket.
Mga manok sa hardin.	Chickens in the garden.
Mga bulaklak sa hardin.	Flowers in the garden.
Mga libro sa estante.	Books on the shelf.
Mga isda sa palengke.	Fish at the market.
Mga puno sa burol.	Trees on the hill.
Mga pera sa pitaka.	Money in the wallet.
Mga sapatos sa ilalim ng kama.	Shoes under the bed.

Now, let's begin with learning complete phrases.

Tagalog	English
Mayroon akong aso.	I have a dog.
Mayroon akong mga aso.	I have dogs.
Ang bahay ay malaki.	The house is big.
Ang mga bahay ay malalaki.	The houses are big.
Nakita mo ba ang kotse?	Did you see the car?
Nakita mo ba ang mga kotse?	Did you see the cars?

Exercise: Break down each phrase word by word and provide the meaning:

- Breakdown: Naglalaro ang mga bata sa lugar.
  Naglalaro -
  ang -
  mga -
  bata -
  sa -
  lugar -
  Meaning:

- Breakdown: Nagluto kami ng mga pagkain.
  Nagluto -
  kami -

ng -
mga -
pagkain -
Meaning:

- Breakdown: Nagha-hike kami sa mga burol / bundok.
  Nagha-hike -
  kami -
  sa -
  mga -
  bundok -
  Meaning:

- Breakdown: Naglinis sila ng kanilang mga kwarto.
  Naglinis -
  sila -
  ng -
  kanilang -
  mga kwarto -
  Meaning:

- Breakdown: Nagturo sila ng mga leksyon.
  Nagturo -
  sila -
  ng -
  mga leksyon -
  Meaning:

Solution:

- Breakdown: Naglalaro ang mga bata sa lugar.
  Naglalaro - playing
  ang - the (subject marker)
  mga - (plural marker)
  bata - children
  sa - in
  lugar - place

Meaning: The children are playing in the place.

- Breakdown: Nagluto kami ng mga pagkain.
  Nagluto - cooked
  kami - we
  ng - of (object marker)
  mga - plural marker
  pagkain - meals
  Meaning: We cooked meals.

- Breakdown: Nagha-hike kami sa mga bundok.
  Nagha-hike - hiking
  kami - we
  sa - in/on
  mga - (plural marker)
  bundok - mountains
  Meaning: We are hiking the mountains.

- Breakdown: Naglinis sila ng kanilang mga kwarto.
  Naglinis - cleaned
  sila - they
  ng - their (object marker)
  kanilang - their
  mga kwarto - rooms
  Meaning: They cleaned their rooms.

- Breakdown: Nagturo sila ng mga leksyon.
  Nagturo - taught
  sila - they
  ng - of (object marker)
  mga leksyon - lessons
  Meaning: They taught lessons.

Lesson 42 - Linker

Linkers (or ligatures) are used to connect words, especially when an adjective, verb, or pronoun modifies a noun, or to link adverbs to adjectives.

Linkers in Tagalog serve to connect:

- Adjectives to the nouns they describe
- Verbs to their direct objects
- Enumerations or lists of words
- Phrases or clauses

The primary linkers are "na" and "ng."

Linker	Description
Na	Used to describe nouns or add details. It connects adjectives to nouns, as in "Malaking bahay" (big house) or structures a description, like "Bahay na malaki" (a house that is big). It also links adverbs to verbs, e.g., "Mabilis na tumakbo" (ran fast), integrates additional information such as "Gusto kong uminom ng kape na may gatas" (I like to drink coffee with milk), and is used in lists, like "Nagdala siya ng mansanas, saging, at ubas na prutas para sa piknik" (He brought apples, bananas, and grapes for the picnic).
Ng	Marks the object of an action, indicating what is being acted upon, as in "Kumain ng mansanas" (ate an apple). It shows ownership or a relationship between two things, such as "Libro ng guro" (the teacher's book), links a noun to a number or quantity, like "Tatlong tasa ng bigas" (three cups of rice), and connects two nouns where the second describes the first, for example, "Kulay ng rosas" (rose-colored).

In short, use "na" to add descriptions or details to nouns and "ng" for showing possession, marking objects, or dealing with numbers, along with the examples provided.

Here are several phrases showcasing the usage of "na" and "ng", along with their English translations:

Tagalog	English
Masayang bata	Happy child
Masayang bata na naglalaro.	A happy child playing.
Malinis na kwarto	Clean room
Malinis na kwarto na may bintana.	A clean room with a window.
Magandang bulaklak	Beautiful flower
Magandang bulaklak na kulay pula.	A beautiful red flower.
Mabait na guro	Kind teacher
Mabait na guro na mahilig magturo.	A kind teacher who loves to teach.
Mahabang daan	Long road
Mahabang daan na bako-bako.	A long, bumpy road.
Kulay ng bahay	Color of the house
Kulay ng bahay ay asul.	The color of the house is blue.
Pinto ng kotse	Car door
Pinto ng kotse na nakabukas.	The car door that is open.
Larawan ng pamilya	Family picture
Larawan ng pamilya na nakasabit sa dingding.	A family picture hanging on the wall.
Takip ng bote	Bottle cap
Takip ng bote na nawawala.	The bottle cap that is missing.
Libro ng estudyante	The student's book
Libro ng estudyante na nasa mesa.	The student's book on the table.

Lesson 43 - Use of Adjectives

Adjectives (pang-uri) serve to describe nouns (pangngalan) by providing information about their qualities, quantities, or states. This lesson will explore how to use adjectives effectively, focusing on their forms, placement, and the specific linkers used to connect them with nouns.

Types of Adjectives:

Type of Adjective	Description & Examples
Descriptive Adjectives (Pang-uring	Describe the appearance, condition, or other qualities of nouns.

Panlarawan)	Examples: "maganda" (beautiful), "matalino" (intelligent), "malaki" (big).
Quantitative Adjectives (Pang-uring Pamilang)	Indicate the number or amount of nouns. They can be specific ("isa" [one], "dalawa" [two], "tatlo" [three]) or indefinite ("ilang" [some], "marami" [many]).
Demonstrative Adjectives (Pang-uring Panturo)	Point out specific nouns. These include "ito" (this), "iyan" (that, near listener), and "iyon" (that, over there).

Placement of Adjectives: Adjectives typically precede the nouns they describe.

- Example: "Mahabang pila" (Long line)

However, for emphasis or stylistic purposes, adjectives can also follow the noun, especially when linked with "ay" to form a predicate.

- Example: "Ang pila ay mahaba." (The line is long.)

Linking Adjectives to Nouns: Na and Ng: These linkers are used to connect adjectives with the nouns they modify.

Na is also used to link multiple adjectives or an adjective phrase to a noun. Multiple adjectives describing a noun are connected by the conjunction "at," which means "and" in English. The use of "at" to connect adjectives, followed by "na" to link these descriptive phrases to the noun, is a common and effective way to add detail in sentences.

- Maganda at matalino na bata.
  A beautiful and intelligent child.
  Here, "maganda" (beautiful) and "matalino" (intelligent) are connected by "at" to collectively describe "bata" (child).

- Malaki at lumang bahay na gawa sa kahoy.
  A big and old house made of wood.

"Malaki" (big) and "lumang" (old) are adjectives linked by "at" before "bahay" (house), followed by the phrase "na gawa sa kahoy" (made of wood) for further description.

- Masarap na prutas na matamis at makatas.
  Delicious fruit that is sweet and juicy.
  "Masarap" (delicious) initially describes "prutas" (fruit), and "matamis" (sweet) and "makatas" (juicy) are linked by "at" for additional details, connected back to "prutas" with "na."

- Mabilis at maingay na kotse.
  A fast and noisy car.
  "Mabilis" (fast) and "maingay" (noisy) are connected by "at" to describe "kotse" (car).

- Malinaw na tubig na malamig at sariwa.
  Clear water that is cold and fresh.
  "Malinaw" (clear) qualifies "tubig" (water), and "malamig" (cold) and "sariwa" (fresh) are connected by "at," further describing "tubig" with the use of "na."

Practice Time: Try to describe something around you using adjectives. For example, if you see a book, you might say, "Makapal na libro" (Thick book).

Here's a list of nouns commonly found in a room, along with adjectives that can be used to describe them.

Nouns and Descriptive Adjectives

Libro (Book)
- Makapal (Thick)
- Manipis (Thin)
- Luma (Old)
- Bago (New)

Mesa (Table)
- Mataas (Tall/High)

- Maikli (Short)
- Malinis (Clean)
- Madumi (Dirty)

Upuan (Chair)
- Komportable (Comfortable)
- Matigas (Hard)
- Malambot (Soft)

Kama (Bed)
- Malaki (Big/Large)
- Maliit (Small)
- Maayos (Neat)
- Magulo (Messy)

Ilaw (Light)
- Maliwanag (Bright)
- Madilim (Dim)

Kurtina (Curtain)
- Makulay (Colorful)
- Maputla (Pale)
- Mahaba (Long)
- Maikli (Short)

Salamin (Mirror)
- Malinaw (Clear)
- Malabo (Blurry)

Larawan (Picture)
- Maganda (Beautiful)
- Nakakatawa (Funny)
- Inspirasyonal (Inspirational)

Almario (Closet)
- Punong-puno (Full)
- Walang laman (Empty)

Telebisyon (Television)

- Malaki (Big)
- Lumang modelo (Old model)
- Moderno (Modern)

Pader (Wall)

- Mataas (High/Tall)
- Kulay-abo (Gray)
- Pininturahan (Painted)

Sahig (Floor)

- Makinis (Smooth)
- Magaspang (Rough)
- Malamig (Cold)

Kisame (Ceiling)

- Mababa (Low)
- Mataas (High)

Pinto (Door)

- Malaki (Big)
- Maliit (Small)
- Nakasarado (Closed)
- Nakabukas (Open)

Bintana (Window)

- Malinis (Clean)
- Madumi (Dirty)
- Malaki (Large)

Carpet (Carpet)

- Makapal (Thick)
- Manipis (Thin)
- Mabalahibo (Furry)

Lampara (Lamp)

- Maliwanag (Bright)
- Madilim (Dim)

- Estilong vintage (Vintage-style)

Orasan (Clock)
- Antigo (Antique)
- Digital (Digital)
- Tumpak (Accurate)

Practice Sentences: Now, let's combine these nouns and adjectives to form descriptive sentences:

Tagalog	**English**
Malaki at moderno na telebisyon.	A big and modern television.
Makulay na kurtina sa bintana.	Colorful curtains on the window.
Lumang larawan sa dingding.	An old picture on the wall.
Mataas na pader na kulay-abo.	A high gray wall.
Makinis na sahig sa kwarto.	A smooth floor in the room.
Malaki at nakasaradong pinto.	A big and closed door.
Maliwanag na lampara sa tabi ng kama.	A bright lamp beside the bed.
Malinis na bintana na may makulay na kurtina.	A clean window with colorful curtains.
Antigong orasan sa ibabaw ng mesa.	An antique clock on top of the table.

Do the same for three items in your room.

Tagalog	**English**

Compact Grammar Guide

In this section, we'll explore a concise overview of Tagalog grammar. Tagalog, like any language, has its unique features and grammatical structures that set it apart from English. Understanding these basics is crucial for grasping the language's flow and constructing sentences accurately.

Tagalog is a language that utilizes a **focus system**, often referred to as voice or trigger system. I prefer the term "focus system" because it most accurately describes how the language operates. When I began learning Cebuano and Tagalog, I was initially puzzled by the different sets of personal pronouns and the varied ways verbs in the same tense were conjugated. It didn't make sense to me until I delved deeper into the grammar, particularly the concept of focus.

The **focus is chosen by the speaker** initiating the conversation and represents the main topic or the element around which the conversation revolves. This focus can be on the actor of an action, known as Actor Focus, or it can be on the object of the sentence, which could be the items or location the action is directed towards or impacted by.

The choice of focus determines which set of pronouns to use, which noun markers are appropriate, and which affixes should be applied in verb conjugations. Therefore, understanding the focus system is crucial for forming grammatically correct sentences. In this grammar section, we will explore the focus system and other essential key areas that are vital for forming grammatically correct sentences.

Case Markers

Case markers are short words or particles that indicate the grammatical function of a noun in a sentence. In most structured sentences, especially those that convey clear relationships between the verb and its subjects or objects, nouns typically appear with case markers to clarify their grammatical role.

Si marker: A name cannot stand alone; it requires a case marker, and the case marker for names is Si. It is used before a singular proper noun (name of a person) or title to indicate the subject of the sentence. For example:

- Matangkad si Paul. - Paul is tall.
- Darating na si Doktor Paul. - Doctor Paul is coming soon.

Sina marker: Used before plural proper nouns (names of people) to indicate the subject of the sentence. Example:

- Sina Paul at Lisa ay magkaibigan. Paul and Lisa are friends.
- Pupunta sina Paul at Lisa sa beach. - Paul and Lisa are going to the beach.

Ang marker: Marks the focus of the sentence, which can be a person, place, or thing. It is used with both singular and plural nouns. Example:

- Ang libro ay nasa mesa. - The book is on the table.

Ng marker: Indicates the possessive case or the object of the action. It's also used after verbs to denote the object or after adjectives to indicate what the adjective is describing. Example:

- Bumili ako ng tinapay. - I bought bread.

Nang marker: Used with adverbs or to connect adjectives or verbs, similar to "when" or "so that" in English. It's also used in place of "ng" in certain expressions to denote manner or cause. Example:

- Umalis siya nang maaga. - He/She left early.

Ni marker: Indicates possession or association with a singular proper noun. Example:

- Ang libro ni Juan. - The book of Juan. / Juan's book.

Nina marker: Similar to "ni" but used for plural proper nouns to indicate possession or association. Example:

- Ang bahay nina Ana at Pedro. - The house of Ana and Pedro.

Sa marker: Denotes direction, location, or recipient, and is used for both specific and nonspecific nouns. Example:

- Pumunta ako sa paaralan. - I went to school.

To summarize, nouns typically do not stand alone; they are accompanied by markers that indicate the noun's role within a sentence. For proper names, the markers are Si (for singular) and Sina (for plural). Ang is used to mark the subject or focus of the sentence. Ng marks the direct object of an action, showing what is being acted upon. Ni (for singular) and Nina (for plural) are used to indicate the possessor or the doer of the action when in an object-focused sentence. Lastly, Sa is utilized for nonspecific locations, directions, or beneficiaries, providing context to the action or state being described.

Focus and Non-Focus Markers

The markers we just learned about are also important for the focus system. They either put a focus or a non-focus on the words they are referring to.

Focus Markers:

Focus-Marker	Description
Ang	Used for the nominative case, marking the subject or focus of the sentence when it is the actor or topic being discussed or described. This marker indicates the entity performing the action (in Actor Focus constructions) or being emphasized in the sentence (focus marker).
Si	Specifically used for singular proper nouns (names of individuals) in the nominative case as the subject or focus of the sentence. This marker is used when referring to a single person who is the subject of the sentence or the entity performing the action.
Sina	Specifically used for plural proper nouns (names of multiple people) in the nominative case as the subject or focus of the sentence. This marker is used when multiple people are the subjects of the sentence or the entities performing the action.

Non-Focus Markers:

Non-Focus-Marker	Description
Ng	Used as a possessive marker or to link the object of the verb in a sentence, marking the direct object of the action or possession. For example, "Kumain ng mansanas" (Ate an apple). It is also used in Object Focus sentences to mark the

	actor performing the action, which is not the focus.
Nang	Functions primarily with adverbs or in certain verbal constructions to link verbs and adverbs or to describe how an action is performed, e.g., "Tumakbo nang mabilis" (Ran quickly). It is not a direct equivalent of "ng" but serves to enhance the description of actions.
Ni/Nina	Used for proper nouns to indicate possession, relationship, or the actor in Object Focus sentences. "Ni" is used for singular and "Nina" for plural. For example, "Libro ni Maria" (Maria's book) and "Mga libro nina Jose at Maria" (The books of Jose and Maria).
Sa	Indicates location, direction, recipient, or beneficiary, providing context for the action but not serving as the focus of the sentence. For example, "Pumunta sa bahay" (Went to the house).

These non-focus markers provide essential grammatical information about the roles of various nouns in a sentence, but they do not mark the sentence's main focus. Instead, they help to clarify who is doing what to whom, where, and for whom, in support of the focus established by the focus markers. We will take a closer look at their usage when we dive into Actor Focus and Object Focus.

The Focus Cases

The focus system, also known as the trigger system, indicates what part of the sentence is being emphasized or what role the focus element plays in the action. Here are the primary focus cases:

1. Actor Focus (AF)
Actor Focus highlights the doer of the action. The verb is conjugated to reflect that the subject (actor/doer) of the sentence is performing the action. Markers for this focus include "ang" for the actor and the Actor Focus affixes for vrb conjugation.

Tagalog	English
Kumakain ang bata.	The child is eating.

2. Object Focus (OF)

Object Focus emphasizes the object receiving the action. This focus is used when the object of the action is the main topic of the sentence. The "ng" marker is used for the actor, and the verb takes the Object Focus affixes for verb conjugation. Example:

Tagalog	English
Kinakain ng bata ang mansanas.	The apple is being eaten by the child.

3. Location Focus (LF)

Location Focus puts emphasis on the location where the action takes place. Verbs in sentences with location focus often take the "pinag-" prefix in the present tense. Example:

Tagalog	English
Pinaglalaruan ng bata ang parke.	The park is where the child plays.

4. Benefactive Focus (BF)

Benefactive Focus highlights the beneficiary or for whom the action is done. This focus uses the "para kay/para sa" construction to indicate the beneficiary. Example:

Tagalog	English
Nagluluto ang nanay para sa pamilya.	The mother is cooking for the family.

5. Instrumental Focus (IF)

Instrumental Focus emphasizes the instrument or means by which the action is carried out. This can include tools, methods, or ways the action is performed. Example:

Tagalog	English
Ipinampupunas ng bata ang basahan.	The rag is being used by the child to wipe.

6. Cause Focus (CF)
Cause Focus is less commonly discussed but involves emphasizing the reason or cause behind an action. Example:

Tagalog	**English**
Ikinatuwa ng magulang ang pag-graduate ng anak.	The parents were made happy by the child's graduation.

In broader terms, Object Focus, Location Focus, Benefactive Focus, Instrumental Focus, and Cause Focus can be collectively referred to under the umbrella of Object Focus in Tagalog grammar discussions. This categorization stems from the fact that, in comparison to Actor Focus (where the focus is on the doer of the action), these other focuses shift the emphasis away from the actor and towards some element of the sentence other than the doer—whether it be the object receiving the action, the location of the action, the beneficiary of the action, the instrument used to perform the action, or the cause or reason for the action.

This broader grouping into Actor Focus and Object Focus helps simplify the understanding of Tagalog's complex verbal system, especially for learners. However, recognizing the distinct types of focuses within what might be broadly called "Object Focus" is crucial for deeper proficiency and accuracy in language use, as each type of focus involves its specific verb conjugations, markers, and sentence structures. Therefore, in this course, we will mainly distinguish between the two main groups referred to as Actor Focus and Object Focus.

Focus in Sentences

Tagalog sentences often center around the concept of "focus." This determines which part of the sentence is being emphasized, such as the doer of an action (actor-focus) or the receiver of an action (object-focus). The focus affects how verbs are conjugated, which markers are used, and the choice of personal pronouns.
When using the Active Voice (Actor-Focus), the emphasis is placed on the individuals performing actions. Conversely, with the Object-Focus (Passive), emphasis shifts to the object being acted upon. The examples below illustrate how

the focus is determined by what or who is being discussed:

- Active → Actor Focus (AF)
  Example: **The man** opens a window.

- Passive → Object Focus (OF)
  Example: **The window** is opened by the man.

The choice between Actor Focus (AF) and Object Focus (OF) is made by the speaker, depending on what the main subject of the conversation is meant to be — essentially, what or who the conversation is really about.

Examples:

Focus	Example	Explanation
AF	The man opens a window.	The main topic/focus of the conversation is the man.)
OF	The window is opened by the man.	The main topic/focus of the conversation is the window.

This distinction between AF and OF allows speakers to highlight different elements of a sentence, guiding the listener's attention to what the speaker deems most important.

Personal Pronouns in Actor Focus

The personal pronouns change form depending on the focus. In Actor Focus (AF), the personal pronouns are used that we learned at the beginning of this course. Actor Focus highlights the doer of the action, and the pronouns used must reflect this focus. Let's explore the Actor Focus personal pronouns:

Tagalog	English
Ako	I
Ikaw / Ka	You
Siya	He/She
Kami	We (exclusive)
Tayo	We (inclusive)

Kayo	You (plural)
Sila	They

Actor Focus Markers

The Actor Focus (AF) construction emphasizes the doer of the action. Understanding the use of markers in AF sentences is crucial for correctly conveying who is performing the action. Let's dive into the markers that are commonly used in Actor Focus sentences.

The "Ang" Marker: The "ang" marker is used to indicate the subject or actor of the sentence in Actor Focus constructions. It precedes the noun or pronoun that is performing the action. Example:

Tagalog	English
Ang bata ay tumatakbo.	The child is running.

The "Si/Sina" Marker: For proper nouns, such as names of people, "si" (for singular) and "sina" (for plural) are used to mark the actor in AF sentences.

Singular/Plural	Tagalog	English
Singular	Kumakain si Juan.	Juan is eating.
Plural	Naglalaro sina Juan at Maria.	Juan and Maria are playing.

The "Ng" Marker: In Actor-Focus sentences, the 'Ng' marker indicates the object of the sentence as Non-Focus.

Tagalog	English
Kumain ng mansanas si Lisa.	Lisa ate an apple.

In this sentence, "ng mansanas" (an apple) is the object marked by "ng", showing it's not the focus. The focus is on Lisa, who performed the action, indicated by "si Lisa".

Tenses and Expressing Time of Actions

Expressing time and the nature of actions (whether completed, ongoing, or intended to happen) doesn't rely on tenses in the same way as in English (past, present future). Instead, Tagalog uses aspects to convey these ideas. Let's dive into an easy guide to understand these concepts.

Aspects: Tagalog verbs are primarily concerned with aspect — the state of completion of an action. There are three main aspects:

1. Completed Aspect: This shows that the action has been finished.

Tagalog	English
Nagluto ng adobo ang nanay kahapon.	The mother cooked adobo yesterday.

This sentence indicates a completed action where the subject (the mother) has finished cooking.

2. Started, but not completed (Ongoing Aspect): This indicates that the action is currently happening.

Tagalog	English Translation
Nagluluto ang nanay ng adobo ngayon.	The mother is cooking adobo now.

This sentence shows an ongoing action where the subject is in the process of cooking.

3. Planned, not started yet (Contemplated/Future Aspect): This indicates that the action will occur or is planned for the future.

Tagalog	English
Magluluto ang nanay ng adobo bukas.	The mother will cook adobo tomorrow.

Here, the action is planned for the future, indicating the mother's intention to cook.

Command: The command aspect is used to give orders or make requests. Commands in Tagalog are straightforward and use the imperative form of the verb.

Tagalog	English
Lutohin mo ang adobo.	Cook the adobo.

Note: In this course, the aspects and tenses will be referred to as Completed, Ongoing, Future.

Aspect / Time	Alternative Nomenclature	Description
Completed	Perfective, Past, „Done“	Describes actions that are completed or finished.
Ongoing	Imperfective, Present, in Process, currently happening, not completed.	Describes actions that are currently in progress.
Future	Contemplative, will happen, planned. not started.	Describes actions that are expected to occur in the future.

Actor Focus Verb Groups

Conjugating verbs in Tagalog varies across different verb groups. The verb groups associated with Actor Focus are:

Verb Group	Description
Mag- Verbs	Used in Actor Focus to indicate actions initiated by the subject.
Ma- Verbs	Ma- verbs often express a state or condition and can sometimes describe potential or ability.
Um- Verbs	Another group that falls under Actor Focus, showing actions performed directly by the subject.
-Um-/-Mag- Hybrid Verbs	These can be used in Actor Focus depending on the aspect and the context of the sentence.

Verb Conjugation in Actor Focus

In Tagalog, verbs are conjugated according to the focus, the verb group and the aspect of the action—whether it's completed, ongoing, future—or to form commands. When the sentence is in Actor Focus, the verb conjugation highlights who is doing the action. Let's break down how to conjugate verbs in Actor Focus for different aspects and commands.

Mag-Verbs

This section focuses on the verb conjugations that uses the affix "Mag-."

1. Completed Aspect

The completed aspect of Mag-verbs is formed by using the prefix "Nag-" attached directly to the root of the verb. This form indicates that the action has been completed. Example:

- Root: Luto (cook)
- Completed Form: Nag + Luto = Nagluto (cooked)

2. Ongoing Aspect

For the ongoing aspect, "Nag-" is used along with a repetition of the first syllable of the root verb. This structure suggests that the action is currently happening. Example:

- Root: Luto (cook)
- Ongoing Form: Nag + Lu + Luto = Nagluluto (cooking)

3. Future Aspect

The future tense of Mag-verbs employs the prefix "Mag-" combined with the repetition of the first syllable of the root verb. This indicates an action that will occur in the future. Example:

- Root: Luto (cook)
- Future Form: Mag + Lu + Luto = Magluluto (will cook)

Table Summary of Mag-Verb Aspects:

Tense/Aspect	Root	Completed (Past)	Ongoing (Present)	Future
Affixes	-	Nag-	Nag + first	Mag + first

			syllable	syllable
Sample Verb	Luto	Nagluto	Nagluluto	Magluluto
Sample Phrase	-	Nagluto ako.	Nagluluto ako.	Magluluto ako.
English Meaning	-	I cooked.	I am cooking.	I will cook.

Ma-Verbs

Ma-verbs in Tagalog share a similar conjugation pattern with Mag-verbs, but they utilize different prefixes to indicate the aspect of the verb. The prefixes help denote whether the action has been completed, is ongoing, or will happen in the future.

1. Completed Aspect

For Ma-verbs, the completed aspect is formed by adding the prefix "Na-" to the root of the verb. This indicates that the action is finished or has already occurred. Example:

- Root: Tulog (sleep)
- Completed Form: Na + Tulog = Natulog (slept)

2. Ongoing Aspect

The ongoing aspect for Ma-verbs is created by using "Na-" followed by the repetition of the first syllable of the root verb. This shows that the action is currently in progress. Example:

- Root: Tulog (sleep)
- Ongoing Form: Na + Tu + Tulog = Natutulog (sleeping)

3. Future Aspect

To express the future tense of Ma-verbs, the prefix "Ma-" is used along with the repetition of the first syllable of the root verb. This form predicts that the action will take place. Example:

- Root: Tulog (sleep)
- Future Form: Ma + Tu + Tulog = Matutulog (will sleep)

Table Summary of Ma-Verb Aspects:

Tense/Aspect	Root	Completed (Past)	Ongoing (Present)	Future
Affixes	-	Na-	Na + first syllable	Ma + first syllable
Sample Verb	Tulog	Natulog	Natutulog	Matutulog
Sample Phrase	-	Natulog ako.	Natutulog ako.	Matutulog ako.
English Meaning	-	I slept.	I am sleeping.	I will sleep.

Um-Verbs

Um-verbs are a fundamental category in Tagalog verb conjugation, demonstrating distinctive patterns across different tenses or aspects. Using the root verb "kain" (to eat), let's explore how Um-verbs are conjugated in completed, ongoing, and future aspects.

1. Completed Aspect

The completed aspect of Um-verbs is formed by inserting the infix "-um-" immediately after the initial consonant of the root verb. For the verb "kain," the conjugation results in Kumain. Example:

- Root: Kain (eat)
- Completed Form: Kumain = Kumain (ate)

2. Ongoing Aspect

In the ongoing aspect, you start with the first syllable of the root verb as a prefix, followed by inserting the infix "-um-" after the first consonant of the root. For "kain," the ongoing form is Kumakain. Example:

- Root: Kain (eat)
- Ongoing Form: Ka + kain = kakain → Adding infix -um- after the first consonant: k + um + a + kain = Kumakain (eating)

3. Future Aspect

The future tense of Um-verbs is created by doubling the first syllable as a prefix to the root verb. Thus, "kain" becomes Kakain. Example:

- Root: Kain (eat)

- Future Form: Ka + kain = kakain = Kakain (will eat)

Table Summary of Um-Verb Aspects:

Tense/Aspect	Root	Completed (Past)	Ongoing (Present)	Future
Affixes	-	-um- inserted after first consonant	First syllable as prefix + um inserted as infix	First syllable as prefix
Sample Verb	Kain	Kumain	Kumakain	Kakain
Sample Phrase	-	Kumain ako.	Kumakain ako.	Kakain ako.
English Meaning	-	I ate.	I am eating.	I will eat.

Actor Focus Sentences

Now we put it all together for Actor Focus. A common sentence structure in Tagalog is Verb-Subject-Object. We will use this sentence structure as a basis and then apply the proper affixes for the verb conjugation, the Actor Focus personal pronouns, the Non-Focus marker for the Object, and the Object.

Structure:

<table>
<tr><th>Aspect</th><th>Verb Groub</th><th>Prefix</th><th>Root</th><th>Subject</th><th>ng-Marker</th><th>Object</th></tr>
<tr><td>Completed:</td><td rowspan="3">mag-verb</td><td>nag-</td><td rowspan="3">Verb root</td><td rowspan="3">Si + Name

Ako, Ikaw, Siya, Kami, Tayo, Kayo, Sila</td><td rowspan="3">ng</td><td rowspan="3">Object</td></tr>
<tr><td>Ongoing:</td><td>nag + first syllable</td></tr>
<tr><td>Future</td><td>mag + first syllable</td></tr>
</table>

Let's use this framework to make sample sentences:

Aspect	Prefix	Root	Subject	ng-Marker	Object
Com-pleted	Nag-	luto	si Lisa	ng	adobo.
Literal	cooked		Lisa	-	adobo.
Phrase:	Nagluto si Lisa ng adobo.				
Meaning	Lisa cooked adobo.				

Aspect	Prefix	Root	Subject	ng-Marker	Object
Com-pleted	Nag-	luto	ako	ng	adobo.
Literal	cooked		I	-	adobo.
Phrase:	Nagluto ako ng adobo.				
Meaning	I cooked adobo.				

Aspect	Prefix	Root	Subject	ng-Marker	Object
Ongoing	Nag-lu-	luto	si Lisa	ng	adobo.
Literal	is cooking		Lisa	-	adobo.
Phrase:	Nagluluto si Lisa ng adobo.				
Meaning	Lisa is cooking adobo.				

Aspect	Prefix	Root	Subject	ng-Marker	Object
Ongoing	Nag-lu-	luto	ako	ng	adobo.
Literal	is cooking		I	-	adobo.
Phrase:	Nagluluto ako ng adobo.				
Meaning	I am cooking adobo.				

Aspect	Prefix	Root	Subject	ng-Marker	Object
Future	Mag-lu-	luto	si Lisa	ng	adobo.
Literal	will cook		Lisa	-	adobo.
Phrase:	Magluluto si Lisa ng adobo				
Meaning	Lisa will cook adobo.				

Aspect	Prefix	Root	Subject	ng-Marker	Object
Future	Mag-lu-	luto	ako	ng	adobo.
Literal	will cook		I	-	adobo.
Phrase:	Magluluto ako ng adobo				
Meaning	I will cook adobo.				

Exercise: Transform the following phrase into the ongoing and future aspects.

Aspect	Tagalog	English
Completed	Nagbasa siya ng libro.	He/She read a book.
Ongoing		
Future		

Aspect	Tagalog	English
Completed	Bumili kami ng isda.	We bought fish.
Ongoing		
Future		

Aspect	Tagalog	English
Completed	Nagluto ako ng mga pancake.	I cooked pancakes.
Ongoing		
Future		

Solution:

Aspect	Tagalog	English
Completed	Nagbasa siya ng libro.	He/She read a book.
Ongoing	Nagbabasa siya ng libro.	He/She is reading a book.
Future	Magbabasa siya ng libro.	He/She will read a book

Aspect	Tagalog	English
Completed	Bumili kami ng isda.	We bought fish.
Ongoing	Nagbibilí kami ng isda.	We are buying fish.
Future	Bibili kami ng isda.	We will buy fish.

Aspect	Tagalog	English
Completed	Nagluto ako ng mga pancake.	I cooked pancakes.
Ongoing	Nagluluto ako ng mga pan-cake.	I am cooking pancakes.
Future	Magluluto ako ng mga pan-cake.	I will cook pancakes.

Personal Pronouns in Object Focus

Personal pronouns have unique forms depending on the grammatical focus of the sentence. In Object Focus they differ from those used in the Actor Focus constructions. Here is the list of the Object Focus personal pronouns:

Tagalog	English
ko	I, by me
mo	You, by you
niya	He, she, by him/her
namin	We, by us (exclusive)
natin	We, by us (inclusive)
ninyo	You, by you (plural)
nila	They, by them

The reason why we say "by me" (ko) instead of just "I" in certain sentences is because of how the language focuses on different parts of a sentence. When we use "ko," "mo," "niya," in sentences, the focus is usually on whom or what receives the action rather than who performs it. This concept is known as "fo-cus" in the sentence. In English, this is often shown by using "by" and changing the word order. For example, "The song was sung by me" puts emphasis on "The song," not on "me." In contrast, saying "I sang the song" shifts the focus to the doer. This distinction is crucial in understanding how focus works differently in languages like Tagalog compared to English. "Kinain ko ang manok." can be translated as both "I ate the chicken" and "The chicken was eaten by me." However, it's important to note that in Object Focus, the emphasis is on "the chicken." In English, this often results in a passive voice translation, making Object Focus personal pronouns appear as "by me," "by you," etc. Ultimately, the key is the focus and what the speaker intends to emphasize. In Object Focus, it's the receiver of the action that's spotlighted.

Object Focus Markers

Object-Focus markers indicate that the focus of the sentence is on the object of the action rather than who is performing the action. These markers include "ang" for singular objects and "ang mga" for plural objects.

"Ang" Marker: Used to mark the object or entity directly affected by the action in a sentence. Example:

Tagalog	English
Hinawakan ang bola ni Juan.	The ball was held by Juan.

In this sentence, "ang bola" (the ball) is the focus of the action, hence the use of "ang".

"Ang mga" Marker for Plurals: When the object of the action is plural, "ang mga" is used to denote that multiple entities are being acted upon. Example:

Tagalog	English
Binasa ang mga libro ni Ana.	The books were read by Ana.

"Ang mga libro" (the books) signifies that several books are the focus of Ana's action of reading.

In Object-Focus sentences the roles of markers shift slightly to emphasize the object receiving the action. However, elements other than the main focus (the object of the action) still require marking to clarify their roles within the sentence. Here are the markers used for non-focus elements in Object-Focus constructions:

"Ng" or "Nina/Ni": These markers are used for the actor (the one performing the action) in Object-Focus sentences, indicating who is carrying out the action. Example:

Tagalog	English
Kinain ng aso ang buto.	The bone was eaten by the dog.

Here, "ng aso" indicates the dog as the actor who performed the action, which is non-focus in this sentence.

"Sa": "Sa" is used for indicating indirect objects, locations, directions, or beneficiaries that are not the main focus of the action. Example:

Tagalog	English
Ibinigay ang libro sa estudyante.	The book was given to the student.

In this sentence, "sa estudyante" (to the student) marks the beneficiary of the action, a non-focus element.

In Object-Focus sentences, while the object receiving the action is marked by "ang" or "ang mga" (for plural objects) to indicate it as the focus, "ng" or "ni/nina" for proper names and "sa" serve to mark actors and other elements involved in the action as non-focus. These markers help to structure the sentence clearly, ensuring that the focus remains on the object of the action.

Object Focus Verb Groups

The overall Object Focus verb groups can be separated by the specific Object Focus (OF), Locative Focus (LF), and Benefactive Focus. Each of these subgroups has their own verb groups and specific affixes for conjugations. Let's take a look at them.

Focus	Verb Group	Description

Object Focus (OF)	-In Verbs	Typically used in Object Focus constructions, emphasizing the object of the action.
Object Focus (OF)	I- Verbs	Also used for Object Focus, especially when the action is directed towards an object.
Locative Focus (LF)	An Verbs	Often used to denote actions affecting a location or involving movement towards a place.
Benefactive Focus	Pa- Verbs, Magpa- Verbs	These verbs can convey actions done for the benefit of someone, particularly in requests or causing actions to be performed by others.

Verb Conjugation in Object Focus

In-/Hin-Verbs

The verbs in the "In-" and "Hin-" groups in Tagalog are conjugated similarly, using infixes, prefixes, and suffixes to denote various tenses. These verbs exhibit specific patterns based on whether the root word begins with a vowel or a consonant. Here's how to conjugate these verbs across completed, ongoing, and future aspects.

In-/Hin-Verbs Starting with a Consonant:

1. Completed Aspect

For verbs beginning with a consonant, the completed aspect is formed by inserting the infix "-in-" immediately after the first consonant of the root word. Example:

- Root: Sabi (say)
- Completed Form: First consonant (S) + in + rest of the root (abi) = Sinabi (said)

2. Ongoing Aspect

The ongoing aspect involves inserting the infix "-in-" after the first consonant, followed by the vowel of the first syllable, and then the entire root word. Example:

- Root: Sabi
- Ongoing Form: First consonant (S) + in + vowel of the first syllable (a) + rest of the root (abi) = Sinasabi (saying)

3. Future Aspect

The future tense is formed by repeating the first syllable of the root verb followed by the root and ending with the suffix "-in" or "-hin". The choice between "-in" or "-hin" must be memorized as there is no specific rule for it. Example:

- Root: Sabi
- Future Form: First syllable (Sa) + root (sabi) + in/hin = Sasabihin (will say.)

In-/Hin-Verbs Starting with a Vowel:

1. Completed Aspect

For verbs starting with a vowel, the completed aspect involves adding "in-" as a prefix directly to the root word. Example:

- Root: Isip (think)
- Completed Form: in + root (isip) = Inisip (thought)

2. Ongoing Aspect

The ongoing aspect is formed by placing "in-" plus the vowel of the first syllable before the root word. Example:

- Root: Isip
- Ongoing Form: in + vowel of the first syllable (i) + root (isip) = Iniisip (thinking)

3. Future Aspect

Similar to consonant-starting verbs, the future form repeats the first syllable of the root followed by the root word itself, ending with the suffix "-in" or "-hin". Example:

- Root: Isip
- Future Form: First syllable (I) + root (isip) + in/hin = Iisipin (will think)

Summary Tables:

For a consonant-starting root:

Tense/Aspect	Root	Completed (Past)	Ongoing (Present)	Future
Affixes	-	First consonant + in + rest of the root	First consonant + in + vowel of the first syllable + rest of the root	First syllable + root + in/hin
Sample Verb	Sabi	Sinabi	Sinasabi	Sasabihin
Sample Phrase	-	Sinabi ko.	Sinasabi ko.	Sasabihin ko.
English	say	I said.	I am saying.	I will say.

For a vowel-starting root:

Tense/Aspect	Root	Completed (Past)	Ongoing (Present)	Future
Affixes	-	in + root	in + vowel of the first syllable + root	First syllable + root + in/hin
Sample Verb	Isip	Inisip	Iniisip	Iisipin
Sample Phrase	-	Inisip ko.	Iniisip ko.	Iisipin ko.
English	think	I thought.	I am thinking.	I will think.

I-Verbs

I-verbs in Tagalog show a variety of conjugation patterns depending on whether the root word starts with a consonant or a vowel. These patterns are used to express completed, ongoing, and future actions. Here's a detailed look at how to conjugate I-verbs in different tenses.

For Root Words Starting with a Consonant:

1. Completed Aspect

The completed form is achieved by inserting the infix "-in-" after the first consonant of the root word. Optionally, "i-" can be added as a prefix to this form. Example:

- Root: Balik (return)
- Completed Form: (i) + First consonant (B) + infix -in- + rest of root (alik) = Binalik (returned)

2. Ongoing Aspect

To form the ongoing aspect, duplicate the first syllable of the root word, insert the infix "-in-" after the first consonant, and use this construction as a prefix to the root word. An "i-" prefix can also be optionally added. Example:

- Root: Balik
- Ongoing Form: (i) + First letter of the duplicated first syllable (Ba) + in + rest of the syllable (lik) + root word = Binabalik (returning)

3. Future Aspect

The future tense is created by adding the prefix "i-" and then repeating the first syllable of the root verb, followed by the root word. Example:

- Root: Balik
- Future Form: I + first syllable (Balik) + root word = Ibabalik (will return)

For Root Words Starting with a Vowel:

1. Completed Aspect

When the root starts with a vowel, the completed aspect is formed by adding "in-" as a prefix to the verb root. Example:

- Root: Uwi (bring home)
- Completed Form: in + root (Uwi) = Inuwi (brought home)

2. Ongoing Aspect

The ongoing aspect for vowel-starting roots is formed by adding the prefix "in-" plus repeating the first letter (vowel) of the root word, followed by the root word itself. Example:

- Root: Uwi
- Ongoing Form: in + first letter of the root word (U) + root word = Inuuwi (bringing home.)

3. Future Aspect

Similarly, the future tense uses the prefix "i-" followed by the repetition of the first letter (vowel) of the root verb and the root word. Example:

- Root: Uwi
- Future Form: I + first letter (vowel U) + root word = Iuuwi (will bring the home)

Summary Table:

For a consonant-starting root:

Tense/Aspect	Root	Completed (Past)	Ongoing (Present)	Future
Affixes	-	(i) + first consonant of the root word + infix -in- + rest of root	(i) + first letter of the duplicated first syllable + in + rest of the syllable + root word	I + first syllable of the root word + root word
Sample Verb	Balik	Binalik	Binabalik	Ibabalik
Sample Phrase	-	Binalik ko ang libro.	Binabalik ko ang libro.	Ibabalik ko ang libro bukas.
English	-	I returned the book.	I am returning the book.	I will return the book tomorrow.

For a vowel-starting root:

Tense/Aspect	Root	Completed (Past)	Ongoing (Present)	Future
Affixes	-	in + root	in + first letter of the root word + root	I + first letter (vowel) + root word
Sample Verb	Uwi	Inuwi	Inuuwi	Iuuwi
Sample	-	Inuwi ko ang	Inuuwi ko	Iuuwi ko ang

Phrase		payong.	ang payong.	payong bukas.
Tense/Aspect	Root	Completed (Past)	Ongoing (Present)	Future

Note: There are exceptions when the root word starts with L, R, or Y.

Object Focus Sentences

Just like in Actor Focus, Object-Focus also often employs the Verb-Subject-Object (VSO) structure. In any given sentence, understanding the roles of the verb, the subject, and the object helps clarify who is doing what to whom. Let's break down these components using a simple Tagalog sentence: "Niluto ni Lisa ang adobo."

Tagalog	**English**
Niluto	Cooked (verb)
ni Lisa	by Lisa (actor, subject)
ang adobo	the adobo (object)

Let's explore how to determine what the verb, subject, and object in a phrase are:

Component	**Description**
Verb	The verb is the action word in the sentence. It tells us what is being done. In the sample phrase: "Niluto" is the verb, which means "cooked".
Subject	The subject is the person, place, thing, or idea that is doing the action or being described. In the sample phrase: "Lisa" is the subject, but it is indicated in a unique way. In Tagalog, the doer of the action is often marked by the word "ni" preceding the name. This use of "ni" highlights that while Lisa is performing the action, she is not the main focus of the sentence. Instead, "ni Lisa" identifies Lisa as the person who performed the action, but the structure shifts the

	emphasis away from her towards the object of the action.
Object	The object is the entity that is receiving the action. It is the thing being acted upon. In the sample phrase: "ang adobo" is the object. The word "ang" is a direct object marker in Tagalog, pointing out that adobo is what is being cooked by Lisa. The use of "ang" sets the focus on the adobo, making it the central element of the sentence.

Thus, in the sentence "Niluto ni Lisa ang adobo," the action is cooking ("Niluto"), the person doing the cooking is Lisa ("ni Lisa"), but the focus is squarely on what is being cooked, the adobo ("ang adobo").

Verb	**Subject / Actor**	**Object**
Niluto	ni Lisa	ang adobo.
cooked	Lisa	the adobo.
Lisa cooked the adobo. / The adobo was cooked by Lisa.		

Exercise: Transform the following English sentences into Tagalog using the Object-Focus VSO structure (verb-subject-object). The sentences are given in the completed aspect, and your task is to convert them to ongoing and future aspects.

1. The book was read by her.

Aspect	**English**	**Tagalog**
Completed	The book was read by her.	Binasa niya ang libro.
Ongoing	The book is being read by her.	
Future	The book will be read by her.	

2. The fish was bought by us.

Aspect	English	Tagalog
Completed	The fish was bought by us.	Binili namin ang isda.
Ongoing		
Future		

3. The pancakes were cooked by me.

Aspect	English	Tagalog
Completed	The pancakes were cooked by me.	
Ongoing		
Future		

Solutions:

1. The book was read by her.

Aspect	English	Tagalog
Completed	The book was read by her.	Binasa niya ang libro.
Ongoing	The book is being read by her.	Binabasa niya ang libro.
Future	The book will be read by her.	Babasahin niya ang libro.

2. The fish was bought by us.

Aspect	English	Tagalog
Completed	The fish was bought by	Binili namin ang isda.

	us.	
Ongoing	The fish is being bought by us.	Binibili namin ang isda.
Future	The fish will be bought by us.	Bibilhin namin ang isda.

3. The pancakes were cooked by me.

Aspect	**English**	**Tagalog**
Completed	The pancakes were cooked by me.	Niluto ko ang mga pan-cake.
Ongoing	The pancakes are being cooked by me.	Niluluto ko ang mga pancake.
Future	The pancakes will be cooked by me.	Iluluto ko ang mga pan-cake.

Comparison of Actor and Object Focus

Tagalog phrases can be focused on either the actor who performs the action or the object that receives the action. This distinction changes how the sentence is structured and which part of the sentence is emphasized.

Actor Focus				**Object Focus**		
verb	subject	object		verb	subject	object
Kumain	**ako**	ng tinapay.		Kinain	ko	**ang tinapay.**
Kumain **ako** ng tinapay.				Kinain ko **ang tinapay.**		
I ate a bread.				I ate **the bread**.		

This is articulated through Actor Focus (AF) and Object Focus (OF), which influence verb conjugation, the use of personal pronouns, grammatical markers, and overall sentence structure. Here's a detailed comparison:

1. Markers "ng" and "ang":

Marker	Focus Type	Description
ng	Non-focus, unspecific	Used in Actor Focus to mark the object of the sentence, indicating an indirect or less emphasized element.
ang	Focus, specific	Used in Object Focus to mark the direct object being acted upon, emphasizing it as a specific and definite element.

2. Personal Pronouns:

Actor Focus Personal Pronouns:

Tagalog	English
Ako	I
Ikaw/Ka	You (singular)
Siya	He/She
Kami	We (exclusive)
Tayo	We (inclusive)
Kayo	You (plural)
Sila	They

Object Focus Personal Pronouns:

Tagalog	English
Ko	My, Mine, I, Me
Mo	Your, Yours, You
Niya	His, Her, Hers, He, She
Namin	Our, Ours, We (exclusive)
Natin	Our, Ours, We (inclusive)
Ninyo	Your, Yours, You (plural)
Nila	Their, Theirs, They

3. Verb Affixes:
Specific verb groups are associated with the focus:

Focus Type	Description	Example
Actor Focus (AF)	Utilizes affixes or verb groups like "um-", "mag-" or "ma-".	Kumain (from "kain" - to eat)
Object Focus (OF)	Uses affixes or verb groups such as "in-", "hin", "i-" to emphasize the action performed on the object.	Kinain (from "kain" - to eat)

4. Sentence Structure:

Focus Type	Description	Example
Actor Focus (AF)	Typically follows the VSO (Verb-Subject-Object) structure, highlighting who is performing the action.	Kumain ako ng tinapay. **I** ate bread.
Object Focus (OF)	Also typically follows the VSO (Verb-Subject-Object) structure, but emphasizes the object affected by the action.	Kinain ko ang tinapay. I ate **the bread**. **(The bread** was eaten by me.)

How to know the Verb Group?

Understanding which verb group a verb belongs to requires familiarity with the verb itself, as there isn't a universal rule that applies to all verbs for determining their group. However, there are strategies and cues you can use to make educated guesses:

1. Familiarize with Common Affix Patterns
Understanding common affix patterns for mag-, um-, -in, i-, and others is a good start. Over time, recognizing these patterns helps predict how a root word might conjugate.

2. Consider the Verb's Meaning

The inherent meaning of a root word can sometimes suggest its typical affixes:

- Action or Activity: Root words denoting deliberate actions often take mag- or um-.
- Receiving Action: If the root word suggests something typically done to an object, it might take -in or i-.
- States: Emotional states typically use the ma- verb group.
- Potential or Capability: Root words describing a state, ability, or condition often use maka-.

3. Usage and Context

The way a verb is commonly used in sentences can give clues:

- Actor Focus: If the root word usually refers to an action performed by a subject (actor), try mag- or um-.
- Object Focus: If the action typically highlights the object receiving the action, consider -in or i-.

4. Conjugation Table

When in doubt, consult the conjugation table at the end of this book.

5. Learn from Examples

Exposure to Tagalog through reading, listening, and practice is invaluable. Noticing how verbs are used in different contexts helps build an intuitive sense of which affixes fit various root words.

6. Trial and Error

Experiment with conjugating the root word in sentences, then check if it sounds correct or look it up. Learning from corrections is a powerful tool.

Overview:

Root Word Characteristic	Affix	Typical Use	Example Verbs
Action or Activity	mag-	Used for verbs that denote deliberate actions or ongoing activities.	magluto (to cook), magsulat (to write)
	um-	Also used for actions,	uminom (to

		particularly those that are habitual or natural.	drink), umalis (to leave)
Receiving Action	-in	Appended to roots suggesting actions typically done to an object.	kainin (to eat something), buksan (to open something)
	i-	Used similarly to -in for object-focused actions.	itago (to keep or hide something), ilipat (to transfer something)
Potential or Capability	maka-	Attached to verbs describing a state, ability, or condition to perform something.	makakita (to be able to see), makalangoy (to be able to swim)
State (being in a state)	ma-	Used for verbs describing a passive or inherent state, especially emotional states.	matakot (to be afraid)

Example Exercise Given the root word "aral" (study): To help you better understand the application of various affixes as "Trial and Error" approach, we will involve experimenting with different verb forms and contexts to see how the root can be adapted using affixes.

1. Deliberate Action:

   If the context is about someone studying in a deliberate manner, you can use:

   Mag-aral (to study, generally) - using the "mag-" prefix for actor-focus verbs that denote voluntary actions.

   Nag-aaral (is studying, ongoing) - "nag-" prefix for ongoing actions in present tense.

2. Receiving Action:

   If the context is about someone being taught or instructed, you might consider:

   Aralin (to study something specific, to be studied) - using the "-in" suffix for object-focus verbs.

   Pag-aralan (to study something in-depth, often for making decisions or deeper understanding) - "pag-" prefix for deliberate and focused study of a topic.

3. Potential or Capability:

    If the context involves the ability or capacity to study:
    Maka-aral (to be able to study) - using the "maka-" prefix which denotes capability or potential.

4. Causing Action:

    If the context involves causing someone else to study or facilitating studying, you might use:
    Paaralin (to have someone study, to send to school) - using the "pa-" prefix which implies causing someone else to undertake the action.
    Ipapaaral (to have something studied by someone, often used by parents talking about their children's education) - "ipa-" prefix used for causing an external action through another agent.

Each root word in Tagalog can have multiple verb forms depending on the focus and aspect of the action being described. This list showcases a variety of common actions and their primary associated verb groups.

Root	English	Focus	Group	Example	English
Aral	Study	AF/OF	Mag-/In-	Nag-aaral ako / In-aaral ko ang lek-syon	I am studying / I am studying the lesson
Basa	Read	AF/OF	Mag-/In-	Nagbabasa ako / Binabasa ko ang libro	I am reading / I am reading the book
Bili	Buy	AF/OF	Um-/In-	Bumibili ako / Binili ko ang pag-kain	I am buying / I bought the food
Bukas	Open	AF/OF	Mag-/In-	Nagbubukas ako / Binubuksan ko ang pinto	I am opening / I opened the door
Gawa	Make / Do	AF/OF	Um-/In-	Gumagawa ako / Ginagawa ko ang proyekto	I am making / I made the project
Guhit	Draw	AF/OF	Mag-/In-	Nagguhit ako / I-ginuhit ko ang	I am drawing / I drew the picture

				larawan	
Hagis	Throw	AF/OF	Mag- /In-	Naghahagis ako / Ihinagis ko ang bola	I am throwing / I threw the ball
Hiram	Borrow	AF/OF	Um- /In-	Humihiram ako / Hiniram ko ang libro	I am borrowing / I borrowed the book
Kain	Eat	AF/OF	Um- /In-	Kumakain ako / Kinain ko ang pagkain	I am eating / I ate the food
Labas	Go out	AF/OF	Um- /In-	Lumalabas ako / Nilabas ko ang bahay	I am going out / I went out of the house
Lakad	Walk	AF/OF	Mag- /In-	Naglalakad ako / Nilakad ko ang daan	I am walking / I walked the path
Linis	Clean	AF/OF	Mag- /In-	Naglilinis ako / Nilinis ko ang kwarto	I am cleaning / I cleaned the room
Luto	Cook	AF/OF	Mag- /In-	Nagluluto ako / Niluto ko ang pagkain	I am cooking / I cooked the food
Punta	Go	AF/OF	Um- /In-	Pumupunta ako / Pinuntahan ko ang lugar	I am going / I went to the place
Sabi	Say/Tell	AF/OF	Mag- /In-	Nagsasabi ako / Sinabi ko ang katotohanan	I am telling / I told the truth
Sara	Close	AF/OF	Mag- /In-	Nagsasara ako / Isinara ko ang bintana	I am closing / I closed the window
Sulat	Write	AF/OF	Mag- /In-	Nagsusulat ako / Sinulat ko ang liham	I am writing / I wrote the letter
Tago	Hide	AF/OF	Mag- /In-	Nagtatago ako / Itinago ko ang regalo	I am hiding / I hid the gift

Many verbs can function in both Actor Focus (AF) and Object Focus (OF) depending on the form the verb takes, which is determined by the affixes attached to the root word. This allows for a flexible expression of focus, where the speaker can choose to emphasize either the doer of the action (Actor Focus) or the receiver/object of the action (Object Focus). However, the capability of a root word to function in both foci depends on the verb and the context.

From the list provided, most of the verbs have forms that can be used in both AF and OF contexts. For instance:

- "Bili" as "Bumibili" for AF and "Binili" for OF.
- "Linis" as "Naglilinis" for AF and "Nilinis" for OF.

Some verbs, however, are more commonly used or traditionally categorized under one focus due to their usual roles in sentences or the actions they describe. For example:

- "Gawa" (made) is typically associated with AF when someone is doing or making something. But it can also take an OF form in certain constructions, though it's less common.
- "Hiram" (borrow) and "Tanggap" (to accept or to receive) are typically in OF because the emphasis is usually on the object being borrowed or received.

At the end of this book is a Tagalog verb conjugation table as a useful reference and resource.

Command

Imperative - Commands or requests are formed by using the root form of the verb or with the prefix mag- for the imperative form of the verb.

Tagalog	English
Kain!	Eat!
Laba!	Wash!

Using the root form of the verb is common for informal commands. Since the imperative directly addresses the listener, the subject is implied (you) and typically not explicitly stated. However, here's how you can structure an Actor-Focus command phrase:

Tagalog	English
Maglinis ka ng kwarto.	Clean your room.

In this command, "Maglinis" is the imperative form of the verb to clean, "ka" represents the implied subject (you), and "ng kwarto" specifies the object (the room). This construction directly addresses the listener with a command, fitting the Actor-Focus orientation by emphasizing the action to be performed.

Ability or Potential

Expressing ability, possibility, capability or potential involves specific verb forms. xpressing ability or capability often involves the use of specific affixes attached to verbs. These affixes transform the verb to convey the ability to perform the action denoted by the verb. Here are the most common affixes used to express ability in Tagalog:

Prefix	Meaning	Examples	English
Maka-	Used to indicate the potential or ability to do something.	Makakain, Makatulog	Able to eat, Able to sleep
Makapag-	Similar to "maka-," but used before verbs that start with a vowel or involve an object or complex action.	Makapagsulat, Makapaglaro	Able to write, Able to play
Ma-	Denotes the ability to do something, often used in a more general sense.	Mabasa, Marinig	Able to read, Able to hear

Sample phrases:

Tagalog	English
Makakain ako nito.	I can eat this.

Makapagsulat siya ng tula.	She can write a poem.
Marinig mo ba ang ingay?	Can you hear the noise?

Explanations:

- Makakain ako nito.
  Maka- is used here with the root verb "kain" (to eat), indicating the ability to perform the action. The phrase means "I am able to eat this," showing personal capability.
- Makapagsulat siya ng tula.
  Makapag- is used with the root verb "sulat" (to write), tailored to express the capability of performing a more complex action, which in this case is writing a poem. The phrase translates to "She is able to write a poem."
- Marinig mo ba ang ingay?
  Ma- is used with the root verb "rinig" (to hear), commonly used to ask about someone's ability to perform a sensory action. The phrase means "Can you hear the noise?" which inquires about the listener's potential to hear something.

Modal Verbs - Ability, Permission & Obligation

Modal verbs can express ability, permission, or obligation, similar to moods in other languages.

Tagalog	English	Description
Puwede	can, may	Expresses permission or possibility.
Kailangan	need, must	Expresses necessity or obligation.

Sample phrases:

Tagalog	English
Puwede akong kumain ng mansanas.	I can eat an apple.
Kailangan kong kumain ng mansanas.	I need to eat an apple.

Sentence Structure

Having gained an overview of focus and verb conjugation, it's essential to understand how these elements come together in the structure of sentences. Tagalog sentence structure offers flexibility comparable to English, presenting a variety of expressions. However, for non-native speakers, this flexibility can sometimes be challenging due to the unpredictability of sentence construction. **Fundamental Differences in Sentence Structure:** In English, the typical sentence structure for main sentences, which are grammatically complete, follows the Subject-Verb-Object (SVO) order. The verb usually occupies the second position in these sentences. Conversely, in Tagalog, the standard structure often begins with the verb, placing the Actor (the acting person/subject) in the second position, followed by the object, and sometimes by the location or other sentence elements (VSO sentence structure)

Examples Demonstrating Sentence Structures: To illustrate the differences between Tagalog and English sentence structures, let's examine a few examples:

Tagalo: Verb + Subject + Object	English: Subject + Verb + Object
Kakain ako sa bahay.	I will eat at home.
Nagtuturo ang guro sa mga bata.	The teacher is teaching the children.
Nananalangin siya sa simbahan.	He/She is praying in the church.

Understanding these structures is key to mastering the language. Here, we'll explore four primary sentence structures: Verb-Subject-Object (VSO), Subject-Verb-Object (SVO), Ang-Verb-Ay (AVA) for Objects, and the use of Stressed Pronouns.

1. Verb-Subject-Object (VSO) Sentence Structure: The VSO structure is the most common in Tagalog. It places the action at the forefront, followed by who or what is performing the action, and finally, the recipient of the action. Sample:

Tagalog		
Kumakain ang bata ng mansanas.		
Kumakain	ang bata	ng mansanas.

Verb	Subject	Object
is eating	the child	an apple
The child is eating an apple.		

2. Subject-Verb-Object (SVO) Sentence Structure: While less common, SVO is used in Tagalog, especially for emphasis on the subject or in more formal or literary contexts. It mirrors the English sentence structure, starting with the subject. The particle "ay" is used to switch the typical verb-subject-object (VSO) order to a subject-verb-object (SVO) order.

Tagalog	**English**
Ang guro ay nagtuturo ng Aralin.	The teacher is teaching a lesson.

Explanation:

- Subject: Ang guro (The teacher)
- ay: "ay" serves as a linking particle that allows the sentence to place the subject at the beginning, followed by the verb.
- Verb: nagtuturo (is teaching)
- Object: ng Aralin (a lesson)

Why use "ay"? Using "ay" allows Tagalog speakers to frame sentences in a way that highlights the subject or aligns with a more English-like structure, making the sentence potentially clearer or more emphatic about who is performing the action. Without "ay" the sentence would typically follow the VSO order: "Nagtuturo ng aralin ang guro," where the verb comes first.

3. Ang-Verb-Ay (AVA) for Objects: The AVS structure is sometimes used, especially when emphasizing an object or a specific individual as the subject. "Ang" introduces the focus, "Si" precedes proper names, and the verb articulates the action.

Tagalog	**English**
Ang kinakain ni Lisa ay mangga.	What Lisa is eating is a mango.

Explanation:

- Focus Marker: Ang (The) — marks what is being discussed or the focus of the sentence.
- Verb: kinakain (is eating) — describes the action being performed.
- Subject Marker: ni Ana (by Ana) — indicates who is performing the action.
- "ay" links this part of the sentence to what follows, emphasizing that the next part is specifically about what Lisa is eating.
- Object: mangga (mango) — the object of the action.

4. Stressed Pronouns (Emphatic Pronouns): Stressed pronouns are used at the beginning of a sentence to add emphasis.

Tagalog	**English**
Ako mismo ang maglilinis ng kwarto.	I myself will clean the room.

Here, "Ako mismo" (I myself) emphasizes personal action.

Tagalog	**English**
Ikaw ba ang kumain ng cake?	Was it you who ate the cake?

In this question, "Ikaw ba" places emphasis on "you," making it a pointed inquiry.

Noun Sentence

Constructing sentences with nouns as the main focus allows you to describe things, people, or situations without necessarily using verbs. This structure is helpful for stating facts, identifying objects or people, and describing states or conditions.

Understanding Noun Sentences: Noun sentences in Tagalog often rely on the word "ay", which functions as a linker between the subject and the predicate, though it can sometimes be omitted in casual conversation.

Structure: Subject + "ay" + Predicate

This structure is used to emphasize the predicate or to make the sentence sound more formal.

Tagalog	English
Ang pusa ay itim.	The cat is black.

Explanation:

- Formal: "Ang pusa ay itim." (The cat is black.)
- Explanation:
- Subject: Ang pusa (The cat)
- Linker: ay
- Predicate: itim (black)

Dropping "ay" for a more conversational tone, often used in everyday speech. Examples. This changes the structure of the noun sentence to: Predicate + Sub ject

Tagalog	English
Itim ang pusa.	The cat is black.

Explanation:

- Casual: "Itim ang pusa." (The cat is black.)
- Predicate: Itim (black)
- Subject: ang pusa (the cat)

Practice: Let's practice constructing noun sentences with both structures.

Describe an object:

Tagalog	English
Formal: "Ang libro ay makapal."	The book is thick.
Casual: "Makapal ang libro."	The book is thick.
Formal: "Si Maria ay guro."	Maria is a teacher.
Casual: "Guro si Maria."	Maria is a teacher.

Learning Tip: Starting with the VSO Sentence Structure
When embarking on your journey to learn Tagalog, it might feel overwhelming

to grasp all the different sentence structures at once. A practical approach to streamline your learning process is to initially focus on the Verb-Subject-Object (VSO) sentence structure.

Here's why: The VSO structure is fundamental and widely used in everyday Tagalog communication. By prioritizing this structure, you simplify your learning path, allowing you to quickly start forming sentences and engaging in basic conversations.

What is VSO?: In VSO sentences, the verb comes first, indicating the action. Next is the subject, who or what performs the action, followed by the object, the recipient of the action.

Examples: Kumakain (eating) + ang bata (the child) + ng mansanas (an apple). Translated: "The child is eating an apple."

Tagalog	English
Kumakain ako ng mansanas.	I am eating an apple.

Lesson 44 - Important Nouns

This concise list provides you with key Tagalog nouns, arranged alphabetically, alongside their English translations.

Tagalog	English
aktor	actor
almusal	breakfast
ama	father
anak na babae	daughter
anak na lalaki	son
anak sa labas	stepson
apelyido	last name
araw	day
asawa	wife
asin	salt
aso	dog
babae	woman
baboy	pig
bahay	house
baka, karne ng baka	cow, beef
balita	news
bangka	boat
banyo	bathroom. toilet
baso	glass
bata	child
bigas	rice (uncooked)
bisita	visitor
biyahe	trip
botika	pharmacy
buhok	hair
bundok	mountain
bus	bus
buwan	month
damdamin	feeling
damit	dress

dentista	dentist
Disyembre	December
doktor	doctor
drayber	driver
dugo	blood
edad	age
Enero	January
eroplano	airplane
estudyante, mag-aaral	student, pupil
gabi	evening
gamot	medicine
gatas	milk
gulay	vegetable
guro	teacher
hagdan	stairs
halimbawa	example
hangin	air
hapunan	dinner
hayop	animal
Hunyo	June
Huwebes	Thursday
ina, nanay	mother
inhinyero	engineer
inumin	drink
isda	fish
istasyon	station (e.g., bus station)
kaibigan	friend
kalabasa	pumpkin
kalye	street
kama	bed
kamatis	tomato
kamay	hand
kanin	rice (cooked)
kape	coffee
kapitbahay	neighbor
karamdaman	illness

karne	meat
kasama	companion
kasintahan	boyfriend / girlfriend
katas	juice
katotohanan	truth
kawali	pan
keso	cheese
kilikili	armpit
kulay	color
kusina	kitchen
kutsara	spoon
kutsilyo	knife
kuwintas	necklace
kwarto	room
lagnat	fever
lalaki	man
lamok	mosquito
lapis	pencil
laro	game
leeg	og - neck
libro	book
linggo	week
lola	grandma
lolo	grandpa
Lunes	Monday
lungsod	city
lungsod, siyudad	city
lupa	land, earth
magulang	parents
malamig	on - cold
mangga	mango
manok	chicken
mansanas	apple
Marso	March
Martes	Tuesday
Mayo	May

melon	melon
mesa	table
minuto	minute
Miyerkules	Wednesday
mukha	face
Nobyembre	November
Oktobre	October
opisina	office
oras	time, hour
ospital	hospital
paaralan	school
pagdiriwang, pista	celebration, festival
pagkain	food
pakwan	watermelon
pamasahe	fare
pamilya	family
panahon	weather
pangalan	name
pantalon	pants
papaya	papaya
Pebrero	February
pera	money
prutas	fruit
prutas	fruit
pulis	policeman
pusa	cat
puso	kasing - heart
relo	watch
saging	banana
sala	living room
sapatos	shoes
serbesa	beer
Setyembre	September
sigarilyo	cigarette
silangan	east
simbahan	church

sinehan	cinema
sugat	wound
sulok	corner
susi	key
tanghali	noon
tanghalian	lunch
tanong	question
tao	person
taon, edad	years, age
timog	south
tinapay	bread
tindahan	store
trangkaso	flu
tubig	water
tuyong isda	dried fish
ubo	cough
ulo	head
umaga	morning
upuan	chair

Exercise: Pick 5 nouns that relate to your daily life and learn them.

Lesson 45 - Important Adjectives

Tagalog	English
bago	new
basa	wet, moist
bata	young
bawat isa	each
berde	green
bughaw, asul	blue
buhay	alive
gwapo	handsome
hilaw	raw
hinog	ripe
iba	different
itim	black
kaliwa	left
kayumanggi	brown
labas	outside
lahat	all, everything
maaga	early
maalat	salty
maanghang	spicy
maasim	sour
mabagal	slow
mabigat	heavy
mabuti	good
madilim	dark
magaan	light (weight)
maganda	beautiful
magkatulad	similar, same
mahal	expensive
mahangin	windy
mahina	weak
mainit	hot, warm
makapal	thick

makinis	smooth
malabnaw	dilute
malakas	strong
malaki	big
malambot	soft
malamig	cold
malapit	near
malawak	wide
malayo	far, distant
maliit	small
maliwanag	bright
mamaya	later
mapait	bitter
marami	many
marumi	dirty
mas maaga	earlier
masama	evil
masarap	delicious
masaya	joyful, happy
masikip	tight
masipag	industrious
matalino	intelligent
matamis	sweet
matigas	hard
mura	cheap
nalilito	confused
nauuhaw	thirsty
pandak, maikli	short
patay	dead
payat	thin, slim
pula	red
puti	white
sariwa	fresh
susunod	next
tama	right
tamad	lazy

totoo	true
walang lasa	bland
wasak, sira	destroyed

Exercise: Pick 5 adjectives that relate to your daily life and learn them.

Lesson 46 - Important Verbs

Verbs are listed here in their root form. To conjugate, affixes are used, which depend on the time, mode, and focus. Here, the verbs are initially introduced in their root form. At the and of this book you find a verb conjugation table with their related affixes.

Tagalog	English
abot	reach
akyat	climb
alala	remember
alam	know
alis	leave
aral	study, learn
ayos	fix
balik	return
basa	read
basag	break
bayad	pay
benta	sell
bigay	give
bili	buy
bukas	open
dala	bring
dating	come, arrive
dinig	listen
gamit	use
gastos	spend
gawa	make, do
gising	wake up
halik	kiss
hanap	search
higa	lie (as in lying down)
hintay	wait
hinto	stop

hipo	touch
hugas	wash
hulog	fall
inom	drink
intindi	understand
isip	think
iyak	cry
kailangan	need
kain	eat
kanta	sing
kita	see
kuha	take
laba	wash clothes
lagay	place
lakad	walk, stroll
lakbay	travel
langoy	swim
laro	play
libang	entertain
ligo	bathe, shower
limot	forget
linis	clean
lipat	move
luto	cook
magkasakit	get sick
magkwento, sabihin	tell
magsalita	speak
magtayo	build
mahal	love
mamatay	die
mangyari	happen
masakit	hurt
ngiti	smile
nood	watch, look at
padala	send
pahinga	rest

pakilala	introduce
pasok	enter
patayin	kill
pili	choose, select
punta	go
putol	cut
rinig	hear
sabi	say, tell
sagot	answer
sakay	ride, drive (as a passenger)
sama	accompany
sara	close
sayaw	dance
sigaw	shout, scream
simula	start, begin
sulat	write
tago	hide
takbo	run
talon	jump
tamaan	hit
tanggap	receive
tanim	plant
tanong	ask
tapak	step on
tapos	finish, complete something
tawa	laugh
tawag	call
tayo	stand
tingin	look
tira	live, reside
tiwala	believe
trabaho	work
tulog	sleep
tulong	help
turo	teach
ulan	rain

upo	sit
uwi	go home
yakap	hug

Exercise: Pick 5 verbs that relate to your daily life and learn them.

Lesson 47 - Pseudoverbs

Pseudoverbs are words that express actions or states without the need for conjugation. They are similar to verbs but are often inherently adjectives or expressions that function without verb affixes. These words are essential in conveying desires, abilities, necessities, and existence.

List of Pseudoverbs:

Tagalog	English
Gusto	Want or like
Kailangan	Need or require
May/Mayroon	Have or there is/are
Pwede	Can or possible
Ayaw	Do not or don't (for expressing negation or prohibition)

Usage of Pseudo Verbs: Pseudo verbs can stand alone or be used alongside other verbs. They do not change form regardless of tense or aspect and can be used with pronouns and nouns to express a complete thought.

Examples of Pseudo Verbs in Use:

Gusto:

Tagalog	English
Gusto ko ng kape.	I want coffee.
Gusto niya umalis.	He/She wants to leave.

Kailangan:

Tagalog	English
Kailangan ko ng tubig.	I need water.
Kailangan nila mag-aral.	They need to study.

May/Mayroon:

"May" and "mayroon" both mean "have" or "there is/are", but they're used a bit differently. "May" is used directly before a noun, like in "May aso ako" ("I have a dog"). "Mayroon" can add emphasis or be used in more complex sentences. It's often used with "ng" or when affirming existence, as in "Mayroon akong libro (akong = ako ang)" ("I have a book"). While their meanings overlap, the choice between them can depend on emphasis or sentence structure.

Tagalog	English
May aso ako.	I have a dog.
Mayroon silang pasok bukas.	They have class tomorrow.

Pwede:

Tagalog	English
Pwede ba akong sumama?	Can I come along?
Pwede mong gamitin ito.	You can use this.

Ayaw:

Tagalog	English
Ayaw ko ng gulo.	I don't want trouble.
Ayaw niyang kumain.	He/She doesn't want to eat.

Forming questions with pseudo verbs: Here are multiple examples for each of the pseudo verbs discussed.

Tagalog	English
Gusto ko ng mangga.	I want mango.
Gusto nilang maglaro ng basketball.	They want to play basketball.
Gusto mong manood ng sine?	Do you want to watch a movie?
Kailangan ko ng pera.	I need money.
Kailangan nating umalis ngayon.	We need to leave now.
Kailangan mong kumain ng gulay.	You need to eat vegetables.
May aso kami.	We have a dog.
Mayroon bang klase bukas?	Is there a class tomorrow?
May pasok sa Lunes.	There are classes on Monday.

Pwede bang magtanong?	Can I ask a question?
Pwede ka bang tumulong sa akin?	Can you help me?
Pwede tayong kumain dito.	We can eat here.
Ayaw ko ng ampalaya.	I don't like bitter gourd.
Ayaw niyang pumunta.	He/She doesn't want to go.
Ayaw kong mag-isa.	I don't want to be alone.

Exercise: Forming sentences using two pseudo verb. Think about what you want, need, have, can do, or don't want to do. Translate those thoughts into Tagalog using the pseudo verbs listed above.

For example:

- I want to sleep early tonight.
- I can cook pasta now.

Tagalog	**English**

Potential Solution:

Tagalog	**English**
Gusto kong matulog nang maaga ngayong gabi.	I want to sleep early tonight.
Pwede mo ba akong pahiramin ng bolpen?	Can you lend me a pen?
Kaya ko nang magluto ng pasta ngayon.	I can cook pasta now.

Lesson 48 - Forming Questions with Pseudo Verbs

Forming questions with pseudo verbs—such as "gusto" (want or like), "kailangan" (need or require), "may/mayroon" (have or there is/are), "pwede" (can or possible), and "ayaw" (do not or don't for expressing negation or prohibition)—is straightforward. You typically place the pseudo verb at the beginning of the sentence, and if it's a yes-no question, you might add "ba" after the pseudo verb for clarification or emphasis. Here's a simple formula for these questions:

1. Start with the pseudo verb.
2. Add "ba" if it's a yes-no question.
3. Follow with the subject (often implied in the verb conjugation) and the rest of the sentence.

When forming a "ba" question with a pseudo verb and the personal pronoun "you", the order slightly adjusts to accommodate the pronoun. The typical structure would be: Pseudo Verb + ba + Personal Pronoun "you" + (Rest of the Sentence).

Now, let's see some examples in a table: Pseudo Verb + ba + Subject + (Rest of the Sentence)

Tagalog	English
Gusto mo ba ng mangga?	Do you want mango?
Kailangan ba natin mag-aral ngayon?	Do we need to study today?
May aso ba kayo?	Do you have a dog?
Pwede ba akong sumama?	Can I come along?
Ayaw mo ba ng ampalaya?	Don't you like bitter gourd?

You can form non-yes/no questions using pseudo verbs by incorporating interrogative words such as "ano" (what), "sino" (who), "kailan" (when), "saan" (where), "bakit" (why), and "paano" (how) into the sentence. These questions aim to gather specific information rather than just a confirmation or denial. The pseudo verb still plays a central role in the sentence, but the interrogative word dictates the flow of the question. Here's the formula:

1. Start with the interrogative word related to the information you seek.

2. Follow with the pseudo verb (and the subject if necessary).
3. Complete the sentence with the relevant information.

Let's see some examples:

Tagalog	**English**
Ano ang gusto mong kainin?	What do you want to eat?
Saan kayo pwede magkita?	Where can you meet?
Kailan mo kailangan ang libro?	When do you need the book?
Paano ka mag-aaral kung walang kuryente?	How will you study if there's no electricity?
Bakit ayaw mo ng ampalaya?	Why don't you like bitter gourd?

Exercise: Translate it to Tagalog.

Tagalog	**English**
	What do you want to drink?
	When do you want to eat?
	Why do you need the car?

Solution:

Tagalog	**English**
Ano ang gusto mong inumin?	What do you want to drink?
Kailan mo gustong kumain?	When do you want to eat?
Bakit mo kailangan ang kotse?	Why do you need the car?

Lesson 49 - Modifying Words with Affixes

Affixes in Tagalog can be attached to root words to form verbs, adjectives, nouns, and adverbs, significantly changing or specifying their meanings. This lesson provides an overview about typical affixes.

Affix	Explanation	Example
Mag-	Indicates an actor-focused action.	laro (play) → maglaro (to play)
-um-	An infix for forming simple actor-focused verbs.	tawa (laugh) → tumawa (laughed)
-in	Transforms verbs to focus on the object or outcome.	sulat (write) → sulatin (to be written)
I-	Directs the action towards an object.	dala (carry) → idala (to carry something)
Pa-	Indicates causation or request.	hiram (borrow) → pahiram (to let someone borrow)
Ma-	Turns root words into adjectives indicating a quality or state.	init (heat) → mainit (hot)
Pinaka-	Denotes the superlative degree.	ganda (beauty) → pinakamaganda (most beautiful)
Ka-...-an / -han	Forms nouns denoting collective or relational concepts.	trabaho (work) → katrabaho (coworker)
Pan- /Pang-	Creates nouns related to tools or instruments.	luto (cook) → pangluto (cooking utensil)
-an	Indicates a location or manner.	bahay (house) → bahayan (residential area)
Maka- / Makapag-	Emphasizes potential or capacity.	tulong (help) → makatulong (to be able to help)
Ma-	Also indicates the ability or potentiality alongside its use for adjectives.	kita (see) → makakita (to be able to see)

Examples in Sentences:

Tagalog	English
Maglalaro kami ng basketball bukas.	We will play basketball tomorrow.
Mainit ang panahon ngayon.	The weather is hot now.
Makakasama ka ba sa amin sa pagpunta sa Baguio?	Will you be able to join us in going to Baguio?
Pahiram ng ballpen mo, please.	Please let me borrow your pen.

Ang kanyang pinakamagandang katangian ay ang kanyang kabaitan.	Her most beautiful trait is her kindness.

Lesson 50 - Specific & Nonspecific

In Tagalog, like in many languages, the distinction between specific and non-specific nouns plays a crucial role in constructing meaningful sentences. This concept is particularly important when it comes to choosing the right articles and constructing sentences with proper focus. Let's break it down into more understandable parts.

Specific Nouns: A noun is considered specific when it refers to a particular member of a group or class. It's known, defined, and identifiable. In English, specific nouns are often accompanied by the definite article "the" or possessive pronouns like "my," "your," etc.

Tagalog Example:

Tagalog	Meaning	Explanation
Ang mansanas	The applee	Here, 'ang' is a marker used for specific nouns. You're not talking about any apple, but a particular apple.

"Ang mansanas" (The apple) – Here, 'ang' is a marker used for specific nouns. You're not talking about any apple, but a particular apple.

Nonspecific Nouns: Nonspecific nouns refer to any member of a group or class, not identified particularly. These nouns are general, undefined, and could be any one of the category mentioned. In English, such nouns are often preceded by "a" or "an" or used without articles in the case of plural or uncountable nouns.

Example:

Tagalog	Meaning	Explanation
Isang mansanas	One apple (un-specific)	Specifies a quantity of one in a general sense, not referring to a specific item (Ang-Maker, Focus, specific)
Ng mansanas	An apple (un-specific)	Used to indicate the object of an action or possession, without specifying which one (Ng-Marker, Non-Focus, unspecific)

Nonspecific phrases: Here's a table with simple nonspecific phrases in Tagalog and their English translations, focusing on the usage of nonspecific nouns:

Tagalog	English
Bumibili ako ng isang mansanas.	I am buying one apple.
Kumakain ako ng mansanas.	I am eating an apple.
May nakita akong aso.	I saw a dog.
Uminom ako ng tubig.	I drank water.
Gusto ko ng keyk.	I want cake.
Naglalaro siya ng laro.	He is playing a game.
Nagsusulat ako ng liham.	I am writing a letter.
Nagbabasa siya ng libro.	She is reading a book.
Kumakanta ako ng kanta.	I am singing a song.
Bumibili ako ng damit.	I am buying clothes.
Naghahanap ako ng trabaho.	I am looking for a job.

Here's the breakdown of "Bumibili ako ng isang mansanas.":

- "Bumibili" is the verb in Actor Focus form, indicating the action of buying being performed by the subject.
- "ako" means "I," referring to the subject performing the action.
- "ng" is a marker used before the object of the action.
- "isang mansanas" means "one apple," specifying the object being bought.

Specific phrases: The proper way to convey specificity in Tagalog involves using the markers "ang" for "the," "ito" for "this," "iyan" (or "yan") for "that" near the speaker, and "iyon" (or "yon") for "that" far from both speaker and listener, along with possessive pronouns.

Vocabulary

Tagalog	English
ang	Focus-Marker, Specific, The
ito	this
iyan (or yan)	that (near speaker)
iyon (or yon)	that (far from both speaker and listener)
ko	I, my, mine (object focus)
mo	you, your (singular)
niya	he/she, him/her
natin	we, our, ours, us
namin	we, our, ours, us
ninyo	you, your (plural)
nila	they, their, theirs, them

Phrases:

Tagalog	English
Kinuha niya ang susi.	She took the key.
Binili niya ang libro.	She bought the book. / The book was bought by her.
Kinain ko ang mansanas.	I ate the apple. / The apple was eaten by me.
Ininom niya ang kape.	He drank the coffee. / The coffee was drunk by him.
Binasa ko ang sulat.	I read the letter. / The letter was read by me.
Kinain niya ang aking mansanas.	He/she ate my apple. / My apple was eaten by him/her.
Gusto ko itong keyk.	I want this cake.
Nilalaro niya iyong laro.	He is playing that game.
Isinulat ko itong liham.	I wrote this letter.
Binabasa niya iyong libro.	She is reading her book.
Kinanta ko itong kanta.	I sang this song.
Binili ko iyang damit.	I bought that piece of clothing.

Exercise: Choose a specific and an unspecific phrase from the lesson, write them down, learn and practice them.

Specific phrase:

Tagalog	English

Unspecific phrase:

Tagalog	English

Lesson 51 - Choosing the Focus

In Tagalog, the focus of a sentence is crucial because it influences how verbs are conjugated and which part of the sentence is highlighted. This concept may be unique to speakers of languages without grammatical focus. Let's dive into how to choose between Actor Focus and Object Focus.

Actor Focus (AF): In Actor Focus, the subject of the sentence performs the action. This focus is used when the actor or the doer of the action is the point of interest. For example, in the sentence "Kumakain ako ng mansanas" (I am eating an apple), the focus is on "ako" (I), indicating that the action of eating is being performed by the subject.
When to use Actor Focus: When highlighting who is performing the action. When the actor is more important than the action or the object receiving the action.

Object Focus (OF): Object Focus, on the other hand, highlights the object receiving the action. The subject of the sentence is the object affected by the action. For instance, "Kinakain ang mansanas" (The apple is being eaten), the focus is on "mansanas" (apple), the object receiving the action.
When to use Object Focus: When the object of the action is more important

than who is performing the action.
To emphasize the action being done to the subject or object.

Choosing the Focus: Determine what is more important: What do you want to highlight? Is it the person doing the action or the object receiving it? Your answer will guide your focus choice.

- Context matters: Sometimes, the context of your conversation will dictate the focus. If you're talking about a person and what they're doing, Actor Focus might be more appropriate. If you're discussing an object and what's happening to it, Object Focus could be the way to go.

- Consider the specificity: If you want to be specific about the receiver of the action (e.g., a particular apple), Object Focus can serve you well. Actor Focus is more suitable when the actor's identity is the main point, regardless of the action's specifics.

Let's explore the difference between focusing on the doer of an action versus the receiver of that action through two sentences: "I eat an apple" and "The apple is eaten by me." In the first sentence, the spotlight is on the actor - me, the one eating the apple. Here, the action's receiver, the apple, is mentioned in a general way, not specifying which apple. This is an example of Actor Focus because it's all about who is performing the action.
On the other hand, in the second sentence, "The apple is eaten by me," attention shifts to the apple, which is now receiving the action. This sentence specifies "the apple," making it clear that we're talking about a particular apple. This specificity about the receiver of the action marks it as an Object Focus sentence.

To simplify, if the sentence is specific about who is doing the action but general about who or what is receiving it, it's using Actor Focus. And if the sentence is precise about who or what is receiving the action, it's an example of Object Focus.

A practical way to grasp this concept is by practicing with examples and transforming sentences from one focus to another. This method illuminates how the shift changes the sentence's emphasis or meaning.
Let's consider an example. Take the sentence "Nagluto si Maria ng adobo" which, with an Actor Focus (AF), highlights Maria as the one performing the action, translating to "Maria cooked adobo." Here, the emphasis is on Maria

cooking.

Now, transform this to an Object Focus (OF) sentence: "Niluto ni Maria ang adobo." This version shifts the spotlight to the adobo itself, being cooked by Maria, and translates to "The adobo was cooked by Maria." The emphasis here is on the adobo, the object receiving the action.

By practicing with such transformations, you can see how changing the focus affects what part of the sentence is highlighted—whether it's the person doing the action or the item the action is being done to.

Exercise: Comple the phrases (specisic, non-specific) in the table.

AF / Unspecific	English	OF / Specific	English
Nagluto si Paul ng pansit.	Paul cooked pan-sit.	Niluto ni Paul ang pansit.	Paul cooked the pansit.
Nagsulat si	Ana wrote a let-ter.	Isinulat ni Ana	Ana wrote the letter.
Nagbasa	Pedro read a book.	Binasa	Pedro read the book.
Naglinis	Tina cleaned a house.	Nilinis	Tina cleaned the house.
Naglaba	Nora washed clothes.	Nilaba	Nora washed the clothes.
Nagbiyahe	Marko traveled by airplane.	Ibinabiyahe	Marko traveled by the airplane.
Nagluto	Leah cooked sinigang.	Niluto	Leah cooked the sinigang.
Nag-ayos	Sam arranged a room.	Inayos	Sam arranged the room.
Bumili	Lisa bought a fish.	Binili	Lisa bought the fish.
Bumili	Lisa bought bread.	Binili	Lisa bought the bread.

Solution:

AF / Unspecific	English	OF / Specific	English
Nagluto si Paul ng pansit.	Paul cooked pan-sit.	Niluto ni Paul ang pansit.	Paul cooked the pansit.
Nagsulat si Ana ng liham.	Ana wrote a let-ter.	Isinulat ni Ana ang liham.	Ana wrote the letter.
Nagbasa si Pedro ng libro.	Pedro read a book.	Binasa ni Pedro ang libro.	Pedro read the book.
Naglinis si Tina ng bahay.	Tina cleaned a house.	Nilinis ni Tina ang bahay.	Tina cleaned the house.
Naglaba si Nora ng damit.	Nora washed clothes.	Nilaba ni Nora ang damit.	Nora washed the clothes.
Nagbiyahe si Marko ng eroplano.	Marko traveled by airplane.	Ibinabiyahe ni Marko ang eroplano.	Marko traveled by the airplane.
Nagluto si Leah ng sinigang.	Leah cooked sinigang.	Niluto ni Leah ang sinigang.	Leah cooked the sinigang.
Nag-ayos si Sam ng kuwarto.	Sam arranged a room.	Inayos ni Sam ang kuwarto.	Sam arranged the room.
Bumili si Lisa ng isda.	Lisa bought a fish.	Binili ni Lisa ang isda.	Lisa bought the fish.
Bumili si Lisa ng tinapay.	Lisa bought bread.	Binili ni Lisa ang tinapay.	Lisa bought the bread.

Lesson 52 - Introduction to Conjugation

The way verbs change form, or conjugate, depends on three things: who or what is doing the action, when the action is happening, and the feeling or mood behind the action. Let's look at the first part, the focus of the verb. There are two main types: Actor Focus Verbs and Object Focus Verbs.

With **Actor Focus** verbs, the spotlight is on the person or thing doing the action. For example, if I say "I eat," the focus is on "I," the one doing the eating. It's called Actor Focus because it's all about the actor, or the one performing the action.

On the other hand, **Object Focus** verbs put the emphasis on the person or thing receiving the action. So, if the sentence is "The apple is eaten by me," the apple is the star because it's receiving the action of being eaten. This is why it's known as Object Focus - the object or the recipient of the action is in the limelight.

The mood or **aspect of a verb** adds a special flavor to the action it describes, providing clues about the nature of the action. It tells us whether the action is a one-time occurrence, a temporary situation, an ongoing process, or even a command. For example, a momentary action could be something like a sudden jump or a quick glance – it happens once and then it's over. A temporal action has a limited timeframe; it starts, lasts for a while, and then finishes, like watching a movie. An ongoing, or durative, action stretches out over time, such as living in a city or working at a job – it's continuous. And when we're talking about commands, the mood shifts to tell someone to do something, like "Sit down" or "Please call me." This aspect of verbs adds depth to our understanding of what's happening, painting a clearer picture of the timing and intention behind actions. When considering the mood of verbs, apart from these aspects there are mainly two scenarios:

1. Conjugating verbs according to the three aspects (completed, ongoing, future), to indicate the time frame and nature of the action;
2. Employing the verb in the imperative mood to issue commands or requests.

Understanding the **timing of actions** goes beyond the simple concept of tense as known in many other languages. Here, the crucial aspect of verb conjugation revolves around whether the action has already started or not. This approach to action—whether it's about its completion, ongoing process, or anticipation—plays a fundamental role in how verbs are utilized within the language, providing a distinctive temporal framework that's integral to Tagalog's grammatical structure.

Tagalog verbs are categorized into three primary aspects: completed (perfektibo), ongoing (imperpektibo), and contemplated (kontemplatibo).

- The completed aspect (perfektibo) signals that an action has been concluded. It's the tense used to denote actions that have already occurred, marking them as finished.

- The ongoing aspect (imperpektibo) indicates that an action is currently underway or was continuing at a certain point in time. This aspect is crucial for describing actions that are in progress, highlighting the fluidity of ongoing processes.
- Lastly, the contemplated aspect (kontemplatibo) pertains to actions that haven't commenced but are intended or expected to occur in the future. It sets the stage for events that are planned or anticipated, providing a forward-looking perspective on actions. The contemplated aspect in Tagalog is largely equivalent to the future tense in English. It's used to describe actions that have not yet started but are expected or planned to happen in the future. This aspect provides a way to talk about future events or actions with an emphasis on the anticipation or planning of these events. While the term "contemplated aspect" might not directly translate to "future tense," the function it serves in conveying future actions aligns with how the future tense is used in English and many other languages. So to use a familiar word, I will call this tense future.

This focus on whether an action has begun offers Tagalog a unique temporal lens, distinct from the tense-based frameworks (past, present, future) prevalent in languages like English. In Tagalog, the primary concern isn't merely when an action takes place but rather its state concerning its initiation and completion. This unique approach enriches the language, offering nuanced ways to express the timing and nature of actions.

Let's summarize what we have just learned:

	Actor Focus	**Object Focus**
Focus	Focus on the doer of the action. (The doer of the action is the Subject of the phrase)	Focus on the recipient of the action. (The recipient of the action is the Subject of the phrase)
Personal Pronouns	Use the Actor Focus set of personal pronouns	Use the Object Focus set of personal pronouns
Verbs	Conjugate the verbs in Actor Focus case.	Conjugate the verbs in Object Focus case.
Tense and Aspect	▪ completed ▪ ongoing	

	▪ future ▪ command

Conjugating Actor Focus Verbs

In our next five lessons, we'll focus on Actor Focus verbs. We'll start with an introduction to the basics, then explore the associated verb groups, and conclude with a practical exercise to solidify your understanding. This sequence will help you master the use of Actor Focus verbs effectively.

Lesson 53 - Introduction

In English, verbs change form based on the subject and tense. For example, we say "I eat" but change the verb for "he" to say "he eats." English has regular and irregular verbs, plus transitive verbs that need an object.

Tagalog verbs, on the other hand, don't change with the subject or pronoun. Whether it's "I," "you," or "they," the verb form stays the same. But verbs are conjugated according to the focus and the aspect or tense. The language uses Actor Focus for actions done by the subject and Object Focus for actions received by the object. So, while English verbs vary with the subject and time, Tagalog verbs adapt based on who or what is the focus of the sentence and when the action happens.

In Tagalog, verbs are categorized into different groups based on their affixes, which affect how they are conjugated for Actor Focus (often referred to as "focus or the doer" of the action). These affixes include -um-, mag-, ma-, mang-, maki-, and magpa-. Each group has its own set of rules for conjugation. Here's an overview:

Affix Verb Group	Tense of Affix	Example Verb	Actor Focus Conjugation	English Translation
-um-	Basic action, present tense	kumain	Kumakain	(Someone) is eating.
mag-	General	magluto	Nagluluto	(Someone) is

	action, present tense			cooking.
ma-	State or condition, present	matulog	Natutulog	(Someone) is sleeping.
mang-	Action involving other objects/people, present	mangisda	Nangisda	(Someone) went fishing.

As a beginner learning Tagalog, it's most effective to focus initially on the "mag-" and "-um-" affixes for Actor Focus verbs. Here's why:

mag- Affix
Broad Usage: "mag-" is versatile and applies to a wide range of actions, making it essential for building a foundational vocabulary. It's used for both transitive and intransitive verbs, from general actions like "mag-aral" (to study) to activities like "maglakad" (to walk).
Ease of Understanding: Because of its general applicability, mastering "mag-" can help beginners quickly expand their ability to express actions in various contexts.

-um- Affix
Intrinsic Actions: The "-um-" affix is crucial for expressing basic, often self-contained actions like "kumain" (to eat) and "umalis" (to leave). These verbs are fundamental to everyday conversation.
Pattern Recognition: Learning the "-um-" affix helps beginners get accustomed to the unique aspect of verb conjugation, where infixes are inserted into the word, enhancing understanding of verb formation.

Lesson 54 - Mag-Verbs

Tagalog verbs have a root form, conjugated with affixes to denote action aspects: completed, ongoing, and future. The verbs of the Mag-Group uses specific affixes for different tenses.

Mag-Verb Aspects:

- **Completed:** A completed action for Mag-Verbs is formed by adding the prefix nag to the root form of the verb: Nag + luto = Nagluto.

- **Ongoing:** An ongoing action for Mag-Verbs is formed by using "Nag-" followed by the repetition of the first syllable of the root verb: Nag + lu + luto = nagluluto.

- **Future:** The future tense of Mag-Verbs involves using "Mag-" along with the repetition of the first syllable of the root verb, indicating an action that will occur: Mag + lu + luto = Magluluto

Overview and examples:

Tense/Aspect	**Root**	**Completed (Past)**	**Ongoing (Present)**	**Future**
Affixes	-	Nag-	Nag + first syllable + root	Mag + first syllable
Sample Verb	Luto	Nagluto	Nagluluto	Magluluto
Sample Phrase	-	Nagluto ako.	Nagluluto ako.	Magluluto ako.
English	-	I cooked.	I am cooking.	I will cook.

Common Mag-Verbs are shown in the following list:
Mag-Verbs are action-oriented and often signify the start or the act of doing something. Here's a list of common Mag-Verbs:

Root Word	**Mag-Verb**	**English**
Aral	Mag-aral	To study
Lakad	Maglakad	To walk
Luto	Magluto	To cook
Trabaho	Magtrabaho	To work
Basa	Magbasa	To read
Turo	Magturo	To teach

Laro	Maglaro	To play
Ehersisyo	Mag-ehersisyo	To exercise
Maneho	Magmaneho	To drive
Linis	Maglinis	To clean
Sulat	Magsulat	To write
Biyahe	Magbiyahe	To travel
Tanim	Magtanim	To plant
Bili	Magbili	To buy
Benta	Magbenta	To sell

Note: See also the verb conjugation table at the end of this book.

Lesson 55 - Ma-Verbs

Ma-Verbs are very similar conjugated like Mag-Verbs.

- **Completed:** A completed action for Ma-Verbs is formed by adding the prefix "na-" to the root form of the verb: Na + tulog = Natulog.

- **Ongoing:** An ongoing action for Ma-Verbs is formed by using "Na-" followed by the repetition of the first syllable of the root verb: Na + tu + tulog = Natutulog.

- **Future:** The future tense of Ma-Verbs involves using "Ma-" along with the repetition of the first syllable of the root verb, indicating an action that will occur: Ma + tu + tulog = Matutulog.

Overview and examples:

Tense/Aspect	**Root**	**Completed (Past)**	**Ongoing (Present)**	**Future**
Affixes	-	Na-	Na + first syllable	Ma + first syllable
Sample Verb	Tulog	Natulog	Natutulog	Matutulog
Sample	-	Natulog ako.	Natutulog ako.	Matutulog ako.

Phrase				
English Meaning	-	I slept.	I am sleeping.	I will sleep.

Common Ma-Verbs are shown in the following list:

Root Word	**Ma-Verb**	**English**
Tulog	Matulog	To fall asleep
Lungkot	Malungkot	To be sad
Tuwa	Matuwa	To be happy
Galit	Magalit	To be angry
Kita	Makita	To see
Dinig	Makinig	To listen
Nood	Manood	To watch
Halata	Mahalata	To notice, to become obvious
Wala	Mawala	To get lost, to disappear
Uhaw	Mauhaw	To become thirsty
Gutom	Magutom	To become hungry
Upo	Maupo	To sit
Ligo	Maligo	To bathe
Talo	Matalo	To be defeated
Panalo	Manalo	To win

Note: See also the verb conjugation table at the end of this book.

Lesson 56 - Um-Verbs

For "Um-Verbs" the root "kain" (to eat) provides a perfect example to illustrate the conjugation across different aspects or tenses. Here's how "Um-Verbs" are typically conjugated:

- **Completed:** The completed aspect is formed by inserting the infix "-um-" after the initial consonant of the root verb. For "kain," it becomes Kumain.

- **Ongoing:** For the ongoing aspect, add the prefix, which is the first syllable of the root verb and then insert the infix "-um-" after the first consonant of the root. So, "kain" becomes Kumakain: Ka + kain = kakain → Adding the infix -um- after the first consonant: k + um + a + kain = kumakain.

- **Future:** The future tense is formed by doubling the first syllable as a prefix to the verb root. Therefore, "kain" turns into Kakain: ka + kain = kakain.

Overview and examples:

Tense/Aspect	**Root**	**Completed (Past)**	**Ongoing (Present)**	**Future**
Affixes	-	Um- as infix, inserted in first syllable	First syllable as prefix + Um inserted as infix	First syllable as prefix
Sample Verb	Kain	Kumain	Kumakain	Kakain
Sample Phrase	-	Kumain ako.	Kumakain ako.	Kakain ako.
English Meaning	-	I ate.	I am eating.	I will eat.

Common Um-Verbs are shown in the following list:

Root Word	**Um-Verb**	**English**
Puntá	Pumuntá	To go
Kain	Kumain	To eat
Inom	Uminom	To drink
Tawa	Tumawa	To laugh
Iyak	Umiyak	To cry
Laro	Lumaro	To play
Akyat	Umakyat	To climb
Tulong	Tumulong	To help

Sayaw	Sumayaw	To dance
Talon	Tumalon	To jump
Takbo	Tumakbo	To run
Ligo	Lumigo	To bathe
Upo	Umupo	To sit
Higa	Humiga	To lie down
Bili	Bumili	To buy

Note: See also the verb conjugation table at the end of this book.

Lesson 57 - Exercice

Exercise: Conjugate the Mag-Verb Lakad - To Walk:

Tense/Aspect	**Root**	**Completed (Past)**	**Ongoing (Present)**	**Future**
Verb	Lakad			
Sample Phrase with ako	-			
English	-			

Exercise: Conjugate the Ma-Verb Nood - To Watch:

Tense/Aspect	**Root**	**Completed (Past)**	**Ongoing (Present)**	**Future**
Verb	Nood			
Sample Phrase with ako	-			
English	-			

Exercise: Conjugate the Um-Verb Bili - To Buy:

Tense/Aspect	Root	Completed (Past)	Ongoing (Present)	Future
Verb	Bili			
Sample Phrase with ako	-			
English	-			

Solution: Conjugate the Mag-Verb Lakad - To Walk:

Tense/Aspect	Root	Completed (Past)	Ongoing (Present)	Future
Affixes	Lakad	Naglakad	Naglalakad	Maglalakad
Sample Phrase with ako	-	Naglakad ako.	Naglalakad ako.	Maglalakad ako.
English	-	I walked.	I am walking.	I will walk.

Solution: Conjugate the Ma-Verb Nood - To Watch:

Tense/Aspect	Root	Completed (Past)	Ongoing (Present)	Future
Verb	Nood	Nanood	Nanonood	Manonood
Sample Phrase with ako	-	Nanood ako.	Nanonood ako.	Manonood ako.
English	-	I watched.	I am watching.	I will watch.

Solution: Conjugate the Um-Verb Bili - To Buy:

Tense/Aspect	Root	Completed (Past)	Ongoing (Present)	Future
Verb	Bili	Bumili	Bumibili	Bibili
Sample Phrase with ako	-	Bumili ako.	Bumibili ako.	Bibili ako.
English	-	I bought.	I am buying.	I will buy.

Conjugating Object Focus Verbs

In our upcoming four lessons, we'll concentrate on Object Focus verbs. We'll begin with an introduction to the basics, continue by exploring the verb groups associated with Object Focus, and finish with a practical exercise to apply what you've learned.

Lesson 58 - Introduction

In Tagalog, verbs can also be conjugated to emphasize the object of the action, known as Object Focus. These verbs often involve different affixes than those used for Actor Focus. Here's an overview of some common Object Focus verb groups, their meanings or tenses, example verbs, their conjugations in Object Focus, and English translations:

Affix	Tense of Affix	Example Verb	Object Focus Conjugation	English Translation
-in	Basic action, often past tense or completed	kainin	Kinain	(The food) was eaten
i-	Action involving movement or transfer	ilipat	Inilipat	(The thing) was transferred
-an	Action targeting a specific location or	sulatan	Sinulatan	(Someone) was written to (a

	providing a service			letter)

As a beginner learning Tagalog, **focusing on the "-in/-hin" verb group** for Object Focus verbs can provide a solid foundation due to their frequency of use and relative ease of understanding. Here's why:
Broad Usage: The "-in" affix is widely used for actions directly affecting objects, making it highly practical for everyday conversations. Learning this affix helps you form sentences focusing on what action is done to an object, which is a common necessity.
Example & Application: With verbs like "kainin" (to eat something specific), you get to practice forming sentences that are very common in daily use, such as "Kinain ko ang mansanas" (I ate the apple).

Lesson 59 - In-/Hin-Verbs

Verbs of the In- and Hin-Verg group are conjugated very similar. Let's take a look how to conjugate them.

- **Completed:** The completed aspect is formed by inserting the infix -in- after the first consonant of the root word: First consonant + in + rest of the root word.
  If the root word starts with a vowel in- is added as a prefix to the root word: in + root.

- **Ongoing:** The ongoing aspect is usually formed by inserting the infix -in- after the first consonant of the root word followed by the vowel of the first syllable of the root verb and the root word: First consonant + in + vowel of the first syllable + the root word.
  If the root word starts with a vowel, then the in plus the vowel of the first syllable of the root word is added before the root word: in + vowel of the first syllable + root.

- **Future:** The future tense is formed by repeating the first syllable of the root verb, followed by the root word and the suffix -in or hin: First syllable + root + in/hin. There is no rule if the suffix is -in or -hin. It just needs to be remembered and learned.

Example for a root word starting with a consonant:

Tense/Aspect	Root	Completed (Past)	Ongoing (Present)	Future
Affixes	-	First consonant + in + rest of the root word.	First consonant + in + vowl of the first syllable + rest of the root word.	First syllable + root + in/hin.
Sample Verb	sabi	sinabi	sinasabi	sasabihin
Sample Phrase	-	Sinabi ko.	Sinasabi ko.	Sasabihin ko.
English	say	I said.	I am saying.	I will say.

Example for a root word starting with a vowel:

Tense/Aspect	Root	Completed (Past)	Ongoing (Present)	Future
Affixes	-	in + root word.	in + vowel of the first syllable + root word.	First syllable + root + in/hin.
Sample Verb	isip	inisip	iniisip	iisipin
Sample Phrase	-	Inisip ko.	Iniisip ko.	Iisipin ko.
English	think	I thought.	I am thinking.	I will think.

Common In-/Hin-Verbs:

Verb Root	In-/Hin-Verb	English Verb
Gamit	Ginamit	To use
Gawi	Ginawi	To do
Isip	Inisip	To think
Sabi	Sinabi	To say
Dalhin	Dinala	To bring, to carry

Tawag	Tinawag	To call
Kilala	Kinilala	To get to know or to recognize
Hingi	Hiningi	To ask for
Tanggap	Tinanggap	To accept
Limot	Nilimot	To forget
Ulit	Inulit	To repeat
Luto	Niluto	To cook
Bili	Binili	To buy
Kain	Kinain	To eat
Gamit	Ginamit	To use

Note: See also the verb conjugation table at the end of this book.

Lesson 60 - I-Verbs

Let's take a look how to conjugate I-Verbs.

- **Completed:** If it root word starts with a vowel: The completed aspect is formed by inserting the infix -in- after the first consonant of the root word. Optionally i- can be added as prefix to the completed form of the verb: (i) + first consonant of the root word + infix -in- + rest of the root word.
  If it root word starts with a vowel: The completed aspect is formed by adding in- as prefix to the verb root: in + root.

- **Ongoing:** If it root word starts with a consonant: Duplicate the first syllable of the root word, then insert the infix -in- after the first consonant and add all this as prefix to the root word. Optional an i- prefix can be added to the ongoing verb form: (i) + first letter of the duplicated first syllable of the root word + in + rest of the duplicated syllable + root word.
  If it root word starts with a vowel: The ongoing aspect is usually formed by adding the prefic in- plus repeating the first letter (vowel) of the root word, followed by the root word: in + first letter of the root word + root word.

- **Future:** If it root word starts with a consunant: The future tense is formed by adding the prefix i- and then repeating the first syllable of the root verb, followed by the root word: I + first syllable of the root word + root word.
  If it root word starts with a vowel: The future tense is formed by adding the prefix i- and then repeating the first letter (vowel) of the root verb, followed by the root word: I + first letter (vowel) + root word.

Example for a root word starting with a consonant:

Tense/Aspect	Root	Completed (Past)	Ongoing (Present)	Future
Affixes	-	(i) + first consonant of the root word + infix -in- + rest of root	(i) + first letter of the duplicated first syllable + in + rest of the syllable + root word	I + first syllable of the root word + root word
Sample Verb	Balik	Binalik	Binabalik	Ibabalik
Sample Phrase	-	Binalik ko ang libro.	Binabalik ko ang libro.	Ibabalik ko ang libro bukas.
English		I returned the book.	I am returning the book.	I will return the book tomorrow.

Example for a root word starting with a vowel:

Tense/Aspect	Root	Completed (Past)	Ongoing (Present)	Future
Affixes	-	in + verb root	in + first letter of the root word + root	I + first letter (vowel) + root word
Sample Verb	Uwi	Inuwi	Inuuwi	Iuuwi
Sample Phrase	-	Inuwi ko ang payong.	Inuuwi ko ang payong.	Iuuwi ko ang payong bukas.
English		I brought the	I am bringing	I will bring the

		umbrella home.	the umbrella home.	umbrella home tomorrow.

Note: There are exemptions when the root word starts with L, R or Y.

List of useful I-Verbs:

Root	I-Verb	English Verb
Balik	Ibalik	To return something
Tago	Itago	To hide something
Isara	Isara	To close something
Lipat	Ilipat	To transfer something
Akyat	Iakyat	To bring up something
Uwi	Iuwi	To bring something home
Dagdag	Idagdag	To add something

Note: See also the verb conjugation table at the end of this book.

Lesson 61 - Exercise

Exercise: Conjugate the verb root Dagdag - To add something as per the table below.

Tense/Aspect	Root	Completed (Past)	Ongoing (Present)	Future
Affixes	-	(i) + first consonant of the root word + infix -in- + rest of root	(i) + first letter of the duplicated first syllable + in + rest of the syllable + root word	I + first syllable of the root word + root word
Sample Verb	Dagdag			
Sample	-			

Phrase with ko and asukal				
English				

Solution: Conjugate the verb root Dagdag - To add something as per the table below.

Tense/Aspect	**Root**	**Completed (Past)**	**Ongoing (Present)**	**Future**
Affixes	-	(i) + first consonant of the root word + infix -in- + rest of root	(i) + first letter of the duplicated first syllable + in + rest of the syllable + root word	I + first syllable of the root word + root word
Sample Verb	Dagdag	Dinagdag	Dinadagdag	Idadagdag
Sample Phrase with ko and asukal	-	Dinagdag ko ang asukal.	Dinadagdag ko ang asukal.	Idadagdag ko ang asukal mamaya.
English		I added the sugar.	I am adding the sugar.	I will add the sugar soon.

Lesson 62 - Commands

Here's a simple guide on how to give commands and make requests. How to form a command depends not only on the root verb but also on the verb group to which the verb belongs. Each verb group has its specific rules for forming commands or imperative forms. Here's a brief overview of how different verb groups typically form commands.

Verb Group	**Focus**	**Example Root**	**Command Form**	**English**

Mag-	Actor	luto (cook)	**Mag**luto! (formal) / Luto! (informal)	Cook!
-um-	Actor	inom (drink)	Inom!	Drink!
-in	Object	sulat (write)	Sulat**in** mo!	Write it!
I-	Object	dala (carry)	**I**dala mo!	Carry it!

Structure: Commands typically follow the structure of the verb followed by the pronoun, if necessary.

Commands:
Direct commands often use the base form of the verb. Example:

Tagalog	English
Tumakbo ka!	Run! (You run!)

Examples:

Tagalog	English	Explanation
Umalis ka na.	Leave now.	Direct command, simple and straightforward.

Learning Tip: When giving commands in Tagalog, start with the root form of the verb. This approach serves as an informal way to issue commands for both "mag-" and "um-" verbs, covering a wide range of everyday situations.

Exercise: Try using these structures to form your own commands and. For example:

- How would you tell someone to “sit down”

Sample solution:

Tagalog	English
Umupo ka!	Sit down! (You sit down!)

Lesson 63 - Requests

forming polite requests often involves the use of the prefix "paki-" combined with the verb. This prefix effectively turns the verb into a request. For adding extra politeness, the word "po" is also frequently included. "Po" is a marker of respect and can be used with anyone, especially those older or in a formal setting. Additionally, the Tagalog word for "please," which is "pakiusap," is sometimes used to enhance the politeness of a request, particularly in more formal or traditional settings. This combination of linguistic elements helps express courtesy and respect in communication.

Key Forms for Requests:

Category	Usage	Example
Polite requests or favors with paki-	The prefix "paki-" in Tagalog is commonly used to turn statements into polite requests or favors. Paki- is derived from the word "pakiusap," which means "a request" or "a favor." The prefix serves to transform a verb into a request form, making the sentence courteous and less direct.	Paki-abot ng asin. Please pass the salt.
Polite Requests with po	Adding po can soften commands into more polite requests, making them sound less direct and more courteous.	Paki-ulit po. Please repeat.
Express hope or a softer suggestion with sana	"Sana" is primarily used to express hope or a wish about a situation. When combined with requests, "sana" helps soften the tone, making the request sound less demanding and more like a hopeful suggestion	Sana makapunta ka. I hope you can come.

Structure: Requests in Tagalog typically follow the structure of the verb followed by the pronoun, if necessary. The inclusion of polite particles like po and modal particles like sana helps in softening the command or making the request more respectful.

Requests:
Adding paki- before the verb is a common way to make polite requests. Example:

Tagalog	English
Paki-dala ito.	Please bring this.

To soften the request further, add po (for respect) and sana (to express hope). Example:

Tagalog	English
Paki-dala po sana ito.	Please bring this, if you could.

Examples:

Tagalog	English	Explanation
Umalis ka na.	Leave now.	Direct command, simple and straightforward.
Paki-ayos po ng mesa.	Please fix the table.	Polite request, using paki- and po to show respect.

Learning Tip: For making requests or when you want to be polite, remember to use "paki-" and "po." These additions help soften your request and show respect to the listener.

Exercise: Try using these structures to form your own requests. For example:

- How would you tell someone to “sit down” in both a direct and a polite way?
- How would you ask someone to “close the door” politely?
- How would you ask someone to close the door politely?

Answers:

Tagalog	English
Paki-upo po.	Please sit down.
Paki-sara po ng pinto.	Please close the door.
Paki-sara ng pinto.	Please close the door.

Lesson 64 - Expressing Ability & Possibility

Expressing abilities and possibilities is often done through the use of specific affixes attached to verbs. These affixes help convey whether someone can do something, whether something is possible, or whether someone has the potential to do something in the future. Here's a simple guide on how to use these affixes effectively in Tagalog.

Prefix	Usage	Example
Maka-	This prefix is used to express the ability or capability to perform an action.	Makakain (can eat)
Makapag-	Similar to maka-, but often used with actions that are slightly more complex or involve an object.	Makapag-aral (can study)
Ma-	This prefix is generally used to denote the potential or general ability.	Marinig (ability to hear)

The word "marinig" is derived from the root word "rinig" which means "to hear." When the prefix "ma-" is added to "rinig," forming "marinig," it transforms the verb into a form that denotes the potential or general ability to hear. This can refer to the ability to hear something specific in a particular instance or more generally, the capability of hearing. Example Usage:

Tagalog	English
Marinig mo ba ako?	Can you hear me?
Gusto kong marinig ang iyong opinyon.	I want to hear your opinion.

Structure: The structure often follows the Verb-Subject-Object (VSO) order, especially in simple sentences that involve these prefixes. Here's how you can construct sentences:

Component	Description
Verb	Start with the prefix and the root verb.
Subject	Follow with the subject, e.g., a personal pronoun or name.
Object	End with the object, if there is one.

Examples:

Tagalog	English
Makakain ako ng mansanas.	I can eat an apple.

Breakdown: Makakain (can eat) + ako (I) + ng mansanas (an apple)

Tagalog	English
Makapag-aral tayo sa susunod na Biyernes.	We can study next Friday.

Breakdown: Makapag-aral (can study) + tayo (we) + sa sunod (next) + Biyernes (Friday).

Tagalog	English
Marinig mo ba ang musika?	Can you hear the music?

Breakdown: Marinig (can hear) + mo (you) + ba (question marker) + ang musika (the music)

Exercise: Translate the phrases:

Tagalog	English
	Can you sleep?
	We can cook dinner.

	She can see a bird.
	You can read this letter.
	We can study tomorrow.
	The child can swim.

Solution:

Tagalog	**English**
Makatulog ka ba?	Can you sleep?
Makapagluto tayo ng hapunan.	We can cook dinner.
Makakita siya ng ibon.	She can see a bird.
Mabasa mo ang sulat na ito.	You can read this letter.
Makapag-aral kami bukas.	We can study tomorrow.
Makalangoy ang bata.	The child can swim.

Explanations:

Phrase	**Explanations**
Makatulog ka ba?	Uses Maka- with "tulog" (sleep) and the question marker ba asking about the possibility of sleeping.
Makapagluto tayo ng hapunan.	Uses Makapag- with "luto" (cook), stating a collective capability to cook dinner.
Makakita siya ng ibon.	Uses Maka- with "kita" (see), indicating the ability to see a bird.
Mabasa mo ang sulat na ito.	Uses Ma- with "basa" (read), asking if the listener can read the letter, implying the capability to do so.
Makapag-aral kami bukas.	Uses Makapag- with "aral" (study), expressing the possibility of studying the next day.
Makalangoy ang bata.	Uses Maka- with "langoy" (swim), expressing that the child has the capability to swim.

Lesson 65 - Verbification

In Tagalog, a fascinating feature of the language is the ability to transform adjectives and nouns into verbs. This process is known as "pagpapandiwa" or verbification. It allows speakers to express dynamic actions or states using words that typically describe qualities or objects. This lesson will guide you through the concept of verbification, including how it works and how to use it effectively. **What is Verbification?** Verbification is the process of converting non-verbs, such as adjectives and nouns, into verbs. In Tagalog, this is commonly achieved by adding appropriate verb affixes to the root word. This allows the language to dynamically express actions or states that are usually static. **How Verbification Works:** To verbify an adjective or noun in Tagalog, you typically add affixes that indicate the focus (actor or object) and aspect (completed, ongoing, future) of the action. Here are the most common affixes used:

Affix Type	Description and Tense/Aspect
Mag-	Often used for actor-focus verbs, typically in future or present tense.
Um-	Common prefix for actor-focus verbs, used across completed, present, and future actions, inserted within the root.
In-	Used for object-focus verbs, commonly for completed actions.
-in	A suffix for object-focus verbs, often used for completed actions.

Examples of Verbification:

Liban (absent)

Tagalog	Tense	Focus	English
Lumiban	Completed	Actor-focus	Was absent
Lumiliban	Ongoing	Actor-focus	Is being absent

Payat (thin)

Tagalog	Tense	Focus	English

Magpayat	Future tense	Actor-focus	Will become thin
Nagpayat	Past tense	Actor-focus	Became thin

Takot (fear)

Tagalog	**Tense**	**Focus**	**English**
Takutin	Future tense	Object-focus	Will scare
Tinakot	Past tense	Object-focus	Scared someone

Saya (happiness)

Tagalog	**Tense**	**Focus**	**English**
Pasayahin	Future tense	Object-focus	Will make happy
Pinasaya	Past tense	Object-focus	Made happy

Exercise: Choose an adjective like "bago" (new), libang (absent) galit (angry)c, sama (bad), laki (big), anak (birth) and verbify them using different affixes.

Tagalog	**English**

Sample solutions:

Tagalog	**English**
Lumiban siya sa klase.	He was absent from class.
Nagagalit siya sa ingay.	He is getting angry because of the noise.
Sumama ang panahon.	The weather became bad.
Lumaki ang puppy.	The puppy grew big.
Nanganak ang kanyang aso.	Her dog gave birth.
Nag-anak siya ng kambal.	She gave birth to twins.
Lumalakas ang ulan.	The rain is getting stronger.
Nagpapayat si Maria.	Maria is losing weight.

Lumilibang siya tuwing gabi.	He entertains himself every evening.
Nagpapasama siya sa doktor.	He is asking someone to accompany him to the doctor.

Lesson 66 - Usage of Markers and Pronouns

In Tagalog, pronouns change form depending on their role in the sentence. There are Actor Focus pronouns, indicating that the pronoun is the doer of the action, and Object Focus pronouns, which are used when the action is being done to the pronoun, showing it as part of the context but not the main focus.

AF (Actor Focus)	OF (Object Focus)	English
Ako	Ko	I/me (by me)
Ka/Ikaw	Mo	You (singular) (by you)
Siya	Niya	He/She (by him/her)
Kami/Tayo	Namin/Natin	We (exclusive/inclusive) (by us)
Kayo	Ninyo	You (plural) (by you plural)
Sila	Nila	They (by them)

Just as we have subject markers to identify the subject of a sentence, there are also object markers that precede objects in a sentence, indicating the recipient of the action or the entity involved in the action. Understanding these markers is essential for constructing clear and grammatically correct sentences.

Object Markers for Names

Tagalog	English
ni	of (singular); indicates possession or target of an action towards a person
nina	of (plural); indicates possession or target of an action towards people

Example:

Tagalog	English
Ang libro ni Juan.	The book of Juan. / Juan's book.
Kumain ako ng mansanas ni Maria.	I ate Maria's apple.

Object Markers for Non-Personal Nouns

For all other objects that are not personal names, the object marker "ng" is used. This includes inanimate objects, ideas, or anything that is not a person. The marker "ng" serves a similar function to "of" in English or indicates the object of the action.

Tagalog	English
ng	ng-marker, marks the noun as non-focus and unspecific; indicates the object of the action or possession for non-person entities.

Example:

Tagalog	English
Kumain ako ng mansanas.	I ate an apple.

In this sentence, "ng" is used before "mansanas" (apple) to indicate that the apple is the object of the action (eating).

Here's a table categorizing markers into Actor Focus and Object Focus, as per their usage with names, objects, subjects, and personal pronouns:

Description	Actor Focus Markers	Object Focus Markers
Names	si (singular)	ni (singular)
	sina (plural)	nina (plural)
Objects	-	ng
Subjects	ang	-
Personal Pronouns	Ako (I)	Ko (by me)
	Ka/Ikaw (You)	Mo (by you)
	Siya (He/She)	Niya (by him/her)
	Kami/Tayo (We)	Namin/Natin (by us)
	Kayo (You, plural)	Ninyo (by you, plural)

	Sila (They)	Nila (by them)
Demonstrative Pronouns		ito (this)
		iyan, yan (that, near the speaker)
		iyon, yon (that, far from both the speaker and listener)

This table reflects the distinction between Actor Focus markers, which are used to emphasize who is performing the action, and Object Focus markers, which highlight the recipient or target of the action. Note that for objects, "ng" is the primary marker used in Object Focus constructions, and there's no direct equivalent in Actor Focus since the subject marker "ang" or personal pronouns are used based on the focus of the sentence.

Here's a table that illustrates the difference between Actor Focus (AF) and Object Focus (OF). This table contrasts Actor Focus phrases, where the action performed by the subject is the main focus, with Object Focus phrases, where the emphasis shifts to the object or recipient of the action. Note that the translation and conjugation shift slightly in Tagalog to reflect these focus changes, providing clarity on what or whom the sentence is primarily about.

Actor Focus	**English**	**Object Focus**	**English**
Nagmamaneho si Lisa ng kotse.	Lisa is driving a car.	Iminamaneho ni Lisa ang kotse.	Lisa is driving the car.
Nagmamaneho si Lisa ng kotse mo.	Lisa is driving your car.	Iminamaneho ni Lisa ang iyong kotse.	Lisa is driving your car.
Umiinom si Paul ng kape.	Paul is drinking coffee.	Iniinom ni Paul ang kape na inihanda ko.	Paul is drinking the coffee that I prepared.
Kumain ako ng mansanas.	I ate an apple.	Kinain ko ang mansanas na nasa mesa.	I ate the apple that was on the table.
Nagbabasa si Lisa ng libro.	Lisa is reading a book.	Binabasa ni Lisa ang bagong libro niya.	Lisa is reading her new book.
Bumili siya ng manok.	She bought chicken.	Binili niya itong manok.	She bought this chicken.

Exercise: Choose a Object Focus phrase from the lesson, write it down, learn and practice it.

Tagalog	English

Lesson 67 - Sentence Structure

In Tagalog, the structure of sentences often starts with the verb, which is a bit different from the typical subject-verb-object order found in English. This arrangement highlights the action right at the beginning, followed by who is doing the action, and then who or what is receiving the action. A simplified formula for constructing these sentences is: Verb + Doer of the Action (Actor)+ Receiver of the Action.

Verb	Actor / Subject	Receiver / Object
Kumakain ang babae ng mansanas.		
Kumakain	ang babae	ng mansanas
is eating	the woman	an apple
The woman is eating an apple. / The woman eats an apple.		

For instance, consider the English sentence "The woman eats an apple." Translated into Tagalog following the mentioned formula, it becomes "Kumakain ang babae ng mansanas." Here, "Kumakain" (eats) is the verb, "ang babae" (the woman) is the doer of the action, and "ng mansanas" (an apple) is the receiver of the action. "Ng mansanas" is marked as the receiver of the action because it is what is being eaten; it receives the action of the verb "eats" This use of the particle "ng" helps clarify the role of different elements in a sentence, distinguishing the actor from the receiver of the action. This verb-initial structure makes Tagalog fascinating because it puts the focus on what's happening before anything else. I would like to point out that this formula and sentence structure work for both Actor Focus and Object Focus phrases.

For Actor Focus phrases, where the spotlight is on the doer, the formula beautifully lays out the sequence of action. For example, "Nagluluto ang chef ng adobo" (The chef cooks adobo), "Nagluluto" being the verb, "ang chef" the actor, and "ng adobo" the object.

Verb	Actor / Subject	Receiver / Object
Nagluto	ang chef	ng adobo.
cooks / is cooking	the chef	adobo

Similarly, this formula adapts seamlessly to Object Focus phrases, which highlight the action's recipient.

Verb	Actor / Subject	Receiver / Object
Niluto	ng chef	ang adobo.
was cooked	by the chef	the adobo

While the syntax may slightly adjust to mark the object as the focus, the underlying principle remains. In "Niluto ng chef ang adobo." (The adobo was cooked by the chef.), the action still leads, followed by the doer and the receiver, showcasing the flexibility and focus-oriented nature of Tagalog grammar.

Actor Focus	English Meaning	Object Focus	English Meaning
Kumakain ako ng mansanas.	I am eating an apple.	Kinakain ko ang mansanas.	The apple is being eaten by me.
Nagsusulat ako ng liham.	I am writing a letter.	Isinusulat ko ang liham.	The letter is being written by me.
Nagluluto siya ng adobo.	She is cooking adobo.	Niluluto niya ang adobo.	The adobo is being cooked by her.
Umiinom ako ng tubig.	I am drinking water.	Iniinom ko ang tubig.	The water is being drunk by me.

Exercise: Choose a Verb-Actor-Receiver phrase from the lesson, write it down, learn and practice it.

Tagalog	English

Lesson 68 - Forming Sentences

This guide demonstrates how to craft grammatically correct phrases in Tagalog in four straightforward steps, making sentence construction accessible and manageable for learners at any level.

1. Topic and Focus
Identify the main subject to establish the sentence focus:

Actor-Focus: On the action's doer.
Object-Focus: On what the action is directed at.

2. Markers and Pronouns
Choose markers and pronouns based on the focus:

Marker	Function	Examples	Meaning
Ang	Focus subject or object (singular)	Ang mansanas	The apple (singular)
Ang mga	Focus on non-specific objects or subjects (plural)	Ang mga mansanas	The apples (plural)
Si	Focus on a specific person (singular)	Si Juan	Juan (specific person, singular)
Sina	Focus on specific people (plural)	Sina Juan at Maria	Juan and Maria (specific people, plural)
Ni	Possession (singular)	Ni Juan	By Juan / of Juan (singular)
Nina	Possession (plural)	Nina Juan at Maria	By Juan and Maria / of Juan and Maria (plural)
Para Kay	Intended recipient (singular)	Para kay Juan	For Juan (singular)

Para Kina	Intended recipients (plural)	Para kina Juan at Maria	For Juan and Maria (plural)
Ng	Additional details in actor-focus or actors in...	Ng mansanas	Of an apple
Sa	Direction, location, or recipients	Sa bahay	To the house
Actor Focus Pronouns	I, you, he/she, we (inclusive), we (exclusive)...	Ako, ikaw/ka, siya...	I, you, he/she, we (inclusive), we (exclusive)
Object Focus Pronouns	me, you, him/her, us (inclusive)/us (exclusive)...	ko, mo, niya...	me, you, him/her, us (inclusive)/us (exclusive)

3. Verb Aspects/Tenses: Completed, Ongoing, Future

Verb tenses change by affixes for completed, ongoing, or future actions, differing by focus and the verb group:

Group	**Focus**	**Completed**	**Ongoing**	**Future**
mag-	AF	Nag-	Nag + first syllable + root	Mag + first syllable
-um-	AF	Um- as infix, inserted in first syllable	First syllable as prefix + Um inserted as infix	Double first syllable as prefix
in- (consonant)	OF	First consonant + in + rest of the root word.	First consonant + in + vowl of the first syllable + rest of the root word.	First syllable + root + in/hin.
in- (vowel)	OF	in + root word.	in + vowel of the first syllable + root word.	First syllable + root + in/hin.
i- (consonant)	OF	(i) + first consonant of the root word + infix -in- + rest of root	(i) + first letter of the duplicated first syllable + in + rest of the syllable + root word	I + first syllable of the root word + root word
i- (vowel)	OF	in + verb root	in + first letter of the root word +	I + first letter (vowel) + root

			root	word

4. Sentence Structure

Use the VSO (Verb-Subject-Object) structure to assemble sentences. In the VSO (Verb-Subject-Object) structure, the sentence begins with the Verb (what was done), followed by the Subject (by whom), and ends with the Object (who or what received the action). This order highlights the action first, then who did it, then who or what it was done to and finally additional information, e,g, like the location and time words.

Nagluto si Mama ng sinigang sa bahay kahapon.				
Nagluto	si Mama	ng sinigang	sa bahay	kahapon
Verb	Subject	Object	Location	time word
cooked	Mama	sinigang	at home	yesterday
Mama cooked sinigang at home yesterday.				

Applying the guide to form an actor-focus sentence for "Lisa is reading a book now":

1. Identify the Focus

Our focus is on the actor, Lisa, who is performing the action of reading, hence we choose Actor Focus.

2. Choose Markers and Pronouns

Since Lisa is the actor, we use "Si" before her name. For the object "a book" (book being "libro"), we use "ng" as the marker to indicate the object of the action in an actor-focus sentence ("ng" marks the book as non-focus).

3. Determine Verb Tense / Aspect

The action is ongoing. We use "nag-" plus the first syllable of the root verb with the verb "basa" (read), becoming "nagbabasa" to indicate an ongoing action.

4. Assemble the Sentence

Following the VSO structure, our sentence starts with the verb, includes the actor, the object, and ends with the time expression.

Tagalog	**English**

Nagbabasa si Lisa ng libro ngayon.	Lisa is reading a book now.

Applying the guide to form an object-focus sentence, let's create an example with the phrase "The book is being read by Lisa now":

1. Identify the Focus
The main focus is on the object, the book, which is receiving the action of being read. Hence, we choose Object Focus.

2. Choose Markers and Pronouns
For the object "book" (book being "libro"), we use "Ang" as the marker to highlight the object as the focus of the sentence. Lisa, who performs the action, is marked with "ni" to indicate the doer of the action in an object-focus sentence.

3. Determine Verb Tense / Aspect
The action is ongoing. In object-focus sentences for ongoing actions, we typically use the affix "-in-" or "i-" placed within or before the root verb. In this case the infix "-in-" is inserted after the first consonant of the root word, and for ongoing actions, the first syllable of the root is repeated. Hence the verb "read" (basa) can be modified to "binabasa" to indicate that the action is currently happening to the object.

4. Assemble the Sentence
Following a slightly modified structure due to object focus, our sentence emphasizes the object, the doer, and then time.

Tagalog	**English**
Binabasa ni Lisa ang libro ngayon.	The book is being read by Lisa now. / Lisa is reading **the book** now.

Exercise: Form out of these two sentence Tagalog phrases in Actor and Object Focus following the guide above:
1. “Juan is cooking chicken soup now.” (use AF)
2. “The letter is being written by Maria now.” (use OF)

Solution:

Actor Focus Phrase: Juan is cooking chicken soup now.
1. Identify the Focus: Juan is doing the action, so this is Actor Focus.
2. Choose Markers and Pronouns: "Si Juan" for the actor. "Ng" marks "chicken soup" ("tinolang manok") as the non-focus object.
3. Determine Verb Tenses: The action is ongoing, so we use "nagluluto" (is cooking).
4. Assemble the Sentence (VSO): Nagluluto si Juan ng tinolang manok ngayon.

Object Focus Phrase: The letter is being written by Maria now.

1. Identify the Focus: The letter is receiving the action, so this is Object Focus.
2. Choose Markers and Pronouns: "Ang sulat" for the object in focus. "Ni Maria" marks Maria as the doer of the action.
3. Determine Verb Tenses: The action is ongoing. We modify "sulat" (write) to "sinusulat" (is being written).
4. Assemble the Sentence (VSO): Sinusulat ni Maria ang sulat ngayon.

Lesson 69 - Ay & Nga Linking Markers

Linking markers play an essential role in sentence structure and emphasis. The most commonly used linking marker is "ay" while "nga" is less frequent and more formal or emphatic. This lesson will explore how and when to use these markers.

1. "Ay" - The Inversion Marker:
"Ay" is used to invert the usual verb-subject-object (VSO) order of Tagalog sentences to subject-verb-object (SVO) order. This is particularly useful for emphasis or stylistic purposes.

VSO	**SVO**	**English**
Kumakain ang bata.	Ang bata ay kumakain.	The child is eating.

Usage Tips:
- Use "ay" for clarity when the sentence begins with something other than the subject.

- Use "ay" to emphasize the subject or to match the rhythm in written or formal contexts.

2. "Nga" - The Emphatic Linker:
"Nga" is a linking marker used to add emphasis and is often found in formal or literary Tagalog. It can also invert a sentence like "ay" but it adds a nuance of certainty or affirmation.

VSO	SVO with "nga"	English
Magaling ang manunu-lat.	Ang manunulat nga ay magaling.	VSO: The writer is ex-cellent. SVO: Indeed, the writer is excellent.

"Nga" can be shortened to "ng" in casual speech and writing, though this is less formal and less emphatic. However, it's important to note that this "ng" is dis-tinct from the very common particle "ng" (pronounced "nang") used in Tagalog for other grammatical purposes, such as linking adjectives to nouns or serving as a possessive marker (Case Marker). When "nga" is used for emphasis and shortened to "ng" it typically follows pronouns or nouns and is often attached directly to the word it emphasizes. Here's how you can contract "nga" with words:

Tagalog	English
Sila nga ang nanalo.	They indeed won.
Sila ng nanalo.	They indeed won.
Ako nga ang may dala.	I indeed am carrying it.
Ako ng ang may dala.	I indeed am carrying it.

Usage Tips: "Nga" is best used in literary works or when you want to affirm something strongly. It can be used to intensify the meaning of the words it fol-lows.

Exercise: Translate and rearrange the following sentences using "ay" and "nga":

1. The teacher speaks.

Instructions	Tagalog	English
VSO - default order		The teacher speaks.
SVO - using "ay"		
SVO - using "nga" for emphasis		

2. The car is fast.

Instructions	Tagalog	English
VSO - default order		
SVO - using "ay"		
SVO - using "nga" for emphasis		

Solution:
1. The teacher speaks.

Tagalog	Explanation	English
Nagsasalita ang guro.	VSO - default order	The teacher speaks.
Ang guro ay nagsasa-lita.	SVO - using "ay"	The teacher is spea-king.
Ang guro ngâ ay nagsa-salita.	SVO - using "nga" for emphasis	Indeed, the teacher is speaking.

2. The car is fast.

Tagalog	Explanation	English
Mabilis ang kotse.	VSO - default order	The car is fast.
Ang kotse ay mabilis.	SVO - using "ay"	The car is fast.
Ang kotse ngâ ay mabi-lis.	SVO - using "ngâ" for emphasis	Indeed, the car is fast.

Note for Beginners in Tagalog: Start with mastering the Verb-Subject-Object

(VSO) sentence structure. It's the natural order in Tagalog. Once you're comfortable with VSO, you can start adding "ay" for sentence inversion, but focus on VSO first to build a strong foundation.

Lesson 70 - Decoding & Understanding

I learned the method of decoding through the videos and books of Vera F. Birkenbihl (management trainer and the former head of the Institute for Brain-Friendly Working, deceased 2011). In decoding, you translate a sentence from Tagalog word for word into English. This way, you decipher the meaning of the words and the grammar of the language. You not only learn the meaning of individual words but also understand their use in sentence context, sentence structure, conjugations, tenses, prepositions, as well as differences and similarities to English. Therefore, I see this as a good method to develop access to the language. Let's get started.

First, choose a sentence in Tagalog (from this book, the internet, or another source). Then start translating the sentence word for word, as in the following example for "Nagluluto ako ng adobo". It works best to write the meaning under each word. In this Ebook version, you see the decoded information in brackets after the word.

Nagluluto [Nag- is a prefix for ongoing tense, Actor-Focus and luto is “to cook”] ako [I, Actor-Focus personal pronoun] ng [noun marker, non-focus, indefinite] adobo [Adobo, a Filipino dish].
Meaning: I am cooking Adobo.

Nagluluto ako ng adobo.			
Nagluluto	ako	ng	adobo
Nag- is a prefix for ongoing tense, Actor-Focus and luto is 'to cook'	I, Actor-Focus personal pronoun	noun marker, non-focus, indefinite	Adobo, a Filipino dish
I am cooking adobo.			

Example for decoding the phrase: Gusto ko humiram ng payong kay Lilly.

Gusto ko humiram ng payong kay Lilly.						
Gusto	ko	humiram	ng	payong	kay	Lilly
Want	I	to borrow	noun marker, non-focus, indefinite	umbrella	from	Lilly
I want to borrow an umbrella from Lilly.						

Example: Sentence: Marami akong dala na prutas kahapon.

Marami akong dala na prutas kahapon.					
Marami	akong	dala	na	prutas	kahapon
Many	I, by me	brought	that	fruits	yesterday
I brought many fruits yesterday.					

Example: Sentence: Pumunta siya sa merkado at pagkatapos sa opisina.

Pumunta siya sa merkado at pagkatapos sa opisina.							
Pu-munta	siya	sa	mer-kado	at	pag-kata-pos	sa	opisina
Went	he/she	to	market	and	after	to	office
He/She went to the market and then to the office.							

Example: Sentence: Maganda si Lilly.

Maganda si Lilly.		
Maganda	si	Lilly
Beautiful	(a marker for personal names)	Lilly
Lilly is beautiful.		

Example: Sentence: Nagluto si Maria ng adobo.

Nagluto si Maria ng adobo.				
Nagluto	si	Maria	ng	adobo
Cooked	(a marker for personal names)	Maria	(noun marker)	adobo
Maria cooked adobo.				

Exercise: Decode this sentence using the same method: Kumain siya sa restaurant kahapon.

Kumain siya sa restaurant kahapon.				
Kumain	siya	sa	restaurant	kahapon

Exercise: Decode the phrase "Kumain siya sa restaurant kahapon."

Kumain siya sa restaurant kahapon.				

Exercise: Decode this sentence using the same method. Nagluto si Maria ng adobo sa kusina.

Nagluto si Maria ng adobo sa kusina.						

Solution: Sentence: Kumain siya sa restaurant kahapon.

Kumain siya sa restaurant kahapon.				
Kumain	siya	sa	restaurant	kahapon
Ate	he/she	in/at	restaurant	yesterday
He/She ate at the restaurant yesterday.				

Solution: Sentence: Nagluto si Maria ng adobo sa kusina.

Nagluto si Maria ng adobo sa kusina.						
Nagluto	si	Maria	ng	adobo	sa	kusina
Cooked	(a marker for personal names)	Maria	(noun marker)	adobo	in	kitchen
Maria cooked adobo in the kitchen.						

Lesson 71 - Here & There

In English, there are two words for referencing locations. These are here and there. They differ by the distance to the speaker. Here is close to the speaker and there is a location away from the speaker.

Tagalog	English
Dito / Narito	This means "here" and is used to describe a location close to the speaker. - I live here.
Doon / Nandoon	This means "there" and is used for places away from both the speaker and listener. - Paule lives there (e.g. in France).
Diyan / Nandiyan	In Tagalog, "Diyan" and "Nandiyan" both translate to "there" and refer to something that is near the speaker but not immediately adjacent, often within sight but not touchable. "Diyan" is used for pointing out nearby locations, while "Nandiyan" implies something or someone is expected to be at a known nearby location, even if not currently visible.

In Tagalog, there are three instead of two distances because Tagalog distinguishes between different degrees of "there," based on the distance from the speaker. Let's explore how you can talk about where things are, focusing on the words for "here" and "there."

1. Here - Dito/Narito

Tagalog	English
Dito ako nakatira.	I live here.
Narito ang susi.	The key is here.

2. There - Doon/Nandoon and Diyan/Nandiyan
Tagalog distinguishes between different degrees of "there", based on the distance from the speaker.

A. Doon/Nandoon - Used for locations far from both the speaker and the listener.

Examples:

Tagalog	English
Doon ako nag-aral.	I studied there (far away).
Nandoon ang simbahan.	The church is over there (far away).

B. Diyan/Nandiyan - Used for locations relatively near the speaker but possibly far from the listener.

Examples:

Tagalog	English
Diyan lang ako.	I am just there (not far).
Nandiyan sa mesa ang libro.	The book is there on the table (close by).

Practice Tips: Use dito/narito when referring to something close to you, like "Here is my house" - Narito ang bahay ko.

Use doon/nandoon when pointing out something far from both you and your listener, like "The hospital is there (far away)" - Nandoon ang ospital.
Use diyan/nandiyan when the object is away from you but not too far, suitable for instructions, like "Please put it there (not far from me)" - Paki-lagay diyan.

Context	Tagalog	English
Close to the speaker	Narito ang bahay ko.	Here is my house.
Far from both the speaker and listener	Nandoon ang ospital.	The hospital is there (far away).
Not too far from the speaker, suitable for instructions	Paki-lagay diyan.	Please put it there (not far from me).

Exercise: Translate.

Tagalog	English
	The ball is here.
	My friend lives there (far).
	Can you see the cat there (close by)?

Solution:

Tagalog	English
Narito ang bola.	The ball is here.
Doon nakatira ang kaibigan ko.	My friend lives there (far).
Nakikita mo ba ang pusa diyan?	Can you see the cat there (close by)?

Lesson 72 - This & That

In Tagalog, just like in English, there are words to specify items or people close to us or further away. These words are equivalent to "this" and "that". Understanding and using them correctly can help make your communication clear, especially when you're referring to specific things or people in your surroundings. Let's dive into the basics of "this" and "that" in Tagalog.

"This" - Ito

Ito is used to refer to something that is close to the speaker. It indicates that the object or person being referred to is within reach or is being directly interacted with by the speaker. Examples:

Tagalog	English
Ito	This (close to the speaker)
Ito ang libro ko.	This is my book.
Gusto mo ba ito?	Do you like this?

"That" - Iyan and Iyon

There are two equivalents for "that," depending on the object's distance from the speaker.

Tagalog	Context & Usage	Example	English
Iyan (Diyan/Nandiyan)	Used when the object or person is not too far from the speaker but not within immediate reach. Closer than "iyon" but farther than "ito".	Diyan mo ilagay ang libro.	Put the book there (not too far).
Iyon (Doon/Nandoon)	Used for objects or people that are far from both the speaker and the listener.	Nandoon ang simbahan.	The church is over there (far away).

Examples:

Tagalog	English
Iyan ang kotse ni Maria.	That is Maria's car (not too far).
Pakikuha mo nga iyan.	Please get that for me (not too far).
Iyon ang bahay nila.	That is their house (far away).
Sino iyon?	Who is that (far away)?

Ito ang bolpen ko.	This is my pen.
Pakiabot naman ng librong iyan.	Can you hand me that book (close by)?
Maganda ang bundok na iyon sa umaga.	That mountain (far away) looks beautiful in the morning.

Exercise: Translate.

English	**Tagalog**
This is my pen.	
Can you hand me that book (close by)?	
That mountain (far away) looks beautiful in the morning.	

Solution:

English	**Tagalog**
This is my pen.	Ito ang bolpen ko.
Can you hand me that book (close by)?	Pakiabot nga iyan na libro.
That mountain (far away) looks beautiful in the morning.	Maganda ang itsura ng bundok na iyon sa umaga.

Here's the breakdown of "Maganda ang itsura ng bundok na iyon sa umaga." word by word:

- Maganda - Beautiful
- ang - the
- itsura - appearance/look
- ng - Ng-Marker for nouns
- bundok - mountain
- na - that
- iyon - that (far away)
- sa - in
- umaga - morning

Lesson 73 - Have & There Is

In English, "have" and "there is" are used to indicate possession and existence, respectively. Tagalog handles these concepts a bit differently, using specific words that change slightly depending on context. Let's dive into how to express "have" and "there is" in Tagalog.

1. Have - May/Mayroon

May and mayroon (more formal) are used to express possession or the existence of something. Examples:

Tagalog	English
May aso ako.	I have a dog.
Mayroon siyang kotse.	He/She has a car.

2. There is/There are - May/Mayroon

Interestingly, may and mayroon are also used to indicate the existence of something or someone in a particular place, similar to "there is" or "there are" in English. Examples:

Tagalog	English
May tao sa loob.	There is someone inside.
Mayroon kaming pagkain para sa lahat.	We have food for everyone.

Usage Tips: Use may for a more conversational tone and mayroon for a slightly more formal or emphasized statement. The structure for using may/mayroon can be flexible. For instance, you can start with may/mayroon, followed by the object, and then the possessor or location. There's no need to conjugate may/mayroon for number or tense. The context will clarify whether you're talking about one or multiple items and whether it's a current or past situation.

Exercise: Translate the phrases.

Tagalog	English
	I have a friend.
	There is a cat under the table.
	We have three books.

Solution:

Tagalog	English
May kaibigan ako.	I have a friend.
May pusa sa ilalim ng mesa.	There is a cat under the table.
May tatlong libro kami.	We have three books.

Lesson 74 - Numbers

Tagalog numbers are straightforward once you grasp the basics. Let's dive in!

Basic Numbers (0-10)

Tagalog	English	Number
Sero	Zero	0
Isa	One	1
Dalawa	Two	2
Tatlo	Three	3
Apat	Four	4
Lima	Five	5
Anim	Six	6
Pito	Seven	7
Walo	Eight	8
Siyam	Nine	9
Sampu	Ten	10

Numbers 11 through 19 are formed by starting with "labing" followed by the base number.

Tagalog	English	Number
Labing-isa	Eleven	11
Labindalawa	Twelve	12
Labintatlo	Thirteen	13
Labing-apat	Fourteen	14
Labing-lima	Fifteen	15
Labing-anim	Sixteen	16
Labing-pito	Seventeen	17
Labing-walo	Eighteen	18
Labinsiyam	Nineteen	19
Dalawampu	Twenty	20

For multiples of ten from twenty onwards, you use "dalawampu" (20), "tatlumpu" (30), "apatnapu" (40), and so on.

Tagalog	English	Number
Dalawampu	Twenty	20
Tatlumpu	Thirty	30
Apatnapu	Forty	40
Limampu	Fifty	50
Animnapu	Sixty	60
Pitumpu	Seventy	70
Walumpu	Eighty	80
Siyanpu	Ninety	90
Isang daan	One hundred	100

For numbers in between, like 21 or 31, combine the words for the tens and the base numbers with "at" (and), shortened to "'t", in between:

Tagalog	English	Number
Dalawampu't isa	Twenty-one	21
Dalawampu't dalawa	Twenty-two	22
Dalawampu't tatlo	Twenty-three	23

Dalawampu't apat	Twenty-four	24
Dalawampu't lima	Twenty-five	25
Dalawampu't anim	Twenty-six	26
Dalawampu't pito	Twenty-seven	27
Dalawampu't walo	Twenty-eight	28
Dalawampu't siyam	Twenty-nine	29
Tatlumpu	Thirty	30
Tatlumpu't isa	Thirty-one	31

Hundreds, Thousands, and Beyond

- Isang daan / Sandaan - One hundred
- Isang libo / Sanlibo - One thousand
- Isang milyon - One million

To form other hundreds, thousands and milyon, just start with the base number followed by "daan" for hundreds, "libo" for thousands and “milyon” for million:

Tagalog	English	Number
Isang daan	One hundred	100
Dalawang daan	Two hundred	200
Tatlong daan	Three hundred	300
Apat na daan	Four hundred	400
Limang daan	Five hundred	500
Anim na daan	Six hundred	600
Pitong daan	Seven hundred	700
Walong daan	Eight hundred	800
Siyam na daan	Nine hundred	900
Isang libo	One thousand	1000
Isang libo't isang daan	One thousand one hundred	1100
Isang libo't isa	One thousand one	1101
Dalawang libo	Two thousand	2000
Dalawang libo't isang daan	Two thousand one hundred	2100
Dalawang libo't isa	Two thousand one	2101
Sampung libo	Ten thousand	10000
Labing-isang libo	Eleven thousand	11000
Labing-isang libo't isa	Eleven thousand one	11001

Dalawampung libo	Twenty thousand	20000
Isang daang libo	One hundred thousand	100000
Isang milyon	One million	1000000
Isang milyon at isang daan	One million and one hundred	1000100
Isang milyon at isang daan at isa	One million, one hun-dred and one	1000101

Overview:

Tagalog	Number
Isa	1
Dalawa	2
Tatlo	3
Apat	4
Lima	5
Anim	6
Pito	7
Walo	8
Siyam	9
Sampu	10
Labing-isa	11
Labing-dalawa	12
Labing-tatlo	13
Labing-apat	14
Labing-lima	15
Labing-anim	16
Labing-pito	17
Labing-walo	18
Labing-siyam	19
Dalawampu	20
Tatlumpu	30
Apatnapu	40
Limampu	50
Animnapu	60
Pitumpu	70
Walumpu	80

Siyamnapu	90
Isang daan	100
Isang libo	1000
Sampung libo	10000
Isang milyon	1000000

Exercise: Translate the following into Tagalog.

Tagalog	**English**
	Thirty-two books.
	One hundred fifty students.
	Two thousand and twenty-one.

Solution: Translate the following into Tagalog.

Tagalog	**English**
Tatlumpu't dalawang libro.	Thirty-two books.
Isang daan at limampung estu-dyante.	One hundred fifty students.
Dalawang libo at dalawampu't isa.	Two thousand and twenty-one.

Note: For large numbers, Tagalog speakers often switch to English, especially in casual conversation or scientific contexts. In prices and dates, English numbers are commonly used, but it's still useful to know the Tagalog numbers for cultural understanding and formal settings.

Lesson 75 - Quantities

This lesson covers basic expressions to help you communicate quantities

Basic Quantity Terms

Tagalog	English
Isa	One
Ilan	How many
Marami	Many
Konti	Few
Kaunti	Few
Sobra	Too much
Kulang	Lacking
Tama	Just right

Fractions

Tagalog	English
Kalahati	Half
Katlo	Third
Kapat	Quarter

Units of Measure

Tagalog	English
Kilogram	Kilogram
Tonelada	Ton
Gramo	Gram
Miligrama	Milligram
Liter	Liter
Galon	Gallon
Milliliter	Milliliter
Bote	Bottle
Piraso	Piece
Unit	Unit
Bahagi	Portion
Sako	Bundle
Kaha	Box
Supot	Bag
Metro	Meter
Sentimetro	Centimeter

Metrokuwadradong	Square meter
Milimetro	Millimeter
Kilometro	Kilometer
Talampakan	Foot
Pulgada	Inch
Porsyento	Percentage

Phrases for Expressing Quantities with Units

Tagalog	**English**
Ilan ang gusto mo?	How many do you want?
Gusto ko ng kalahating kilo ng ma-nok.	I want half a kilo of chicken.
Dalawang piraso ng mangga, please.	Two pieces of mango, please.
Isang bungkos ng saging.	One bundle of bananas.
Maaari ba akong makakuha ng isang bahagi ng cake?	Can I get one portion of cake?
Kalahating kilo ng bigas.	Half a kilo of rice.
Tatlong bungkos ng kangkong.	Three bundles of water spinach.
Isang piraso ng tinapay.	One piece of bread.
Dalawang porsyon ng spaghetti.	Two portions of spaghetti.

Practice Using Fractions and Units

Tagalog	**English**
Kalahating kilo ng bigas.	Half a kilo of rice.
Tatlong bungkos ng kangkong.	Three bundles of water spinach.
Isang piraso ng tinapay.	One piece of bread.
Dalawang porsyon ng spaghetti.	Two portions of spaghetti.

Practice Tip: To practice, think of scenarios where you might need to use these terms. For example, shopping at a market or dividing food among friends. Try forming sentences like

Tagalog	**English**

Gusto ko ng .... kilo/piraso ng ...	I want .... kilo/pieces of ...

Lesson 76 - Exchanging Money

This lesson is about exchanging money (pagpapalit ng pera).

Vocabulary

Tagalog	**English**
Pera	Money
Palit	Exchange
Salapi	Currency
Palitan ng Halaga	Exchange Rate
Dayuhang Salapi	Foreign Currency
Piso ng Pilipinas	Philippine Peso
Magpalit ng pera	To exchange money
Bangko	Bank
Magkano	How much

Useful Phrases,

Tagalog	**English**
Saan ako makakapagpalit ng pera?	Where can I exchange money?
Ano ang palitan ng halaga ngayon?	What is the exchange rate today?
Gusto kong magpalit ng dolyar sa piso.	I want to exchange dollars for pesos.
Magkano ang makukuha ko sa isang daang dolyar?	How much will I get for $100?
May bayad ba sa pagpapalit ng salapi?	Is there a fee for currency exchange?

Dialogue: At the Currency Exchange

Tagalog	English
Magandang araw, saan ako makakapagpalit ng pera dito?	Good day, where can I exchange money here?
Magandang araw din! Dito po sa aming bangko, maaari kayong magpalit ng pera. Anong klase ng salapi ang nais ninyong ipalit?	Good day as well! Here in our bank, you can exchange money. What type of currency would you like to exchange?
Gusto ko sanang magpalit ng dolyar sa piso. Ano po ang palitan ng halaga ngayon?	I would like to exchange dollars for pesos. What is the exchange rate today?
Ang palitan ngayon ay limampu't limang piso sa bawat dolyar. Magkano ang nais ninyong ipalit?	The exchange rate is fifty-five pesos for every dollar. How much would you like to exchange?
Magpapalit ako ng isang daang dolyar. Magkano po ang bayad sa serbisyo?	I will exchange one hundred dollars. How much is the service fee?
Walang bayad sa serbisyo. Makakakuha po kayo ng limang libo't limang daang piso sa inyong isang daang dolyar.	There is no service fee. You will receive five thousand five hundred pesos for your one hundred dollars.

Lesson 77 - Bank & Transactions

This lesson aims to provide a foundation for understanding and discussing basic financial matters.

Part 1: Introduction to Money and Banking (Pera at Bangko)

Vocabulary:

Tagalog	English
Bangko	Bank
Pera	Money
Mag-ipon	To save
Akawnt	Account
Deposito	Deposit

Mag-withdraw	Withdraw

Useful Sentences:

Tagalog	English
Gusto kong magbukas ng akawnt sa bangko.	I want to open an account at the bank.
Magkano ang dapat kong ideposito?	How much money should I deposit?
Kailangan kong mag-withdraw ng pera.	I need to withdraw money.

Part 2: Getting a Credit Card (Pagkuha ng Credit Card)

Vocabulary:

Tagalog	English
Credit Card	Credit Card
Mag-apply	To apply
Limit ng Credit	Credit Limit
Taunang Bayad	Annual Fee
Rate ng Interes	Interest Rate

Useful Sentences:

Tagalog	English
Gusto kong mag-apply para sa credit card.	I want to apply for a credit card.
Ano ang mga kinakailangan?	What are the requirements?
Kailan ang petsa ng aking pagbabayad?	When is my due date?

Part 3: Sending and Transferring Money (Pagpapadala at Paglilipat ng Pera)

Vocabulary:

Tagalog	English
Paglilipat ng Pera	Money Transfer
Magpadala ng Pera	To send money
Tatanggap	Recipient
Transaksyon	Transaction
Bayad	Fee

Useful Sentences:

Tagalog	English
Gusto kong magpadala ng pera sa aking pamilya.	I want to send money to my family.
Paano ako makakapaglipat ng pera?	How can I transfer money?
May bayad ba sa pagpapadala ng pera?	Is there a fee for sending money?

Dialogue: Engaging in Financial Transactions

Tagalog	English
Customer: Magandang araw, gusto ko sanang magbukas ng akawnt at mag-apply para sa credit card.	Customer: Good day, I would like to open an account and apply for a credit card.
Bank Teller: Magandang araw! Masaya kaming tumulong. Anong klase ng akawnt ang nais ninyong buksan?	Bank Teller: Good day! We're happy to help. What type of account would you like to open?
Customer: Gusto ko ng savings account. At sa credit card, interesado ako sa may mababang taunang bayad.	Customer: I want a savings account. And for the credit card, I'm interested in one with a low annual fee.
Bank Teller: Naiintindihan, maari ko bang malaman ang ilang detalye para sa inyong aplikasyon?	Bank Teller: Understood, may I know some details for your application?
Customer: Oo, syempre. Gusto ko rin sana magtanong kung paano magpadala ng pera sa aking pamilya sa probinsya.	Customer: Yes, of course. I would also like to inquire about how to send money to my family in the province.
Bank Teller: Para sa pagpapadala ng	Bank Teller: For sending money, you

pera, maaari ninyong gamitin ang aming online banking services o mag-direct deposit sa kanilang akawnt. Simple lang ang proseso.	can use our online banking services or make a direct deposit into their account. The process is straightforward.

Lesson 78 - Direction & Places

This lesson will introduce you to basic terms and phrases related to directions and places, making it easier for you to get around or understand directions given.

Essential Vocabulary for Directions

Tagalog	English
Kanan	Right
Liko sa kanan	Turn right
Kaliwa	Left
Liko sa kaliwa	Turn left
Diretso	Straight
Likod	Back
Harap	Front
Itaas	Up
Ibaba	Down
Tabi or Gilid	Beside
Pagitan	Between
Malapit	Close
Malayo sa	Far from
Katapat	Opposite
Pasulong	Forward
Kalye or Dalan	Street
Daan or Karsada	Road
Highway	Highway
Kanto or Eskina	Corner
Interseksyon	Intersection
Sa loob	Inside

Sa labas	Outside

Common Places

Tagalog	English
Bahay	House
Paaralan	School
Simbahan	Church
Palengke	Market
Ospital	Hospital
Istasyon ng bus	Bus Station
Parke	Park

Useful Phrases for Navigation and Requests

Tagalog	English
Saan ang [place]?	Where is [place]?
Malayo ba dito?	Is it far from here?
Malapit ba?	Is it close?
Paano ako makakapunta sa [place]?	How do I get to [place]?
Saan ako sasakay ng jeep/bus?	Where do I catch the jeepney/bus?
Magkano ang pamasahe?	How much is the fare?
Saan ako bababa?	Where do I get off?
Pakisulat ang address.	Please write down the address.

Giving Directions

Tagalog	English
Kumanan ka sa susunod na kanto.	Turn right at the next corner.
Kaliwa pagkatapos ng simbahan.	Left after the church.
Diretso lang, malapit lang.	Just go straight, it's near.
Nasa likod ng paaralan ang bahay ko.	My house is behind the school.
Paki-kaliwa sa susunod na intersek-syon.	Please turn left at the next intersec-tion.

Tumigil, Paki-tigil sa puting bahay.	Stop, Please stop at the white house.
Pakihintay dito.	Please wait here.

Exercise: Choose a phrase from the lesson, write it down, learn and practice it.

Tagalog	English

Lesson 79 - Transportation & Movement

This lesson covers basic vocabulary and phrases related to transportation and movement, making it easier for you to get around.

Vocabulary for Transportation:

Tagalog	English
Sasakyan	Vehicle
Kotse	Car
Jeepney	Jeepney
Bus	Bus
Tricycle	Tricycle
Bisikleta	Bicycle
Tren	Train
Bangka	Boat
Eroplano	Airplane
Scooter	Scooter
Motorbike	Motorbike

Vocabulary for Movement:

Tagalog	English
Umalis	To leave
Dumating	To arrive
Sumakay	To ride
Bumaba	To get off
Magmaneho	To drive
Maglakad	To walk
Hintay	To wait

Sample Phrases

Tagalog	English
Paano ako makakapunta sa palengke?	How can I go to the market?
Sumakay ako ng bus papuntang trabaho.	I rode a bus going to work.
Magkano ang pamasahe sa jeepney?	How much is the fare for the jeepney?
Magmaneho ka ba o maglalakad?	Will you drive or walk?
Bumaba ako sa susunod na istasyon.	I will get off at the next station.

Asking for Directions:

Tagalog	English
Saan ang sakayan ng tricycle?	Where is the tricycle terminal?
Paano pumunta sa istasyon ng tren?	How to go to the train station?
Ilang oras ang biyahe mula dito hanggang Baguio?	How many hours is the journey from here to Baguio?

Useful phrases for going by taxi:

agalog	English
Saan po ba makakakuha ng taxi?	Where can I get a taxi?
Magkano po ang pamasahe papunta	How much is the fare to

sa (destination)?	(destination)?
Magkano po ang fixed na presyo papunta sa (destination)?	What is the fixed price for the drive to the destination?
Gusto ko ang isang taksi na may metro.	I want a taxi with a meter.
Pakihatid po ako sa (destination).	Please take me to (destination).
Pwede po ba tayo magpa-gas sa daan?	Can we stop for gas along the way?
Diretso lang, sasabihin ko na lang po kung saan.	Just go straight, I'll tell you where to turn.
Kaliwa pagkatapos ng simbahan.	Left after the church.
Kumanan ka sa susunod na kanto.	Turn right at the next corner.
Malapit ba?	Is it close?
Malayo ba dito?	Is it far from here?
Paki-ikot lang po, mayroon akong dalaang bagahe.	Please drive around, I have luggage to load.
Paki-pabilisan po, may appointment ako.	Please hurry, I have an appointment.
Paki-patay po ang metro.	Please turn off the meter.
Paki-buksan po ang metro.	Please turn on the meter.
Magkano po ang karagdagang bayad sa bagahe?	How much is the additional fee for luggage?
Maaari ko bang humingi ng resibo?	Can I have a receipt, please?
Pwede po ba tayo huminto sandali?	Can we stop for a moment?
Kailangan ko bumili ng kailangan.	I need to buy something.
Pwede po ba tayo huminto saglit?	Can we stop for a pause?
Kailangan ko dumaan sa CR.	I need to go to the CR.
May shortcut ba dito?	Is there a shortcut here?
Pakisakay po dito.	Please stop here.
Magkano po?	What is the price?
Ang tira ay tip lamang.	The rest is tip only.
Paki-bigay po ang sukli.	Please give me the change.
Salamat sa paghatid.	Thanks for the ride.

Exercise: To prepare for your next taxi ride, insert you desired destination below:

Tagalog	English
Magandang araw, pwede po bang mag-taxi?	Good day, can I get a taxi?
Magkano po papunta sa [destinasyon]?	How much is it to [destination]?
[Destinasyon], po.	[Destination], please.
Magkano po ang pamasahe?	How much is the fare?
Sige, tara na po.	Okay, let's go.

Lesson 80 - At the Market

Visiting a local market is a vibrant, essential experience in the Philippines. This lesson will introduce you to basic phrases and vocabulary you'll need for shopping at the market, helping you navigate transactions and interactions smoothly.

Key Vocabulary

Tagalog	English
Pamilihan	Market
Tindahan	Store
Magkano	How much
Presyo	Price
Mahal	Expensive
Mura	Cheap
Tawad	Bargain
Bili	Buy
Tinda	Sell
Gulay	Vegetables
Prutas	Fruits
Karne	Meat
Isda	Fish
Bayad	Payment
Sukli	Change (money)

Sample Phrases

Tagalog	English
Magkano ito?	How much is this?
Masyadong mahal. Pwede bang mag-tawad?	It's too expensive. Can I bargain?
Saan ang tindahan ng gulay?	Where is the vegetable stall?
Gusto kong bumili ng prutas.	I want to buy fruits.
Pwede bang makahingi ng sukli?	Can I get the change?

At the Market Dialogue

Tagalog	English
Customer: Magkano ang mangga?	Customer: How much are the man-goes?
Vendor: Limampung piso bawat isa.	Vendor: Fifty pesos each.
Customer: Masyadong mahal. Pwede bang gawing beinte pesos na lang bawat isa?	Customer: Too expensive. Can you make it twenty pesos each instead?
Vendor: Naku, hindi kaya ng beinte. Pero para sa iyo, gawin natin tatlum-pung piso na lang bawat isa.	Vendor: Oh, twenty is too low. But for you, let's make it thirty pesos each.
Customer: Salamat! Bibili ako ng tatlo.	Customer: Thank you! I'll buy three.

Exercise: Form questions based on the template.

Tagalog	English
Gusto kong bumili ng...?	I want to buy...?
Magkano ang...?	How much are the ...?

Sample solution:

Tagalog	English
Gusto kong bumili ng saging.	I want to buy bananas.
Magkano ang mga saging?	How much are the bananas?

Lesson 81 - In the Shopping Mall

This lesson introduces essential phrases and vocabulary you might need when visiting a shopping mall, making your experience smoother and more enjoyable.

Key Vocabulary

Tagalog	English
Mall (Pamilihan)	Shopping Mall
Tindahan	Store
Damit	Clothes
Pagkain	Food
Sinehan	Cinema
Libangan	Entertainment
Palabas	Show/Movie
Kainan	Restaurant/Eatery
Pasukan	Entrance
Labasan	Exit
Hagdan	Stairs
Eskalator	Escalator
Elevator	Elevator

Sample Phrases

Tagalog	English
Saan ang pinakamalapit na kainan?	Where is the nearest eatery?
Magkano ang damit sa tindahang ito?	How much are the clothes in this store?
Nasaan ang sinehan?	Where is the cinema?
Gusto kong manood ng palabas.	I want to watch a show/movie.
Saan ang pasukan sa mall?	Where is the entrance to the mall?
Paano ako makakapunta sa escalator?	How can I get to the escalator?

In the Shopping Mall Dialogue

Tagalog	English
Ana: Excited ako mag-shopping nga-yon. Saan ba tayo magsisimula?	Ana: I'm excited to go shopping to-day. Where should we start?
Ben: Pwede tayong magsimula sa tindahan ng damit sa ikalawang pal-apag.	Ben: We can start at the clothing store on the second floor.
Ana: Maganda! Gusto ko rin sana manood ng sine mamaya.	Ana: Great! I also want to watch a movie later.
Ben: Sige, titingnan natin kung ano ang palabas pagkatapos natin mag-shopping.	Ben: Okay, we'll see what's showing after we shop.

Let's take a look at some additional useful phrases:

Tagalog	English
Saan ang parking lot?	Where is the parking lot?
May libreng WiFi ba dito?	Is there free WiFi here?
Saan ang pinakamalapit na kainan?	Where is the nearest eatery?
Kailan mag-sasara ang mall?	When does the mall close?
Saan ko mahahanap ang librohan?	Where can I find the bookstore?
Pwede bang magpalit ng nabiling i-tem?	Can I exchange a purchased item?
Mayroon ba kayong size na mas ma-laki?	Do you have a bigger size?
Magkano ang renta para sa stroller ng bata?	How much is the rent for a child's stroller?
Pwede bang magpareserba ng seats sa sinehan?	Can I reserve seats in the cinema?
Mayroon bang play area para sa mga bata?	Is there a play area for children?
Saan ang customer service?	Where is customer service?
Kailangan ko ng tulong, mayroon bang first aid station dito?	I need help, is there a first aid sta-tion here?
Saan ang pinakamalapit na ka-pehan?	Where is the nearest coffee shop?
Pwede ba akong magbayad gamit ang electronic wallet?	Can I pay using an electronic wallet?

Magkano ang halaga ng valet parking?	How much does valet parking cost?
Mayroon bang lugar para sa mga pets?	Is there a place for pets?
Saan maaaring kumain na may kasamang alagang hayop?	Where can one eat with a pet?
May charger station ba dito?	Is there a charger station here?

Exercise: Break down the sentence "Mayroon ba kayong size na mas malaki?" word by word:

- Mayroon -
- ba -
- kayong -
- size -
- na -
- mas -
- malaki -
- English meaning:

Solution: Breaking down the sentence "Mayroon ba kayong size na mas malaki?" word by word:

- Mayroon - Have/There is
- ba - (a particle used for questions, no direct translation)
- kayong - you (plural/formal)
- size - size (English term commonly used in Tagalog)
- na - that
- mas - more
- malaki - big/large
- Put together in English, this sentence means: "Do you have a bigger size?"

Lesson 82 - Clothing

This lesson introduces basic vocabulary and phrases related to clothing.

Vocabulary for Clothing

Tagalog	English
Damit	Clothes
Pantalon	Pants
Kamiseta	T-shirt
Blusa	Blouse
Sapatos	Shoes
Medyas	Socks
Sumbrero	Hat
Shorts	Shorts
Palda	Skirt
Belt	Belt
Underwear, Panloob na damit	Underwear
Jaket	Jacket
Panyo	Handkerchief
Relo	Watch

Sample Phrases

Tagalog	English
Magkano ang pantalon na ito?	How much are these pants?
May iba pa bang kulay ang kamiseta?	Are there other colors for this t-shirt?
Pwede ko bang isukat ang sapatos?	Can I try on the shoes?
Masikip ang blusa. May mas malaking sukat ba kayo?	The blouse is tight. Do you have a larger size?
Pwede ko bang isukat ito?	Can I try this on?
Nasaan ang fitting room?	Where is the fitting room?

Describing Clothing

Tagalog	English
Bagay sa iyo ang damit na yan.	That dress suits you.
Mahangin ngayon, magdala ka ng jaket.	It's windy today, bring a jacket.
Gusto ko ang disenyo ng panyo mo.	I like the design of your handker-chief.
Kailangan ko ng bagong sapatos para sa trabaho.	I need new shoes for work.

Shopping for Clothing

Tagalog	English
Naghahanap ako ng pantalon para sa kasal.	I'm looking for pants for a wedding.
May sale ba kayo ngayon?	Do you have a sale right now?
Pwede bang magbayad gamit ang credit card?	Can I pay with a credit card?
Pwede ba akong humingi ng dis-count?	Can I ask for a discount?
Kukuha ako ng isa nito sa itim.	I'll take one of these in black.

Exercise: Translate.

Tagalog	English
Naghahanap...	I am looking for pants.
	I want to buy a T-shirt.

Solution

Tagalog	English
Naghahanap ako ng pantalon.	I am looking for pants.
Gusto kong bumili ng T-Shirt.	I want to buy a T-shirt.

Lesson 83 - Food

Diving into the rich and vibrant world of Filipino cuisine? This lesson focuses solely on food, providing you with the fundamental vocabulary to talk about various food items. This foundational knowledge will serve you well, whether you're shopping for groceries, exploring local markets, or simply discussing your favorite vegetables. In the Philippines, you can find food in a wide variety of places, each offering different types of experiences and cuisines. Here's a comprehensive list of locations where you can get food:

Traditional & Everyday Locations

Tagalog	**English**
Pagkain	Food
Pamilihan	Traditional markets offering fresh produce, meat, fish, and other ingredients.
Tindahan	Small neighborhood stores selling basic groceries and snacks.
Supermarket	Larger stores with a wide range of food products, including international items.
Palengke	Larger than traditional markets, offering a vast selection of goods.
Sari-sari Store	Small, community-based retail outlets selling a variety of items in smaller quantities.

Eating Out

Tagalog	**English**
Kainan / Karinderia	Small, often informal eateries serving home-cooked Filipino meals at affordable prices.
Restaurant	Establishments serving a wide range of local and international dishes.
Fast Food Chain	Quick-service restaurants offering ready-to-eat food.
Street Food Vendors	Stalls or carts found on the streets selling a variety of snacks and quick meals.
Food Parks	Outdoor areas with a variety of food stalls or trucks, offering diverse cuisines.

Café / Coffee Shop	Places offering coffee, tea, pastries, and sometimes light meals.
Buffet Restaurant	Restaurants where a fixed price allows you to eat as much as you want from a variety of dishes.
Panaderya (Bakery)	Specializes in baked goods like bread, cakes, and pastries.
Talipapa	Smaller markets specializing in fresh seafood, sometimes also selling fruits and vegetables.
Food Court	A large area within a shopping center or complex where various food vendors are located, offering a wide range of options in one place.

Food Categories and Examples

Navigating through Filipino cuisine and grocery shopping becomes easier when you know the basic food categories and some common items within each. Below is a list organized by food type.

Vegetables (Mga Gulay)

Tagalog	**English**
Gulay	Vegetable
Kamatis	Tomato
Talong	Eggplant
Sitaw	String Beans
Kalabasa	Squash
Ampalaya	Bitter Gourd
Patatas	Potato
Sibuyas	Onion
Bawang	Garlic
Karot	Carrot
Luya	Ginger
Pipino	Cucumber
Repolyo	Cabbage
Labanos	Radish
Kangkong	Water Spinach
Pechay	Bok Choy
Mustasa	Mustard Greens

Okra	Okra
Sigarilyas	Winged Bean
Upo	Bottle Gourd
Sayote	Chayote
Malunggay	Moringa Leaves
Talbos ng Kamote	Sweet Potato Leaves
Tagalog Word	English Translation
Gulay	Vegetable
Kamatis	Tomato

Fruits (Mga Prutas)

Tagalog	**English**
Prutas	Fruit
Saging	Banana
Mansanas	Apple
Bayabas	Guava
Mangga	Mango
Papaya	Papaya
Pinya	Pineapple
Niyog	Coconut
Atis	Sugar Apple/Custard Apple
Chico	Sapodilla
Pakwan	Watermelon
Melon	Melon/Cantaloupe
Lansones	Langsat
Durian	Durian
Rambutan	Rambutan
Lanzones	Longan
Guyabano	Soursop
Avocado	Avocado
Kamias	Bilimbi
Siniguelas	Spanish Plum
Dalandan	Orange
Kalamansi	Calamondin
Suha	Pomelo
Santol	Cottonfruit

Meat

Tagalo	English
Baboy	Pork
Baka	Beef
Manok	Chicken
Kambing	Goat
Tupa	Lamb
Pato	Duck
Liempo	Pork Belly
Tadyang ng Baka	Beef Ribs
Paa ng Manok	Chicken Feet
Leeg ng Manok	Chicken Neck
Isaw	Intestines (often grilled)
Balun-balunan	Gizzard
Atay	Liver
Buntot	Tail (often refers to ox tail)

Fish

Tagalog	English
Isda	Fish
Hito	Catfish
Tilapia	Tilapia
Bangus	Milkfish
Hipon	Shrimp
Alimango	Crab
Tuna	Tuna
Pusit	Squid

Convenience Food

Tagalog	English
Convenience Food	Convenience Food
Instant Noodles	Instant Noodles
Canned Goods	Canned Goods (de-latang pagkain)

Tocino	Cured pork
Longganisa	Philippine sausage
Daing	Dried fish

Animal Products

Tagalog	**English**
Itlog	Eggs
Keso	Cheese
Gatas	Milk
Yogurt	Yogurt
Mantikilya	Butter
Krema	Cream

Grains (Butil)

Tagalog	**English**
Kanin	Rice (cooked rice)
Bigas	Uncooked rice
Mais	Corn
Trigo	Wheat
Barley	Barley (Sebada)
Tinapay	Bread
Pasta	Pasta
Cereal	Cereal
Pancit	Noodles (Filipino dishes)
Lugaw	Porridge or Congee

Legumes

Tagalog	**English**
Lentil (commonly used)	Lentils
Garbanzos	Chickpeas
Itim na Beans (commonly used)	Black Beans
Kidney Beans (commonly used)	Kidney Beans

Pinto Beans (commonly used)	Pinto Beans
Navy Beans (commonly used)	Navy Beans
Soybeans (commonly used)	Soybeans
Mani	Peanuts
Green Peas (commonly used)	Green Peas
Black-eyed Peas (commonly used)	Black-eyed Peas
Monggo	Mung Beans

Cooking Ingredients

Tagalog	**English**
Asin	Salt
Paminta	Pepper
Asukal	Sugar
Toyo	Soy sauce
Suka	Vinegar
Mantika	Oil
Patis	Fish sauce
Dahon ng Laurel	Bay leaves
Kalamansi	Calamondin (or Philippine lime)
Malunggay	Moringa

Sweets

Tagalog	**English**
Tsokolate	Chocolate
Kendi	Candy
Ice Cream (commonly used English term)	Ice Cream
Keyk	Cake
Biskwit	Biscuits/Cookies
Leche Flan	A type of caramel custard
Halo-halo	A popular Filipino cold dessert that includes shaved ice, milk, various fruits, and sweet beans
Turon	A sweet snack made from banana

	(or jackfruit) wrapped in spring roll wrapper and deep-fried
Puto	Steamed rice cake

Discussing Food Preferences

Tagalog	**English**
Gusto ko ng...	I like/I want...
Gusto ko ng gulay.	I like vegetables.
Ayoko ng...	I don't like...
Ayoko ng karne.	I don't like meat.
Allergic ako sa...	I'm allergic to...
Allergic ako sa hipon.	I'm allergic to shrimp.
Paborito ko ang...	My favorite is...
Paborito ko ang mangga.	My favorite is mango.

Sample Phrases for Food Conversations

Tagalog	**English**
Anong paborito mong prutas?	What's your favorite fruit?
Masarap ba ang isdang ito?	Is this fish delicious?
Saan ako makakabili ng sariwang gulay?	Where can I buy fresh vegetables?
Pwede ba akong makahingi ng recipe para sa adobo?	Can I have a recipe for adobo?

Exercise: Choose a phrase from the lesson, write it down, learn and practice it.

Tagalog	**English**

Lesson 84 - Beverages

This lesson introduces basic vocabulary related to beverages, types of drinks, and essential phrases for ordering or discussing your preferences.

Basic Vocabulary

Tagalog	English
Inumin	Beverage/Drink
Baso	Glass
Tasa	Cup (for hot beverages)
Bote, Botelya	Bottle
Pambukas ng Botelya	Bottle Opener
Mainit	Hot
Malamig	Cold
Yelo	Ice Cubes

Water

Tagalog	English
Tubig	Water
Tubig mula sa gripo	Tap Water
Mineral na Tubig	Mineral Water
Tubig na nasa bote	Bottled Water

Juice

Tagalog	English
Katas	Juice (when referring to natural fruit juice)
Prutas na Inumin	Fruit Drink (more generic, can include flavored beverages)
Buko Juice	Coconut Water
Sago't Gulaman	Tapioca and Jelly Drink
Kalamansi Juice	Calamondin Juice

Soda

Tagalog	English
Soda	Soda
Softdrinks	Soft Drinks

Hot Beverages

Tagalog	English
Kape	Coffee
Kape na may gatas	Coffee with milk
Kape na may asukal	Coffee with sugar
Tsaa	Tea
Mainit na Tsokolate	Hot Chocolate

Alcoholic Beverages

Tagalog	English
Alak	Alcohol (generic term)
Serbesa	Beer
Bino	Wine
Tagay	A shot or drink (often in a communal context)

Others (Shakes, etc.) - Tipically the English terms are used.

Tagalog	English
Shake	Shake
Smoothie	Smoothie
Milkshake	Milkshake

Sample Phrases

Tagalog	English
Pwede ba akong humingi ng malamig na tubig?	Can I have some cold water, please?

Isa pong kape, mainit.	One coffee, hot, please.
Gusto ko ng katas ng mangga na may yelo.	I'd like mango juice with ice.
Anong klaseng serbesa ang mayroon kayo?	What kind of beer do you have?
Pwede ba akong mag-order ng smoothie na strawberry?	Can I order a strawberry smoothie?

Practice: Try using these words and phrases the next time you order a drink Gusto ko ng ... (I'd like ...).

Lesson 85 - In the Kitchen

Here's a list of common kitchen vocabulary

Kitchen Essentials

Tagalog	English
Ref	Refrigerator (Ref is hort for "Refrigerator")
Aparador	Cabinet
Kahon	Drawer
Istante	Shelf
Saksakan ng kuryente	Power Outlet
Switch ng ilaw	Light Switch
Kalan	Stove
Lutuang kalan	Cooking Stove
Oven	Oven (Commonly used in Tagalog)
Microwave	Microwave (Commonly used in Tagalog)
Mesa	Table
Lugar na paggawaan	Working Area/Countertop
Bintana	Window
Pinto	Door

Additional Items and Actions

Tagalog	English
Pinggan	Dishes
Lababo	Sink
Maghugas	To Wash
Maghugas ng pinggan	To Wash Dishes
Makinang panghugas ng pinggan	Dishwasher
Basura	Garbage
Walis	Broom
Vacuum	Vacuum Cleaner (Commonly used in Tagalog)
Panglinis	Cleaning Agents
Marumi	Dirty
Malinis	Clean
Buksan	Turn on
Patayin	Turn off

Example sentences:

Tagalog	English
Maglalagay ako ng pagkain sa ref.	I will put the food in the fridge.
Maghuhugas ako ng pinggan sa lab-abo.	I will wash the dishes in the sink.
Marumi ang sahig, kailangan kong magwalis.	The floor is dirty, I need to sweep.

Exercise: Form a sample phrase with the given vocabulary.

Tagalog	English

Lesson 86 - Cooking

Let's explore some basic phrases and vocabulary related to cooking, focusing on simple actions you can describe and share with others.

Key Vocabulary:

Tagalog	**English**
Kaldero	Pot
Kawali	Pan
Takip	Lid
Kusina (Stove)	Stove
Gasera	Gas Stove
Mangkok	Bowl
Kutsara	Spoon
Kutsilyo	Knife
Tinidor	Fork
Kubyertos	Cutlery
Sangkalan	Cutting Board
Basura	Trash
Basurahan	Trash Can
Pagluluto	Cooking (Boiling)
Pagprito	Frying
Pagpapasingaw	Steaming
Pagdeep-fry	Deep-frying
Pag-init	Reheating
Tubig	Water
Langis	Oil
Mainit	Hot
Malamig	Cold
Pampalasa	Spices
Asin	Salt
Paminta	Pepper
Sangkap	Ingredients
Luto	Cook
Gutom	Hungry
Masarap	Delicious
Hapunan	Dinner

Handa	Ready

Phrases:

Tagalog	**English**
Magluluto ako	I will cook (AF)
Magluluto ako ng kanin	I will cook rice
Gagawa ako ng adobo	I will make adobo
Lutuin ang manok	Cook the chicken (OF)
Magluluto ako ng sinigang na baboy mamayang gabi.	I will cook pork sinigang tonight.
Kailangan ko ng kaldero	I need a pot
Pakiabot naman ang mga sangkap.	Please give me the ingredients.
Handa na ang hapunan	Dinner is ready
Kumain tayo!	Let's eat!
Masarap ang ulam.	The dish is delicious.

Exercise: Choose a phrase from the lesson, write it down, learn and practice it.

Tagalog	**English**

Lesson 87 - Meals & Eating

This lesson covers typical meal times, essential vocabulary for mealtime items, and phrases to express hunger, satisfaction, and opinions about the food.

Typical Meal Times

Tagalog	**English**	**Description**
Almusal	Breakfast	Usually eaten from 6:00 AM to 9:00 AM.
Tanghalian	Lunch	Typically from 12:00 PM to 1:00 PM.

Meryenda	Snack	Afternoon snack around 3:00 PM or 4:00 PM.
Hapunan	Dinner	Evening meal usually from 6:00 PM to 8:00 PM.

Basic Vocabulary for Meal Items

Tagalog	**English**
Mesa	Table
Plato	Plate
Kubyertos	Cutlery
Tinidor	Fork
Kutsara	Spoon
Kutsilyo	Knife
Baso	Glass
Mantel	Tablecloth
Napkin	Napkin

Talking About Meals

Tagalog	**English**
Gutom na gutom ako.	I am very hungry.
Busog na ako.	I am full.

Discussing Food Quality

Tagalog	**English**
Masarap	Delicious
Hindi masarap	Not delicious
Maanghang	Spicy
Malamig	Cold
Mainit	Hot

Common Phrases

Tagalog	English
Anong gusto mong kainin?	What do you want to eat?
Kain na tayo.	Let's eat.
Masarap ba ang ulam?	Is the dish delicious?
Pwedeng pakilagay ng kaunti pa?	Can I have a little more, please?
Saan tayo kakain?	Where are we going to eat?

Dialogue

Tagalog	English
Gutom na gutom na ako. Anong oras tayo kakain ng tanghalian?	I am very hungry. What time are we eating lunch?
Kain na tayo ngayon. Masarap ang niluto ko na adobo.	Let's eat now. The adobo I cooked is delicious.
Talaga? Excited na akong tikman! Gusto ko rin sana ng malamig na i-numin.	Really? I'm excited to taste it! I would also like a cold drink.
Mayroon akong dala na sariwang mango juice. Masarap yan kapag malamig.	I have fresh mango juice. It's delici-ous.

Exercise: Choose a phrase from the lesson, write it down, learn and practice it.

Tagalog	English

Lesson 88 - In the Restaurant

Eating out at a restaurant is a common and enjoyable experience in the Philippines. This lesson will guide you through essential phrases and vocabulary needed when visiting a restaurant, covering everything from making reservations to commenting on the meal.

Making Reservations

Tagalog	English
Magpareserba	To make a reservation
Mesa para sa dalawa	Table for two
Sa ilalim ng pangalan na...	Under the name of...

Upon Arrival

Tagalog	English
Mayroon ba kayong reserbasyon?	Do you have a reservation?
May reserbasyon ako.	I have a reservation.
Pwede bang mag-request ng mesa sa tabi ng bintana?	Can I request a table by the window?

Calling the Waiter

Tagalog	English
Excuse po.	Excuse me. (Getting the waiter's attention politely)
Miss/Mister, pwede po bang mag-order?	Miss/Mister, can I order?

Asking for the Menu

Tagalog	English
Pwede ko bang makita ang menu?	Can I see the menu?
Mayroon ba kayong menu para sa mga vegetarian?	Do you have a menu for vegetarians?
Ano ang pinakamabenta ninyong pagkain?	What is your best-selling food?

Indicating Readiness to Order

Tagalog	English
Handa na po kami umorder.	We are ready to order.
Pwede na po ba kami mag-order?	Can we order now?

Ordering Food

Tagalog	English
Handa na ba kayong umorder?	Are you ready to order?
Ano ang inyong espesyal ngayon?	What is your special today?
Ano ang irerekomenda mo?	What do you recommend?
Gusto ko po ng...	I would like...
Isang order po ng...	One order of...
Pwede po bang...	Can I have...
Tubig, pakiusap.	Water, please.

Asking for Specialties or Modifications

Tagalog	English
Pwede po bang palitan ang patatas ng french fries?	Can the potatoes be replaced with french fries?
Mayroon po ba kayong vegetarian na pagkain?	Do you have any vegetarian dishes?
Pwede po bang walang karne?	Can it be without meat?

Custom Requests

Tagalog	English
Allergic po ako sa mani. Pwede po ba itong tanggalin?	I am allergic to peanuts. Can this be removed?
Maaari mo bang palitan ang...? May alerhiya ako dito.	Can you replace the...? I am allergic to it.
Gusto ko po sana ng mas maraming gulay.	I would prefer more vegetables.
Pwede bang hindi masyadong	Can it be not too spicy?

maanghang?	

Confirming the Order

Tagalog	English
Tama po ba ang order ko na...?	Is my order correct that...?
Paki-ulit nga po ang order ko.	Please repeat my order.

Asking About Ingredients

Tagalog	English
Anong sangkap ang nasa...?	What ingredients are in...?
Mayroon bang mani dito? Allergic kasi ako.	Does this contain peanuts? I'm aller-gic.
Ginagamitan ba ito ng gatas?	Is this made with milk?
Pwede bang malaman kung paano ginawa ang...?	Can I know how... is made?

Asking for the Price

Tagalog	English
Magkano po ito?	How much is this?
Magkano ang halaga ng...?	How much does... cost?
Pwede bang malaman ang presyo ng...?	Can I know the price of...?

During the Meal

Tagalog	English
Pwedeng pakidagdagan ng kanin?	Can I have more rice, please?
Masarap ang pagkain!	The food is delicious!
Pwede bang magpa-take out?	Can I have this for takeout?

Asking for Assistance

Tagalog	English
Paumanhin, pwede bang mag-tanong?	Excuse me, may I ask?
Pwede bang makahingi ng ka-ragdagang kutsara?	Can I have an extra spoon, please?

Paying the Bill

Tagalog	English
Pwede na po bang humingi ng bill?	Can I have the bill, please?
Pwede bang makuha na ang bill?	May I ask for the bill now, please?
Magkano po lahat?	How much is everything?
Cash o card po?	Cash or card?

Leaving the Restaurant

Tagalog	English
Salamat sa masarap na pagkain.	Thank you for the delicious food.
Babalik kami!	We will come back!

Sample Dialogue I:

Tagalog	English
Customer: Magandang gabi, mesa para sa dalawa po sa ilalim ng pan-galan na Santos.	Good evening, a table for two under the name Santos.
Waiter: Tuloy po kayo. Handa na ba kayong umorder?	Please come in. Are you ready to or-der?
Customer: Oo, isang order ng adobo at sinigang na baboy, at tubig din po.	Yes, one order of adobo and pork si-nigang, and water as well.
Waiter: Magandang pagpili! Ilalabas na po namin ang inyong pagkain.	Good choices! We will bring out your food shortly.

Sample Dialog II:

Tagalog	English
Customer: Excuse po, pwede ko bang makita ang menu?	Excuse me, can I see the menu?
Waiter: Opo, heto po ang menu.	Yes, here is the menu.
Customer: Magkano po ang adobo dito?	How much is the adobo here?
Waiter: Php 250 po ang adobo.	The adobo is Php 250.
Customer: Anong sangkap ang nasa adobo ninyo?	What ingredients are in your adobo?
Waiter: Ang adobo po namin ay may sangkap na manok, toyo, suka, bawang, at paminta.	Our adobo contains chicken, soy sauce, vinegar, garlic, and pepper.
Customer: Mayroon bang mani o anumang seafood? Allergic kasi ako.	Does it contain peanuts or any seafood? Because I am allergic.
Waiter: Wala po, ligtas po ito para sa may allergy sa mani at seafood.	No, it is safe for those with allergies to peanuts and seafood.
Customer: Ready na kami umorder.	We're ready to order.
Waiter: Ano order niyo?	What's your order?
Customer: Sinigang na baboy, pwede fries instead of patatas? May vegetarian dish ba?	Pork sinigang, can I have fries instead of potatoes? Do you have a vegetarian dish?
Waiter: Yes, may pinakbet. Sa sinigang, pwede fries.	Yes, we have pinakbet. For the sinigang, fries are okay.
Customer: Ok, pinakbet at sinigang with fries. Dagdagan ng gulay, less spicy.	Ok, pinakbet and sinigang with fries. Add more vegetables, make it less spicy.
Waiter: Got it. Pinakbet at sinigang with fries, more veggies, less spicy. Tama?	Got it. Pinakbet and sinigang with fries, more veggies, less spicy. Correct?
Customer: Yes. Salamat.	Yes. Thank you.

Exercise: Translate the phrases.

Tagalog	English
	I want to order adobo and a Coke.
	I want to order pork, vegetable, and extra (additional) rice.

Solution:

Tagalog	English
Gusto ko mag-order ng adobo at Coke.	I want to order adobo and a Coke.
Gusto ko mag-order ng baboy, gulay, at dagdag na kanin.	I want to order pork, vegetable, and extra (additional) rice.

Exercise: Break down of "Gusto ko mag-order ng baboy, gulay, at dagdag na kanin.":

- Gusto ko -
- mag-order -
- ng -
- baboy -
- gulay -
- at -
- dagdag na kanin -
- na kanin -

Solution: Break down of "Gusto ko mag-order ng baboy, gulay, at dagdag na kanin.":

- Gusto ko - I want
- mag-order - to order
- ng - Ng-Markr, noun markeer
- baboy - pork
- gulay - vegetable
- at - and
- dagdag na kanin - additional
- na kanin - rice

Lesson 89 - Hotel & Accommodation

This lesson covers essential vocabulary and phrases for a comfortable and enjoyable stay.

Vocabulary for Hotel & Accommodation

Tagalog	**English**
Hotel	Hotel
Kuwarto	Room
Reserbasyon	Reservation
Gabi	Night
Susi	Key
Reception	Reception
Check-in	Check-in
Check-out	Check-out
Paliguan	Bathroom
Kama	Bed
Aircon	Air conditioner
WiFi	WiFi

Sample Phrases

Tagalog	**English**
Mayroon ba kayong bakanteng kuwarto?	Do you have any available rooms?
Magkano ang isang gabi?	How much is it per night?
Gusto ko ng kuwartong may aircon.	I want a room with air conditioning.
Pwede bang mag-check-in ng maaga?	Can I check in early?
Hanggang anong oras ang check-out?	Until what time is check-out?
Pwede bang humingi ng dagdag na tuwalya?	Can I ask for extra towels?
Mayroon ba kayong WiFi?	Do you have WiFi?
Saan ang reception?	Where is the reception?

Making Requests

Tagalog	English
Pwede ko bang makita ang kuwarto muna?	Can I see the room first?
May problema sa aircon, pwede bang palitan?	The air conditioner is not working, can it be replaced?
Pwede bang magpa-reserve ng taxi papuntang airport bukas?	Can you book a taxi to the airport for tomorrow?

At Check-Out,

Tagalog	English
Gusto ko nang mag-check-out.	I would like to check out.
Pwede ko bang makuha ang resibo?	Can I get the receipt?

Lesson 90 - Family Members

This lesson covers basic vocabulary for family members and simple phrases you might use when talking about your family.

Vocabulary for Family Members

Tagalog	English
Pamilya	Family
Nanay / Ina	Mother
Tatay / Ama	Father
Anak	Child
Kapatid	Sibling
Ate	Older sister
Kuya	Older brother
Bunso	Youngest child
Lola	Grandmother

Lolo	Grandfather
Tito	Uncle
Tita	Aunt
Pinsan	Cousin

Talking About Family

Tagalog	**English**
Ilan ang miyembro ng iyong pamilya?	How many members are in your family?
May kapatid ka ba?	Do you have siblings?
Ako ang bunso sa aming magkakapatid.	I am the youngest among my siblings.
Malaki ang pamilya namin.	We have a big family.
Mahal ko ang aking pamilya.	I love my family.
Ang nanay ko ay isang guro.	My mother is a teacher.
Apat kami na magkakapatid.	We are four siblings.
Ang lolo ko ay mahilig magtanim ng gulay.	My grandfather loves to plant vegetables.
Kami ay malapit sa isa't isa.	We are close to each other.

Dialogue

Tagalog	**English**
Teacher: Juan, ilan ang miyembro ng iyong pamilya?	Teacher: Juan, how many members are in your family?
Juan: Lima po kami. Ang tatay ko, nanay, isang kuya, at isang ate, tapos ako.	Juan: We are five. My father, mother, one older brother, one older sister, and then me.
Teacher: Mahilig ba kayong magbakasyon bilang pamilya?	Teacher: Do you like going on vacation as a family?
Juan: Opo, tuwing bakasyon, nagpupunta kami sa probinsya para bisitahin ang lolo at lola ko.	Juan: Yes, every vacation, we go to the province to visit my grandfather and grandmother.

Exercise: Translate the phrases.

Tagalog	English
	The name of my father is ...
	I have one brother and one sister.
	My family lives in the USA.

Solution: Translate the phrases.

Tagalog	English
Ang pangalan ng aking ama ay ...	The name of my father is ...
Mayroon akong isang kapatid na lalaki at isang kapatid na babae.	I have one brother and one sister.
Ang aking pamilya ay nakatira sa America.	My family lives in the USA.

Lesson 91 - Terms for People

Addressing people properly is crucial for showing respect. This lesson focuses on common terms used to denote age, gender, and respect.

Denoting Age and Gender

Tagalog	English
Binata	Young man
Dalaga	Young woman

Terms of Respect and Familiarity

Tagalog	English
Ate	Older sister
Kuya	Older brother

Formal Address

Tagalog	English
Ginoo	Sir or Mister
Binibini or Ginang	Miss or Mrs./Madam

Sample Phrases

Tagalog	English
Magandang umaga, Ginoo.	Good morning, Sir.
Salamat, Ate, sa tulong mo.	Thank you, older sister, for your help.
Kuya, pwede mo ba akong tulungan?	Older brother, can you help me?
Binibini, nawawala ba kayo?	Miss, are you lost?
Ginang, magkano po ito?	Madam, how much is this?
Dalaga na si Maria.	Maria is already a young woman.
Binata na si Juan.	Juan is already a young man.

Lesson 92 - Animals & Pets

This lesson will introduce you to basic animal names in and some phrases related to pets.

Vocabulary

Tagalog	English
Hayop	Animal
alagang hayop	Pet
Aso	Dog
Pusa	Cat
Ibon	Bird
Isda	Fish
Daga	Rat
Kabayo	Horse

Baka	Cow
Baboy	Pig
Manok	Chicken

Phrases

Tagalog	English
May alaga ka ba?	Do you have a pet?
Gusto ko ng aso.	I want a dog.
Ang pusa ay nasa loob ng bahay.	The cat is inside the house.
Mahilig ako sa ibon.	I like birds.
Ang aso ko ay mabait.	My dog is kind.

Dialog

Tagalog	English
A: May alagang hayop ka ba?	A: Do you have a pet?
B: Oo, mayroon akong aso at pusa.	B: Yes, I have a dog and a cat.
A: Anong pangalan ng aso mo?	A: What's your dog's name?
B: Siya ay si Bruno. Mahilig siya sa paglalaro.	B: His name is Bruno. He likes to play.

Exercise: Answer the question.

Tagalog	English
Anong paborito mong alaga?	What is your favorite pet?

Sample solution:

Tagalog	English
Ang paborito kong alagang hayop ay aso.	My favorite pet is a dog.
Gusto ko ang mga aso.	I like dogs.

Lesson 93 - Renovating & Repairing

This lesson provides an introduction to relevant terms and phrases about tools and repairing (mga kasangkapan at pagkukumpuni).

Vocabulary:

Tagalog	**English**
Martilyo	Hammer
Destornilyador	Screwdriver
Liyabe or Yabe	Wrench
Mga Pako	Nails
Mga Tornilyo	Screws
Lagari	Saw
Drill	Drill
Pliers or Pang-ipit	Pliers
Metro	Tape Measure
Antas	Level
Pag-aayos / Renobasyon	Renovation
Mag-ayos / Mag-renovate	To renovate
Konstruksyon	Construction
Kontratista	Contractor
Disenyo ng Interior	Interior Design
Bluprint / Plano	Blueprint
Sukat	Measurement
Tantya	Estimate
Demolisyon	Demolition
Pundasyon	Foundation
Pader	Wall
Sahig	Floor
Kisame	Ceiling
Tile / Baldosa	Tile
Pintura	Paint
Brush / Brotsa	Brush
Magpintura	To paint
Tubero / Plomeriya	Plumbing
Elektrikal	Electrical
Muwebles	Furniture

Dekorasyon	Decoration

Useful Phrases for Repairing

Tagalog	English
Kailangan ko ng mag kasangkapan.	I need tools.
Gusto kong bumili ng hagdan.	I want to buy a ladder.
Naghahanap ako ng I pintura.	I am looking for white paint.
Kailangan ko itong ayusin.	I need to fix this.
Pwede mo ba akong abutan ng martilyo?	Can you hand me the hammer?
Kailangan kong sukatin ito.	I need to measure this.
Maluwag ang tornilyong ito.	This screw is loose.
Kailangan nating mag-drill ng butas dito.	We need to drill a hole here.
Pwede mo bang higpitan ang bolt na ito?	Can you tighten this bolt?

Dialogue in a Repair Situation:

Tagalog	English
Pwede mo ba akong tulungan? Kailangan kong ayusin ang pinto.	Can you help me? I need to fix the door.
Oo, ano ang kailangan nating gawin?	Yes, what do we need to do?
Kailangan nating palitan ang mga lumang tornilyo. Maluwag na kasi.	We need to replace the old screws. They're loose already.
Sige, kukuha ako ng destornilyador at mga bagong tornilyo.	Alright, I'll get a screwdriver and some new screws.
Salamat. Pagkatapos, pwede mo bang sukatin ang taas ng pinto? Parang hindi pantay.	Thank you. After that, can you measure the height of the door? It seems uneven.
Walang problema. Aayusin natin ito.	No problem. We'll fix

Rennovating

Tagalog	English
Kailangan nating ayusin ang kusina.	We need to renovate the kitchen.
Magkano ang magagastos sa pag-aayos?	How much will the renovation cost?
Pwede ba nating makita ang blue-print?	Can we see the blueprint?
Gusto kong palitan ang mga baldosa sa sahig.	I want to change the floor tiles.
Anong kulay ang dapat nating ipinta sa mga pader?	What color should we paint the walls?
Kailangan ba nating kumuha ng elektrisyan?	Do we need to hire an electrician?
Kailan matatapos ang pag-aayos?	When will the renovation be finished?
Dapat tayong bumili ng bagong muwebles para sa sala.	We should buy new furniture for the living room.

Dialogue Example: Discussing a Renovation Plan

Tagalog	English
Gusto kong magpa-renovate ng bahay. Ano ang unang hakbang?	I want to renovate the house. What's the first step?
Unang-una, kailangan nating tignan ang kondisyon ng bahay at gumawa ng plano. Anong parte ba ang gusto mong i-renovate?	First, we need to check the condition of the house and make a plan. Which part do you want to renovate?
Plano kong ayusin ang kusina at banyo. Gusto ko ring palitan ang sahig sa sala.	I plan to fix the kitchen and bathroom. I also want to change the flooring in the living room.
Sige, gagawa kami ng estima sa gastos at plano para sa renovation. Pag-usapan din natin ang disenyo at mga materyales na gagamitin.	Alright, we'll make an estimate of the costs and a plan for the renovation. Let's also talk about the design and materials to be used.

Lesson 94 - Days of the Week

The names for the days of the week are derived from Spanish.

Overview of the Days

Tagalog	English
Linggo	Sunday
Lunes	Monday
Martes	Tuesday
Miyerkules	Wednesday
Huwebes	Thursday
Biyernes	Friday
Sabado	Saturday

Additional Vocabulary:

Tagalog	English
Araw	Day
Linggo	Week (also means Sunday; context distinguishes meaning)
Ngayon	Today
Bukas	Tomorrow
Kahapon	Yesterday

Sample Phrases

Tagalog	English
Anong araw ngayon?	What day is it today?
Lunes ngayon.	It's Monday today.
Sa susunod na Lunes.	Next Monday.
Noong nakaraang Lunes.	Last Monday.
Araw-araw or Bawat araw	Every day
Bukas ay Linggo.	Tomorrow is Sunday.
Magkikita tayo sa Biyernes.	We will meet on Friday.
Anong araw ang paborito mo?	What is your favorite day?

Araw-araw akong nag-eehersisyo.	I exercise every day.
Sa Miyerkules ang kaarawan ko.	My birthday is on Wednesday.

Dialogue

Tagalog	**English**
Ana: Anong araw ngayon?	Ana: What day is it today?
Ben: Martes ngayon. Bakit?	Ben: It's Tuesday today. Why?
Ana: Ah, kala ko Huwebes na. May meeting pala ako sa Biyernes.	Ana: Ah, I thought it was already Thursday. I have a meeting on Friday.
Ben: Ah, mabuti na lang at nagtanong ka. May dalawang araw ka pa para ma-ghanda.	Ben: Ah, it's good that you asked. You still have two days to prepare.

Exercise: Choose a phrase from the lesson, write it down, learn and practice it.

Tagalog	**English**

Lesson 95 - Months

This lesson will introduce you to each month's name, provide some sample phrases for talking about months, and include a short dialogue to help you practice.

Months of the Year in Tagalog

Tagalog	**English**
Enero	January
Pebrero	February
Marso	March

Abril	April
Mayo	May
Hunyo	June
Hulyo	July
Agosto	August
Setyembre	September
Oktobre	October
Nobyembre	November
Disyembre	December

Sample Phrases

Tagalog	English
Anong buwan ngayon?	What month is it now?
Ngayon ay Oktubre.	It is October now.
Kailan ang iyong kaarawan?	When is your birthday?
Ang aking kaarawan ay sa Mayo.	My birthday is in May.
Saang buwan ang Pasko?	In what month is Christmas?
Ang Pasko ay sa Disyembre.	Christmas is in December.

Talking About Seasons and Events

While the Philippines doesn't experience four distinct seasons like temperate countries, Filipinos recognize them in a global context. Here are phrases that might come in handy:

Tagalog	English
Tag-init	Dry season (literally "hot season")
Tag-ulan	Wet season (rainy season)
Tag-lamig	Cold season, usually referring to colder months elsewhere or the Christmas season in the Philippines.

Example:

Tagalog	English

Masarap mag-beach tuwing tag-init, lalo na sa Mayo.	It's nice to go to the beach during the dry season, especially in May.

Word by word reak down of the phrase "Masarap mag-beach tuwing tag-init, lalo na sa Mayo.":

- Masarap - Delicious/nice
- mag-beach - to go to the beach
- tuwing - during
- tag-init - dry season
- lalo na - especially
- sa - in
- Mayo - May

Dialogue

Tagalog	**English**
Carlos: Anong buwan ang pinaka-mainit sa Pilipinas?	Carlos: What is the hottest month in the Philippines?
Mia: Karaniwan, ang pinakamainit ay Abril at Mayo. Iyon ang tag-init.	Mia: Usually, the hottest are April and May. That's the dry season.
Carlos: Ahh, kaya pala maraming nagbabakasyon sa mga buwang iyon.	Carlos: Ahh, that's why many people take their vacations in those months.
Mia: Oo, at marami ring pista sa buong bansa.	Mia: Yes, and there are also many festivals across the country.

Practice: To practice, try to associate each month with an event or personal milestone (like birthdays or anniversaries) that occurs during that month for you. This way, you can remember the Tagalog names more easily and use them in sentences.

Lesson 96 - Time

This lesson will guide you through the basics of telling time, providing you with the necessary vocabulary, sample phrases, and a short dialogue to help you practice.

Basic Vocabulary

Tagalog	English
Oras	Hour/Time
Minuto	Minute
Alas	O'clock (derived from Spanish, used to tell time)
Ng umaga	In the morning (AM)
Ng tanghali	At noon
Ng hapon	In the afternoon (PM)
Ng gabi	In the evening/night (PM)
Kalahating oras	Half hour
Kwarto	Quarter (15 minutes)

Expressing Time
To tell time you often start with "Alas" followed by the number. For half hours, use "kalahati," and for quarters, use "kwarto."

Tagalog	English
Alas-dos ng hapon	2:00 PM
Alas-siyete ng umaga	7:00 AM
Alas-dose ng tanghali	12:00 PM (Noon)
Alas-singko y medya ng hapon	5:30 PM (medya is another term for half)
Alas-kuwatro kinse ng umaga	4:15 AM (kinse for fifteen/quarter)

Sample Phrases

Tagalog	English
Anong oras na?	What time is it?

Alas tres na ng hapon.	It is 3:00 PM now.
Magkikita tayo alas-otso ng umaga.	Let's meet at 8:00 AM.
Alas-diyes y medya na.	It's already 10:30.

Asking About Time

Tagalog	**English**
Ilang oras ang biyahe mula dito hanggang Manila?	How many hours is the journey from here to Manila?
Gaano katagal ang pulong?	How long is the meeting?

Short Dialogue

Tagalog	**English**
Juan: Anong oras na?	Juan: What time is it?
Maria: Alas-dose na ng tanghali. Oras na para sa tanghalian.	Maria: It's noon already. Time for lunch.
Juan: Ah, tama. Tara, kain na tayo.	Juan: Ah, right. Let’s go eat.

Exercise: Choose a phrase from the lesson, write it down, learn and practice it.

Tagalog	**English**

Lesson 97 - Date

This lesson simplifies the concept of dates, providing essential vocabulary, how to form dates, sample phrases, and a brief dialogue.

Basic Vocabulary

Tagalog	English
Petsa	Date
Buwan	Month
Araw	Day
Taon	Year
Ngayon	Today
Bukas	Tomorrow
Kahapon	Yesterday
Anibersaryo	Anniversary
Kaarawan	Birthday

Recall from a previous lesson the months of the year and days of the week, as they often accompany dates in scheduling.

Forming Dates

To express dates start with the day, followed by the month, and then the year. Use "ika-" before the date to signify "nth" as in "ika-1 ng Enero" for "1st of January."

Tagalog	English
Ika-10 ng Pebrero, 2025	February 10, 2025
Ika-25 ng Disyembre	December 25

Sample Phrases

Tagalog	English
Anong petsa ngayon?	What's the date today?
Ngayon ay ika-5 ng Mayo.	Today is May 5th.
Kailan ang iyong kaarawan?	When is your birthday?
Ang aking kaarawan ay sa ika-20 ng Hunyo.	My birthday is on June 20th.

Asking About Important Dates

Tagalog	English
Kailan ang anibersaryo ninyo?	When is your anniversary?
Sa susunod na linggo ang Pasko, di ba?	Christmas is next week, right?

Dialogue

Tagalog	English
Luis: Kailan ang eksam sa Matematika?	Luis: When is the Math exam?
Ana: Sa ika-15 ng Marso. Dapat tayong mag-aral.	Ana: On March 15th. We should study.
Luis: Tama ka. Simulan natin ngayong weekend.	Luis: You're right. Let's start this weekend.

Exercise: Translate the phrases.

Tagalog	English
	When do you want to meet?
	I want to meet you tomorrow.

Solution: Translate the phrases.

Tagalog	English
Kailan mo gustong magkita?	When do you want to meet?
Gusto kong makipagkita sa iyo bukas.	I want to meet you tomorrow.

Lesson 98 - Time Expressions

This lesson introduces basic time expressions, providing a simple guide to expressing past, present, and future times. You'll learn essential vocabulary, sample phrases, and engage in a short dialogue for practice.

Essential Vocabulary

Tagalog	English
Kanina	A while ago
Mas maaga	Earlier
Ngayon	Now
Kararating lang	Just now
Agad-agad	Immediately
Mamaya	Soon
Mamaya pa	Later
LAng	just
May ilang oras	Some time (span of time)
Balang araw	Some day / Some time (unspecified future point.)
Kahapon	Yesterday
Bukas	Tomorrow
Ngayong araw	This day
Kagabi	Last night
Bukas ng umaga	Tomorrow morning
Noong isang araw	The other day
Sa susunod na linggo	Next week
Sa nakaraang buwan	Last month
Ngayong taon	This year
Sa susunod na taon	Next year
Sa susunod	Next
Oras	Time
Sa susunod na pagkakataon	Next time
Oras	Hour
Sa loob ng isang oras	In an hour
Isang oras ang nakalipas	An hour ago

Sample Phrases

Tagalog	English
Anong oras ka dumating kahapon?	What time did you arrive yesterday?
Bukas ko na gagawin.	I will do it tomorrow.
Kanina pa kita hinihintay.	I have been waiting for you for a while.
Mamaya tayo magkita.	Let's meet later.
Ngayong araw ay maganda ang panahon.	The weather is nice today.
Kagabi hindi ako nakatulog ng maayos.	I didn't sleep well last night.
Sa susunod na linggo kami aalis.	We will leave next week.
Noong isang araw, nagpunta kami sa beach.	The other day, we went to the beach.
Sa nakaraang buwan, marami akong trabaho.	Last month, I had a lot of work.
Ngayong taon, plano kong mag-aral ng Tagalog.	This year, I plan to study Tagalog.
Sa susunod na taon, gusto kong magbakasyon sa Pilipinas.	Next year, I want to take vacation in the Philippines.

Using Time Expressions in Questions

Tagalog	English
Kailan ka magbabakasyon ngayong taon?	When are you going on a vacation this year?
Anong gagawin mo bukas ng umaga?	What will you do tomorrow morning?
Kailan tayo magkikita mamaya?	When will we meet later?

Dialogue

Tagalog	English
Leo: Mamaya ka na maglaba, kanina pa maulan.	Leo: Do the laundry later, it has been raining since earlier.
Ana: Sige, bukas na lang ng umaga.	Ana: Okay, just tomorrow morning

Ngayong araw, maglilinis ako ng bahay.	then. Today, I will clean the house.
Leo: Maganda. Mamaya, tulungan kita pagkatapos ko sa trabaho.	Leo: Good. Later, I'll help you after my work.
Ana: Salamat! Sa susunod na linggo, maghahanda tayo para sa kaarawan ni Lola, di ba?	Ana: Thank you! Next week, we're preparing for Grandma's birthday, right?
Leo: Oo, ngayong taon, sa bahay lang tayo magdiriwang.	Leo: Yes, this year, we'll celebrate at home.

Exercise: Break down the sentence "Ngayong taon, plano kong mag-aral ng Tagalog." word by word:

- Ngayong -
- taon -
- plano -
- kong -
- mag-aral -
- ng -
- Meaning:

Solution: Breaking down the sentence "Ngayong taon, plano kong mag-aral ng Tagalog." word by word:

- Ngayong - Now + ng (linking particle)
- taon - year
- plano - plan
- kong - my (a combination of "ko" meaning "my" or "I" and "ng" which is a linking particle)
- mag-aral - to study (a combination of "mag-" which is a prefix indicating an action, and "aral" which means "study" or "learn")
- ng - ng-Marker
- Tagalog - Tagalog (the language)
- Put together in English: "This year, my plan to tudy Tagalog." or more naturally, "This year, I plan to study Tagalog."

Exercise: Add the missing Tagalog time expression.

Tagalog	English
__________, umulan.	It rained a while ago.
___________ _____, kumain ako.	I ate earlier.
__________, nag-aaral ako.	Now, I am studying.
Kararating __________ niya.	He/She just arrived.
_______________, tumugon siya.	He/She responded immediately.
__________, tatawag ako.	Soon, I will call.
___________ ___ ako uuwi.	I will go home later.
___________ _____, magtatagumpay ako.	Someday, I will succeed.
_________, nag-jogging ako.	Yesterday, I went jogging.
_________, magkikita kami.	Tomorrow, we will meet.
___________ _______, masaya ako.	Today, I am happy.
__________, nanood ako ng pelikula.	Last night, I watched a movie.
________ ___ ________, aalis ako.	Tomorrow morning, I will leave.
________ _____ ________, nagkita kami.	The other day, we met.
___ __________ ___ ___________, bakasyon.	Next week, vacation.
___ _________ ________, nagpunta ako sa Baguio.	Last month, I went to Baguio.
_______ _______, gradweyt ako.	This year, I graduate.
___ _________ ___ ________, magtatrabaho na ako.	Next year, I will start working.
___ _____ ___ _____ _____, gusto kong pumunta sa mall.	In an hour, I want to go to the mall.

Solution:

Tagalog	English
Kanina, umulan.	It rained a while ago.
Mas maaga, kumain ako.	I ate earlier.
Ngayon, nag-aaral ako.	Now, I am studying.
Kararating lang niya.	He/She just arrived.
Agad-agad, tumugon siya.	He/She responded immediately.

Mamaya, tatawag ako.	Soon, I will call.
Mamaya pa ako uuwi.	I will go home later.
Balang araw, magtatagumpay ako.	Someday, I will succeed.
Kahapon, nag-jogging ako.	Yesterday, I went jogging.
Bukas, magkikita kami.	Tomorrow, we will meet.
Ngayong araw, masaya ako.	Today, I am happy.
Kagabi, nanood ako ng pelikula.	Last night, I watched a movie.
Bukas ng umaga, aalis ako.	Tomorrow morning, I will leave.
Noong isang araw, nagkita kami.	The other day, we met.
Sa susunod na linggo, bakasyon.	Next week, vacation.
Sa nakaraang buwan, nagpunta ako sa Baguio.	Last month, I went to Baguio.
Ngayong taon, gradweyt ako.	This year, I graduate.
Sa susunod na taon, magtatrabaho na ako.	Next year, I will start working.
Sa loob ng isang oras, gusto kong pumunta sa mall.	In an hour, I want to go to the mall.

Lesson 99 - And, Or, But...

This lesson covers basic yet essential conjunctions and phrases, helping you link your thoughts clearly.

- and

Tagalog	**English**
At	And
Example: Ako at ikaw	Example: You and I

- or

Tagalog	**English**
O	Or
Example: Kape o tsaa	Example: Coffee or tea

- but

Tagalog	English
Ngunit or Subalit	But
Example: Gusto ko maglaro, ngunit busy ako.	Example: I want to play, but I am busy.

- in order to, so that

Tagalog	English
Upang or Para	In order to, so that
Example: Nag-aaral ako upang matuto.	Example: I study in order to learn.

- when

Tagalog	English
Kapag or Pag	When
Example: Kapag umulan, magdala ng payong.	Example: When it rains, bring an umbrella.

- because, due to

Tagalog	English
Dahil or Dahil sa	Because, due to
Example: Masaya ako dahil sa iyo.	Example: I am happy because of you.

- that

Tagalog	English
Na	That, Used to link clauses or as a marker for detail or explanation.

Example: Sabi niya na malapit na siya.	Example: He said that he is close by.

- if

Tagalog	**English**
Kung	If
Example: Kung gusto mo, sumama ka sa amin.	Example: If you want, come with us.

- unless

Tagalog	**English**
Maliban kung	Unless
Example: Hindi ako aalis maliban kung tapos na ang trabaho.	Example: I won't leave unless the work is done.

- not only, but also

Tagalog	**English**
Hindi lamang... kundi pati	Not only, but also
Example: Hindi lamang siya matalino, kundi pati na rin masipag.	Example: Not only is she smart, but also hardworking.

Sample Sentences

Tagalog	**English**
Kumain ako ng agahan at uminom ng kape.	I ate breakfast and drank coffee.
Pumunta ka ba sa party o umuwi ka na?	Did you go to the party or did you go home?
Nais kong maglakbay sa Pilipinas, ngunit kulang ako sa oras.	I want to travel to the Philippines, but I lack the time.
Magtatrabaho ako sa weekend upang makabili ng bagong telepono.	I will work on the weekend in order to buy a new phone.

Kapag pumasa ako sa eksam, mag-diriwang kami.	When I pass the exam, we will celebrate.
Nagkasakit siya dahil sa pagod.	He got sick because of fatigue.
Alam mo ba na umalis na si Ana?	Do you know that Ana has already left?
Kung hindi ka pa handa, pwede tayong maghintay.	If you are not ready yet, we can wait.
Hindi kita sasamahan maliban kung magpapakabait ka.	I won't accompany you unless you behave.
Hindi lamang ako ang nagtatrabaho kundi pati na rin siya.	Not only am I working, but he is also.

Exercise: Choose a phrase from the lesson, write it down, learn and practice it.

Tagalog	**English**

Lesson 100 - For, From, To, ... (Prepositions)

This lesson will guide you through using basic prepositions to describe locations, directions, purposes, and more.

"For" Prepositions

Tagalog	**English**
Para (sa)	For, in order to, intended for someone/something.
Para sa iyo	For you.
Para kay Lisa	For Lisa.
Para sa kanila	For them.
Galing (sa)	From, originating from.
Galing sa Pilipinas	From the Philippines.
Galing kay Maria	From Maria.

"To" Prepositions

Tagalog	English
Sa	To, towards a location or direction.
Pupunta ako sa simbahan	I am going to the church.
Para sa	Can also mean "to" depending on context, similar to "for".
Para sa iyong kalusugan	For your health.

Spatial Prepositions

Tagalog	English
Sa ibabaw ng	On top of.
Sa ibabaw ng mesa	On top of the table.
Sa ilalim ng	Under, beneath.
Sa ilalim ng kama	Under the bed.
Sa harap ng	In front of.
Sa harap ng bahay	In front of the house.
Sa likod ng	Behind.
Sa likod ng paaralan	Behind the school.
Malapit sa	Close to.
Malapit sa palengke	Close to the market.
Sa tabi ng	Beside, next to.
Sa tabi ng bangko	Beside the bank.

Mixed Prepositions

Tagalog	English
Tulad ng	Like, similar to.
Tulad ng isang ibon	Like a bird.
Sa pamamagitan ng	Through, by means of.
Sa pamamagitan ng tren	By train.
Kasama	With (someone).
Kasama ko si Ana	I am with Ana.

Pagkatapos ng	After.
Pagkatapos ng klase	After class.

Sample Sentences

Tagalog	**English**
Para sa kaligtasan, huwag tumawid dito.	For safety, do not cross here.
Galing ako sa opisina ngayon.	I am coming from the office now.
Pupunta ako sa bahay ni Lola bukas.	I am going to Grandma's house tomorrow.
Ang libro ay nasa ibabaw ng lamesa.	The book is on top of the table.
Magkita tayo sa harap ng sinehan.	Let's meet in front of the cinema.
Naglakad kami sa pamamagitan ng parke.	We walked through the park.
Kasama ko ang aking pamilya sa bakasyon.	I am with my family on vacation.
Pagkatapos ng ulan, lumabas ang bahaghari.	After the rain, the rainbow appeared.

Exercise: Choose a phrase from the lesson, write it down, learn and practice it.

Tagalog	**English**

Lesson 101 - Comparing

This lesson focuses on how to compare things, highlight their differences, and emphasize their similarities.

Key Vocabulary:

Tagalog	English
Mas	More, used for comparisons.
Kaysa	Than, used in comparisons.
Pareho or Magkapareho	Both mean "same" or "similar."
Iba	Different.
Katulad or Tulad	Like or similar to.
Isipin	To think

Basic Comparisons: To compare two things, you can use the pattern: "Mas [adjective] ang [subject] kaysa sa [comparative subject]."

Tagalog	English
Mas [adjective] ang [subject] kaysa sa [comparative subject].	[Subject] is more [adjective] than [comparative subject].
Mas mabilis ang pusa kaysa sa aso.	The cat is faster than the dog.

Pointing Out Similarities: When you want to say that two things are similar, you can use "pareho," "magkapareho," or "tulad."

Vocabulary

Tagalog	English
Pareho	Same
Magkapareho	Similar
Tulad	Like

Phrases

Tagalog	English
Pareho ang kulay ng pusa at aso.	The cat and dog are the same color.
Magkapareho ang libro at dyaryo.	The book and newspaper are similar.
Tulad ng mansanas ang peras sa lasa.	The pear is like the apple in taste.

Highlighting Differences: To indicate that something is different, use "iba."

Tagalog	English
Iba	different or another
Iba ang lasa ng kape sa tsaa.	The taste of coffee is different from tea.

Practice Sentences:

Tagalog	English
Pareho kami ng opinyon.	We have the same opinion.
Magkapareho ang kanilang ideya.	Their ideas are similar.
Mas mataas ang gusali kaysa sa bahay.	The building is taller than the house.

Exercise: Translate the phrase.

Tagalog	English
	He is like her father.

Solution: Translate the phrase.

Tagalog	English
Tulad siya ng kanyang ama.	He is like his father.

Lesson 102 - Opinion

This lesson covers essential phrases to help you share your thoughts and inquire about others' viewpoints in various situations.

Vocabulary

Tagalog	English
tingin	look / think
opinyon	opinion

Naniniwala	to belive
think	isip
feel	maramdaman
agree	sumasang-ayon
disagree	hindi sumasang-ayon
Gusto ko ...	I like ...
Ayaw ko ...	I dislike ...
Naniniwala ako ...	I believe ...
Tinatanggihan ko ...	I reject ...
Sumasang-ayon ako ...	I agree ...
Hindi ako sumasang-ayon ...	I disagree ...
Mas gusto ko ...	I prefer ...
Sa palagay ko ...	I think ...
Naniniwala ako ...	I believe ...
Inaakala ko ...	I assume ...

The difference between "tingin" and "isip" pertains to their meanings and usage contexts.

Tagalog	Explanation
Tingin	Typically means "look" or "glance" when referring to the act of looking at something with one's eyes. It can also mean "view" or "opinion" in a different context, such as when expressing one's perspective on a matter ("Ano ang tingin mo?" - "What's your opinion/view?").
Isip	Refers to the mind's cognitive functions, such as "think" or "thought." It's used when talking about the process of thinking or the act of having a thought ("Ano ang iniisip mo?" - "What are you thinking?").

Expressing Your Opinion: To express your opinion, you can start with phrases like:

Tagalog	English
Sa tingin ko, ...	In my opinion, ...
Sa tingin ko, maganda ang pelikulang	In my opinion, this movie is good.

ito.	
Para sa akin, ...	For me, ...
Para sa akin, masarap ang ulam na ito.	For me, this dish is delicious.
Naniniwala ako na, ...	I believe that, ...
Naniniwala ako na mahalaga ang edukasyon.	I believe that education is important.

Asking for Opinions: When asking for someone else's opinion, use these polite inquiries:

Tagalog	English
Ano ang sa tingin mo?	What do you think?
Ano ang sa tingin mo tungkol sa bagong patakaran?	What do you think about the new policy?
Ano ang iyong opinyon?	What's your opinion?
Ano ang iyong opinyon sa isyung ito?	What's your opinion on this issue?
Mayroon ka bang suhestiyon?	Do you have any suggestions?
Mayroon ka bang suhestiyon para sa proyektong ito?	Do you have any suggestions for this project?

Agreeing and Disagreeing: In discussions, agreeing and disagreeing respectfully is crucial. Here's how you can do it:

Tagalog	English
Sumasang-ayon ako.	I agree.
Hindi ako sumasang-ayon.	I disagree.
Sa palagay ko, ... (I think, ...).	To soften a disagreement, you might add: 'I think, ...' before stating your differing viewpoint.

Exercise: Try forming sentences using the phrases above. For example, express your opinion about a book you recently read or a movie you watched. Then, ask a friend for their opinion on the same topic.

Lesson 103 - Express Feelings

Communicating your emotions effectively is crucial for meaningful interactions. This lesson introduces basic Tagalog phrases and vocabulary to express feelings, helping you convey your emotions clearly.

Vocabulary for Feelings

Tagalog	English
Pakiramdam	Feeling
Emosyon	Emotion
Masaya	Happy
Malungkot	Sad
Galit	Angry
Takot	Scared
Excited	Excited
Pagod	Tired
Gutom	Hungry
Uhaw	Thirsty
Nababato	Bored
Kalmado	Calm
Maramdaman	To feel

Sample Phrases

Tagalog	English
Masaya ako.	I am happy.
Malungkot ako ngayon.	I am sad today.
Bakit ka galit?	Why are you angry?
Natatakot ako.	I am scared.
Excited ako para bukas.	I am excited for tomorrow.
Pagod na pagod ako.	I am very tired.
Gutom na ako.	I am hungry.
Uhaw na uhaw ako.	I am very thirsty.
Nababato ako dito.	I am bored here.
Kalmado ang pakiramdam ko.	I feel calm.

Asking about feelings:

Tagalog	English
Anong pakiramdam mo?	How do you feel?
Masaya ka ba?	Are you happy?
Bakit ka malungkot?	Why are you sad?
Gusto mo bang kumain? Gutom ka na ba?	Do you want to eat? Are you hungry?

Dialogue

Tagalog	English
Juan: Anong pakiramdam mo nga-yon, Ana?	Juan: How do you feel now, Ana?
Ana: Masaya ako dahil nakapasa ako sa exam.	Ana: I am happy because I passed the exam.
Juan: Magaling! Excited na ako sa ating selebrasyon bukas.	Juan: Great! I am excited for our cel-ebration tomorrow.
Ana: Ako rin. Salamat sa suporta, ha?	Ana: Me too. Thanks for the sup-port, okay?
Juan: Walang anuman. Palagi kitang susuportahan.	Juan: You're welcome. I will always support you.

Exercise: Translate and write sample phrases how you feel.

Tagalog	English
Anong pakiramdam mo?	
Masaya ako.	
Malungkot ako.	
	I am tired.
	I am hungry.
	I am thirsty.
____________ ___	__ ___ ________

Solution: Translate and write sample phrases how you feel.

Tagalog	English
Anong pakiramdam mo?	How do you feel?
Masaya ako.	I am happy.
Malungkot ako.	I am sad.
Pagod ako.	I am tired.
Gutom ako.	I am hungry.
Uhaw ako.	I am thirsty.

Lesson 104 - Hygiene

This lesson expands on vocabulary and phrases related to hygiene.

Vocabulary

Tagalog	English
Kalinisan	Cleanliness
Banyo or Palikuran	Bathroom
Kasilyas or CR (Comfort Room)	Toilet
Limpyo	Clean
Hugaw	Dirty, filthy
Paglilinis	Cleaning
Paghuhugas	Washing
Paglalaba	Washing clothes
Pagsisinina ng Limpyo	Wearing clean clothes
Pagputol ng Kuko	Cutting nails
Deodorant	Deodorant
Punlas or Shampoo	Shampoo
Tubig	Water
Sabon	Soap
Tuwalya	Towel
Sipilyo	Toothbrush
Toothpaste or Kulgit	Toothpaste
Pahumot	Perfume
Panyo	Handkerchief

Sanitary Napkin	Sanitary pad
Condom	Condom
Mask	Face mask
Dis-impikta	Disinfect
Igpangpatayg kagaw	Disinfectant
Hilamos	Wash
Ligo	Shower, bathe

Sample Phrases

Tagalog	**English**
Saan ang banyo?	Where is the bathroom?
Ang banyo ay nasa kanan ng kusina.	The bathroom is to the right of the kitchen.
Maligo tayo ngayon.	Let's take a bath now.
Maghugas ka ng kamay gamit ang sabon at tubig.	Wash your hands with soap and water.
Isuot ang malinis na damit.	Wear clean clothes.
Putulin ang iyong kuko.	Cut your nails.
Gamitin ang deodorant.	Use the deodorant.
Linisin ang tuwalya.	Clean the towel.
Hugasan ang buhok gamit ang shampoo.	Shampoo the hair.
Malinis ba ang palikuran?	Is the toilet clean?
Hugaw ang banyo.	The bathroom is dirty.
Dis-impektahin ang kwarto.	Disinfect the room.
Maghugas ka ng kamay gamit ang sabon at tubig.	Wash your hands with soap and water.
Maligo araw-araw para manatiling malinis.	Take a bath/shower daily to stay clean.
Gamitin ang tuwalya pagkatapos maligo.	Use a towel after taking a bath/shower.
Magsepilyo ng ngipin tatlong beses sa isang araw.	Brush your teeth three times a day.
Dalhin ang panyo sa tuwing lalabas ng bahay.	Bring a handkerchief whenever you go out of the house.
Linisin ang palikuran upang	Clean the toilet to avoid germs.

maiwasan ang mikrobyo.	
Kailangan ko ng mga panlinis.	I need cleaning agents.

Dialogue I

Tagalog	English
Ana: Kuya, hugaw ang CR. Pwedeng linisin mo?	Ana: Brother, the toilet is dirty. Can you clean it?
Marco: Sige, gagamitin ko ang dis-impikta. Ikaw, pakilinis naman ng banyo.	Marco: Okay, I will use the disinfect-ant. You, please clean the bathroom.
Ana: Oo, maghuhugas din ako ng tu-walya pagkatapos.	Ana: Yes, I will also wash the towels afterward.
Marco: Magandang ideya. Gamitin natin ang bagong sabon.	Marco: Good idea. Let's use the new soap.

Dialog II

Tagalog	English
Ana: Kuya, saan ang sabon?	Ana: Brother, where is the soap?
Juan: Nasa tabi ng lababo. Bakit?	Juan: It's beside the sink. Why?
Ana: Maghuhugas ako ng kamay bago kumain.	Ana: I will wash my hands before eating.
Juan: Magandang gawain yan. Ako rin, pagkatapos kong gamitin ang palikuran.	Juan: That's a good practice. Me too, after using the toilet.

Lesson 105 - Feeling Unwell & Illness

This lesson introduces basic Tagalog vocabulary and phrases related to feeling unwell and illness, enabling you to express health concerns effectively.

Vocabulary for Feeling Unwell

Tagalog	English
Masakit	Painful / It hurts
Lagnat	Fever
Ubo	Cough
Sipon	Cold
Sakit ng ulo	Headache
Sakit ng tiyan	Stomachache
Pagod	Tired
Hilo	Dizzy
Allergy	Allergy
Hika	Asthma

Sample Phrases

Tagalog	English
Masakit ang ulo ko.	My head hurts.
May lagnat ako.	I have a fever.
Umuubo ako.	I am coughing.
May sipon ako.	I have a cold.
Masakit ang tiyan ko.	My stomach hurts.
Pagod na pagod ako.	I am very tired.
Nahihilo ako.	I am dizzy.
May allergy ako.	I have an allergy.
May hika ako.	I have asthma.

Asking for Help or Advice

Tagalog	English
Anong dapat kong inumin?	What should I take?
Kailangan ko bang pumunta sa doktor?	Do I need to see a doctor?
Pwede mo ba akong samahan sa ospital?	Can you accompany me to the hospital?

Dialogue

Tagalog	English
Luis: Kumusta ka na? Mukhang hindi ka maganda ang pakiramdam.	Luis: How are you? You look like you're not feeling well.
Mara: Masakit ang ulo ko at may lagnat ako.	Mara: My head hurts and I have a fever.
Luis: Kailangan mong magpahinga. Gusto mo bang magdala ako ng gamot mula sa botika?	Luis: You need to rest. Do you want me to bring medicine from the pharmacy?
Mara: Oo, sana. Salamat.	Mara: Yes, please. Thank you.

Lesson 106 - Emergencies & Help

This lesson covers basic Tagalog phrases and vocabulary related to emergencies and seeking help.

Vocabulary for Emergencies & Help

Tagalog	English
Tulong	Help
Saklolo	Rescue
Emerhensiya	Emergency
Sunog	Fire
Aksidente	Accident
Pulis	Police
Bumbero	Firefighter
Doktor	Doctor
Ospital	Hospital
Ambulansiya	Ambulance

Sample Phrases

Tagalog	English
Tulong!	Help!

Kailangan ko ng tulong.	I need help.
May emergensiya.	There's an emergency.
May sunog!	There's a fire!
Nasangkot ako sa aksidente.	I was involved in an accident.
Tumawag ng pulis.	Call the police.
Kailangan natin ng bumbero.	We need firefighters.
Dalhin mo ako sa ospital.	Take me to the hospital.
Tumawag ka ng ambulansiya.	Call an ambulance.

Asking for Help or Information

Tagalog	English
Saan ang pinakamalapit na ospital?	Where is the nearest hospital?
Paano ako makakapunta sa presinto?	How do I get to the police station?
May nasaktan ba?	Is anyone hurt?
Anong nangyari?	What happened?

Short Dialogue

Tagalog	English
Carlos: Tulong! Saklolo! May sunog sa kabilang bahay!	Carlos: Help! Rescue! There's a fire in the next house!
Anna: Tumawag ka na ba ng bumbero?	Anna: Have you called the firefighters?
Carlos: Oo, tumawag na ako. Kailangan din nating alertuhin ang mga kapit-bahay.	Carlos: Yes, I have called. We also need to alert the neighbors.
Anna: Sige, ako na ang bahala. Mag-ingat ka.	Anna: Okay, I'll take care of it. Be careful.

Lesson 107 - Accidents

This lesson is divided into two main sections, covering essential vocabulary and phrases for general accidents and car accidents

Part 1: General Accidents (Pangkalahatang Aksidente)

Vocabulary

Tagalog	English
Aksidente	Accident
Madulas	To slip
Mahulog	To fall
Matapilok	To trip
Pinsala	Injury
Dumugo	To bleed
Paso	Burn
Tulong	Help
Emerhensiya	Emergency
Kaligtasan	Safety
Panganib	Danger
Pag-iingat	Caution
Pangunang lunas	First aid

Useful Phrases

Tagalog	English
Kailangan ko ng tulong.	I need help.
Tumawag ng tulong.	Call for help.
Ayos ka lang ba?	Are you okay?
Mag-ingat ka.	Be careful.
Saan ang pinakamalapit na ospital?	Where is the nearest hospital?
Kailangan ko ng pangunang lunas.	I need first aid.

Part 2: Car Accidents (Aksidente sa Kotse)

Vocabulary

Tagalog	English
Kotse	Car
Bumangga	To crash
Banggaan	Collision
Drayber	Driver
Pasahero	Passenger
Trapiko	Traffic
Sira	Damage
Seguro	Insurance
Pulis	Police
Ambulansiya	Ambulance
Talyer / Pagawaan ng kotse	Repair shop
Ipa-tow	To tow
Pagkukumpuni	Repair
Presyo	Price
Magkano	How much
Pagpapagawa	Getting something fixed

Useful Phrases

Tagalog	English
May aksidente sa kotse.	There was a car accident.
Tumawag ng ambulansiya.	Call an ambulance.
Kailangan natin ang pulis.	We need the police.
Nasira ang aking kotse.	My car got damaged.
Ayos lang ba ang lahat?	Is everyone okay?
Kailangan kong i-report ang aksidenteng ito.	I have to report this accident.
Ano ang proseso ng seguro?	What's the insurance procedure?
Kailangan ko ang buong pangalan mo, address, at numero ng telepono.	I need your full name, address, and phone number.
Gumawa tayo ng mga larawan ng aksidente para sa dokumentasyon.	Let's make pictures of the accident for documentation.
Kailangan ipa-tow ang nasira kong	My damaged car needs to be towed

kotse papunta sa talyer.	to the repair shop.
Nasira ang kotse ko sa aksidente.	My car was damaged in an accident.
Kailangan kong ipaayos ang kotse ko.	I need to get my car fixed.
Magkano po ang gastos para sa pag-kukumpuni ng kotse?	How much will the repair of the car cost?
Puwede bang magtanong ng esti-mate para sa mga gastos sa pagpa-pagawa?	Can I ask for an estimate of the re-pair costs?

Dialogue Example: After Any Accident

Tagalog	**English**
Ayos lang ba kayo? May nasaktan ba?	Are you okay? Is anyone hurt?
Sa tingin ko, may ilang nasugatan. Kailangan namin ng ambulansiya.	I think there are some injuries. We need an ambulance.
Tumawag na ako ng ambulansiya at pulis. Tulong na rin ang parating.	I've already called an ambulance and the police. Help is on the way.
Salamat. Paano kaya ito sa seguro ng kotse?	Thank you. What about the car in-surance?
Kapag dumating ang pulis, siguradu-hing kumuha ng kopya ng report para sa seguro.	Once the police arrive, make sure to get a copy of the report for the in-surance.

Lesson 108 - Allergies

This lesson will cover basic vocabulary, phrases related to allergies, and some cultural notes where relevant.

Vocabulary

Tagalog	**English**
Alerhiya	Allergy

Ako ay may alerhiya sa...	I am allergic to...
Pagkain	Food
Gamot	Medicine/Medication
Alikabok	Dust
Polen	Pollen
Kumain	To eat
Balat	Skin
Matindi	Severe

Useful Phrases

Tagalog	**English**
Hindi ako makakain nito, may alerhiya ako.	I can't eat this, I have an allergy.
Mayroon ba kayong pagkain na wa-lang mani?	Do you have anything without nuts?
Kailangan kong uminom ng gamot sa alerhiya.	I need to take allergy medicine.
Nangangati ang balat ko dahil sa a-king alerhiya.	My skin itches because of my al-lergy.
Ako ay may alerhiya sa...	I am allergic to...
Hindi ako makakain ng... dahil sa al-erhiya.	I can't eat... because of allergy.
Pakiusap, walang... ako ay aler-hiyiko.	Please, no... I am allergic.
Mayroon akong matinding alerhiya sa...	I have a severe allergy to...
Maaari mo bang palitan ang...? May alerhiya ako dito.	Can you replace the...? I am allergic to it.
Ako ay alerhiyiko sa mga gamot na...	I am allergic to the medication...
Pakitanggal ang... dahil may alerhiya ako.	Please remove the... because I am allergic.
Ako ay may alerhiya sa balat kapag nakakontak sa...	I have a skin allergy when in contact with...
Mangyaring siguraduhin na walang... ang pagkain.	Please ensure the food is free from...
Alerhiyiko ako sa alikabok at pollen.	I am allergic to dust and pollen.

Kailangan ko ng doktor. Mayroon akong matinding alerhiya.	I need a doctor. I have a serious allergy.

Cultural Notes: In the Philippines, food is a huge part of the culture, with many dishes containing a variety of ingredients that might trigger allergies, such as seafood, nuts, and soy. It's important to be very clear when communicating your allergies, especially since some traditional dishes might not always list all their ingredients openly, similar to many other cuisines worldwide.

Dialogue

Tagalog	English
Pakiusap, walang mani sa ulam. Ako ay may alerhiya.	Please, no nuts in the dish. I am allergic.
Naiintindihan ko. Maghahanda ako ng pagkain na walang mani para sa iyo.	I understand. I will prepare a dish without nuts for you.
Maraming salamat po.	Thank you very much.

Lesson 109 - Body Parts

This lesson covers basic vocabulary for body parts and sample phrases.

Vocabulary for Body Parts

Tagalog	English
Ulo	Head
Mata	Eye
Ilong	Nose
Bibig	Mouth
Tenga	Ear
Kamay	Hand
Braso	Arm

Tiyan	Stomach
Paa	Foot
Binti	Leg
Balikat	Shoulder
Likod	Back
Dibdib	Chest
Daliri	Finger/Toe
Tuhod	Knee

Sample Phrases

Tagalog	**English**
Masakit ang ulo ko.	My head hurts.
Mayroon akong itim na mata.	I have a black eye.
Hinawakan niya ang kanyang tiyan.	He held his stomach.
Nakatayo siya sa kanyang mga paa.	He stood on his feet.
Nagpapalakas ako ng braso.	I am strengthening my arms.

Describing Body Parts

Tagalog	**English**
Malaki ang mata niya.	He/She has big eyes.
Mahaba ang buhok ko.	My hair is long.
Makinis ang balat niya.	His/Her skin is smooth.

Short Dialogue

Tagalog	**English**
Ana: Naku, masakit ang tuhod ko mula sa pagtakbo kanina.	Ana: Oh no, my knee hurts from running earlier.
Ben: Bakit, nadapa ka ba?	Ben: Why, did you fall?
Ana: Hindi, pero parang na-stretch yata ng sobra.	Ana: No, but it seems like it was overstretched.
Ben: Magpahinga ka muna at maglagay ka ng yelo.	Ben: You should rest and apply some ice.

Exercise: Choose or form a phrase from the lesson, write it down, learn and practice it.

Tagalog	English

Lesson 110 - Looking for a Job

lesson will cover those basics, aiming to provide a foundation for navigating the job market.

Vocabulary

Tagalog	English
Trabaho	Job
Maghanap ng trabaho	To look for a job
Aplikasyon	Application
Resume / Curriculum Vitae	Resume / CV
Liham ng Aplikasyon	Cover Letter
Mga Kwalipikasyon	Qualifications
Karanasan	Experience
Panayam	Interview
Empleyador	Employer
Empleyado	Employee
Mga Kasanayan	Skills
Posisyon	Position
Sahod	Salary
Mga Benepisyo	Benefits
Full-time	Full-time
Part-time	Part-time
Kumontrata	To hire
Form ng aplikasyon	Application form

Useful Phrases

Tagalog	English
Naghahanap ako ng trabaho.	I am looking for a job.
Gusto kong mag-apply para sa posisyon ng...	I want to apply for the position of...
Saan ako maaaring magpasa ng aking resume?	Where can I submit my resume?
Ano ang mga kwalipikasyon para sa trabahong ito?	What are the qualifications for this job?
Kailan ang panayam?	When is the interview?
May karanasan ako sa...	I have experience in...
Anong mga kasanayan ang kailangan?	What skills are required?
Ano ang panimulang sahod?	What is the starting salary?
May mga benepisyo ba?	Are there any benefits?

Dialogue Example: Applying for a Job

Tagalog	English
Magandang araw, naghahanap po ako ng trabaho. May bakante po ba kayo?	Good day, I am looking for a job. Do you have any vacancies?
Magandang araw! Oo, may bakante kami para sa posisyon ng sales representative. Naghahanap kami ng may karanasan. May resume ka ba dito?	Good day! Yes, we have a vacancy for a sales representative position. We are looking for someone with experience. Do you have your resume with you?
Opo, narito po ang aking resume at liham ng aplikasyon.	Yes, here is my resume and application letter.
Salamat. Titingnan namin ito at tatawagan ka para sa iskedyul ng panayam. Anong oras ka pwedeng tawagan?	Thank you. We will review it and call you for an interview schedule. What time can we call you?
Pwede po ako sa umaga, mula alas-otso hanggang alas-onse.	I am available in the morning, from eight to eleven.

Lesson 111 - God & Faith

Faith plays a significant role in the lives of many Filipinos, with the country being predominantly Christian alongside other religious beliefs. This lesson introduces basic Tagalog vocabulary and phrases related to God and faith, suitable for respectful discussions or expressions of one's spiritual beliefs.

Vocabulary for God & Faith

Tagalog	English
Diyos	God
Paniniwala	Belief
Dasal	Prayer
Simbahan	Church
Bibliya	Bible
Pagsamba	Worship
Espiritu Santo	Holy Spirit
Anghel	Angel
Milagro	Miracle
Pag-asa	Hope
Pagpapala	Blessing
Pagmamahal	Love

Talking About Faith

Tagalog	English
Naniniwala ako sa Diyos.	I believe in God.
Pwede ba tayong magdasal?	Can we pray?
Pumupunta ako sa simbahan tuwing Linggo.	I go to church every Sunday.
Basahin natin ang Bibliya.	Let's read the Bible.
Naghahanap ako ng pag-asa.	I am looking for hope.
Salamat sa mga pagpapala.	Thank you for the blessings.
Ipakita mo sa akin ang tamang daan.	Show me the right path.
Gusto kong humingi ng tawad kay Hesus.	I want to ask Jesus for forgiveness.

Exercise: Choose a phrase from the lesson, write it down, learn and practice it.

Tagalog	English

Lesson 112 - Weather & Climate

This lesson covers basic vocabulary, common phrases, and a short dialogue to help you talk about the weather in Tagalog.

Vocabulary for Weather

Tagalog	English
Panahon	Weather
Mainit	Hot
maalinsangan	Humid
Malamig	Cold
Umuulan	Raining
Mahangin	Windy
Maulap	Cloudy

Questions and Phrases about the Weather

Tagalog	English
Anong panahon ngayon?	What's the weather like today?
Mainit ba ngayon?	Is it hot today?
Umuulan ba?	Is it raining?
Masyadong maalinsangan ang panahon.	The weather is very humid.
Ano ang temperatura?	What's the temperature?
Malamig sa umaga.	It's cold in the morning.

Talking About Appropriate Clothes for the Weather

Tagalog	English
Umuulan. Magdadala ako ng payong.	It is raining. I will bring an umbrella.
Magsuot ka ng jacket, malamig.	Wear a jacket, it's cold.
Dahil mainit, magsuot ng manipis na damit.	Because it's hot, wear light clothes.
Kapag umuulan, mag-boots ka.	When it rains, wear boots.

Dialogue

Tagalog	English
Ana: Anong panahon ngayon?	Ana: What's the weather like today?
Ben: Mainit ngayon. Pero maulap, baka umulan mamaya.	Ben: It's hot now. But it's cloudy, it might rain later.
Ana: Ah, kaya pala. Dapat pala magdala ako ng payong.	Ana: Ah, I see. I should bring an umbrella then.
Ben: Oo, at magsuot ka rin ng hat para sa init.	Ben: Yes, and also wear a hat for the heat.

Here's the phrase "Ah, kaya pala. Dapat pala magdala ako ng payong." broken down word by word:

- Ah - An interjection expressing realization or understanding.
- kaya - Means "so" or "thus," indicating a reason or explanation.
- pala - Used for realization of something not previously known to the speaker; it can imply "that's why" or "indeed."
- Dapat - Should; indicating an obligation or suggestion.
- pala - (Reiterated for emphasis on realization or newfound understanding.)
- magdala - To bring or carry.
- ako - I; referring to oneself.
- ng - A marker indicating the direct object of the action.
- payong - Umbrella.
- Meaning: Ah, I see. I should bring an umbrella then.

Exercise: Choose a phrase from the lesson, write it down, learn and practice it.

Tagalog	English

Lesson 113 - Seasons

The Philippines, being a tropical country, doesn't experience four seasons like spring, summer, fall, and winter. Instead, it has two main seasons based on precipitation: the dry season (tag-init) and the wet season (tag-ulan).
In Tagalog, the word for "weather" is "panahon", which can also mean "season" depending on the context. Thus, in some contexts, the same word is used for both "weather" and "season." However, the specific word for "season" in the sense of spring, summer, autumn, and winter is "tag-panahon" or sometimes just "panahon" with qualifiers to specify the type of season.

Tagalog	English
Tag-init	Dry Season, Hot Season
Tag-init ang panahon mula Disyembre hanggang Mayo.	The dry season lasts from December to May.
Mainit at maaraw sa tag-init, maganda pumunta sa beach.	It's hot and sunny in the dry season, nice to go to the beach.
Tag-ulan	Wet Season, Rain Season
Tag-ulan naman mula Hunyo hanggang Nobyembre.	The wet season is from June to November.
Madalas ang ulan sa tag-ulan, nagiging berde ang kapaligiran.	The rain is frequent in the wet season, the surroundings become green.

Exercise: Answer the question.

Tagalog	**English**
Ano ang paborito mong tag-panahon?	What is your favorite season?

Sample solution:

Tagalog	**English**
Ano ang paborito mong tag-panahon?	What is your favorite season?
Ang paborito kong panahon ay ang tagtuyot kahit na ito ay napakainit. (SVO)	My favorite season is the dry season although it is very hot.
Kahit na napakainit, ang tagtuyot ay paborito kong panahon. (VSO)	Although it is very hot, the dry season is my favorite.

Here's a breakdown of the sentence "Ang paborito kong panahon ay ang tagtuyot kahit na ito ay napakainit.":

- Ang - The
- paborito - favorite
- kong - my
- panahon - season
- ay - is
- ang - the
- tagtuyot - dry season
- kahit na - although
- ito - it
- ay - is
- napakainit - very hot
- Meaning: "My favorite season is the dry season although it is very hot."

Word by word breakdown of the phrase "Kahit na napakainit, ang tagtuyot ay paborito kong panahon.":

- "Kahit na napakainit" (Although it is very hot) becomes the leading clause, setting the context.
- "ang tagtuyot" (the dry season) is the subject.
- "ay paborito kong panahon" (is my favorite season) acts as the predicate, explaining the subject.
- Meaning: "Although it is very hot, the dry season is my favorite."

This version adheres to the typical VSO structure used in Tagalog, emphasizing the condition (the heat) before stating the main subject (the dry season as the favorite season).

Lesson 114 - Leisure Time

This lesson will introduce you to basic Tagalog phrases and vocabulary related to spending your free time, making it easier for you to talk about your hobbies and leisure activities.

Vocabulary for Leisure Time

Tagalog	English
Libangan	Hobby/Leisure
Oras ng paglilibang	Leisure time
Magbasa	To read
Manood	To watch
Makinig	To listen
Maglakad-lakad	To take a walk
Maglaro	To play
Musika	Music
Libro	Book
Pelikula	Movie
Laro	Game
Ehersisyo	Exercise
Pagpipinta	Painting
Paglalakbay	Traveling
Lumabas	To go out

Talking About Leisure Activities

Tagalog	English
Anong libangan mo?	What are your hobbies?
Gusto kong magbasa ng libro sa aking libreng oras.	I like to read books in my free time.
Mahilig akong manood ng mga pelikula tuwing weekend.	I enjoy watching movies on weekends.
Nag-eehersisyo ako para manatiling malusog.	I exercise to stay healthy.
Making Plans for Leisure Activities	Making Plans for Leisure Activities
Gusto mo bang maglakad-lakad sa parke?	Would you like to take a walk in the park?
Maglaro tayo ng basketball sa Sabado.	Let's play basketball on Saturday.
Samahan mo ako manood ng bagong pelikula.	Join me to watch the new movie.

Expressing Preferences

Tagalog	English
Mas gusto ko ang makinig sa musika kaysa manood ng TV.	I prefer listening to music over watching TV.
Hindi ko hilig ang maglaro ng video games.	I'm not into playing video games.

Let's break down the Tagalog phrase "Mas gusto ko ang makinig sa musika kaysa manood ng TV." into its components for a clearer understanding:

- Mas - More
- gusto - like
- ko - I/my
- ang - the
- makinig - to listen
- sa - to
- musika - music
- kaysa - than
- manood - to watch

- ng - noun marker
- TV - TV

Break down of „Hindi ko hilig ang maglaro ng video games."
- Hindi - No/Not
- ko - I/my
- hilig - fondness/interest
- ang - the
- maglaro - to play
- ng - of
- video games - video games

Sample Dialoge

Tagalog	English
Mark: Anong libangan mo kapag weekend?	Mark: What do you do for fun on weekends?
Lisa: Mahilig ako magbasa ng mga nobela at mag-ehersisyo sa umaga.	Lisa: I enjoy reading novels and exercising in the morning.
Mark: Interesado ka ba sa pagpipinta? May libreng workshop sa Linggo.	Mark: Are you interested in painting? There's a free workshop on Sunday.
Lisa: Oo, gusto ko iyan! Palagi kong gustong subukan ang pagpipinta.	Lisa: Yes, I'd love that! I've always wanted to try painting.

Exercise: Form sentences what you like and want to do in your leisure time. To express "I like to..." and "I want to...", you would use "Gusto ko" for "I like" and "Gusto kong" or "Nais kong" for "I want".

Tagalog	English
Gusto ko maglakbay.	I like to travel.
Gusto kong kumain.	I want to eat.
Gusto ko ...	I like to ...
Gusto kong ...	I want to ...

Lesson 115 - Hobbies

Let's start with some useful words:

Tagalog	English
Libangan	Hobby
Magbasa	To read
Magsulat	To write
Magluto	To cook
Maglaro	To play
Kumanta	To sing
Sumayaw	To dance
Pinta	Paint (verb: magpinta)
Musika	Music
Pelikula	Movie
Aklat	Book
Subukan	To try

Asking About Hobbies: When you want to know about someone's, you can use the following questions.

Tagalog	English
Ano ang iyong libangan?	What is your hobby?
Anong libangan ang gusto mong gawin sa iyong bakanteng oras?	What hobbies do you like to do in your free time?
May libangan ka ba sa pagluluto o pagbabasa?	Do you have hobbies in cooking or reading?

Answering About Hobbies: Here's how you might answer questions about your hobbies:

Tagalog	English	Example
Ang libangan ko ay [libangan].	My hobby is [hobby].	Ang libangan ko ay pagluluto. (My hobby is cooking.)

Gusto kong [verb] tuwing [time or situation].	I like to [verb] during [time or situation].	Gusto kong magbasa tuwing gabi. (I like to read at night.)
Mahilig akong mag-[activity].	I enjoy [activity-ing].	Mahilig akong magpinta. (I enjoy painting.)

Dialogue:

Tagalog	English
Ano ang iyong libangan?	What is your hobby?
Ang libangan ko ay pagbabasa ng mga aklat. Gusto ko rin magluto tuwing weekend.	My hobby is reading books. I also like to cook during weekends.
Talaga? Anong uri ng mga aklat ang gusto mong basahin?	Really? What kind of books do you like to read?
Mahilig ako sa mga nobela at mga libro tungkol sa paglalakbay.	I enjoy novels and books about travel.

Exercise: What is your hobby?

Tagalog	English
Ang libangan ko ay ...	My hobby is ...
Mahilig akong	I like ...
Mahilig akong mag-...	I like to ...

Lesson 116 - Phone Call

This lesson will introduce you to basic vocabulary and phrases for phone calls, making it easier for you to navigate these conversations.

Vocabulary for Phone Calls

Tagalog	English
Tawag	Call
Telepono	Telephone/Phone
Numero	Number
Tumawag	To call
Sagot	Answer
Missed call	Missed call (commonly used in English)
Mensahe	Message
Voicemail	Voicemail (often used in English)
Ringing	Ringing (often used in English)
Speaker	Speaker (for speakerphone function, often used in English)

Sample Phrases

Tagalog	English
Pwede ba kitang tawagan?	Can I call you?
Ano ang iyong numero?	What is your number?
Tatawag ako mamaya.	I will call later.
Hindi ko nasagot ang tawag mo.	I couldn't answer your call.
May missed call ka mula sa akin.	You have a missed call from me.
Pwede bang iwanan mo ng mensahe?	Can you leave a message?
Ipaalam mo sa akin pag tumawag siya.	Let me know when he/she calls.

Making a Phone Call

Tagalog	English
Hello, pwede ko bang makausap si [Pangalan]?	Hello, may I speak to [Name]?
Nandiyan ba si [Pangalan]?	Is [Name] there?
Gusto kong magtanong tungkol sa ...	I want to ask about ...

Receiving a Phone Call

Tagalog	English
Sino po sila?	Who is this?
Sandali lang po, itatawag ko siya.	One moment, I will get him/her.
Wala siya ngayon, gusto mo bang mag-iwan ng mensahe?	He/She is not here right now, would you like to leave a message?

Dialogue

Tagalog	English
Ana: Hello, pwede ko bang makausap si Ben?	Ana: Hello, may I speak to Ben?
Receptionist: Sandali lang po, tatawagan ko po siya. Sino po sila?	Receptionist: One moment, I will call him. Who is this?
Ana: Ako po si Ana. Pakisabi na lang tumawag ako.	Ana: This is Ana. Please just tell him I called.
Receptionist: Sige po, Ms. Ana. Iiwan ko po ang iyong mensahe.	Receptionist: Okay, Ms. Ana. I will leave your message.

Exercise: Choose a phrase from the lesson, write it down, learn and practice it.

Tagalog	English

Lesson 117 - Ordering Food

Let's dive into useful phrases:

Tagalog	English
Gusto ko sana mag-order ng...	I would like to order...
Puwede ba akong mag-order ng...	Can I order...

Magkano po ang...	How much is...
Ilan po ang gusto niyo?	How many would you like?
Para sa ilang tao?	For how many people?
Ano po ang inyong pangalan?	What is your name?
Saan po kayo nakatira?	Where do you live?
Ilang minuto po ang hihintayin?	How many minutes will it take?

Dialog:

Tagalog	**English**
Customer: Hello, gusto ko sana mag-order ng pizza at spaghetti.	Customer: Hello, I would like to order pizza and spaghetti.
Restaurant: Magandang araw! Ilan po ang order niyo ng pizza at spaghetti?	Restaurant: Good day! How many orders of pizza and spaghetti would you like?
Customer: Isa po ng bawat isa. Magkano po ang lahat?	Customer: One of each, please. How much will it be?
Restaurant: Ang total po ay 500 pesos. Saan po kayo nakatira?	Restaurant: The total is 500 pesos. Where do you live?
Customer: Sa 123 Sampaguita Street, Quezon City.	Customer: At 123 Sampaguita Street, Quezon City.
Restaurant: Nakuha ko po. Mga 45 minutos po ang hihintayin. Ano po ang pangalan para sa order?	Restaurant: Got it. It will take about 45 minutes. What's the name for the order?
Customer: Sa pangalan po ni Juan Dela Cruz. Salamat po!	Customer: Under the name Juan Dela Cruz. Thank you!
Restaurant: Salamat din po, Sir Juan. Hintayin niyo na lang po ang delivery.	Restaurant: Thank you too, Sir Juan. Just wait for the delivery.

Exercise: Complete the phrase with your favorite dish:

Tagalog	**English**
Hello, gusto ko sana mag-order ng ...	Hello, I would like to order ...

Lesson 118 - Texting

Let's start with some basic vocabulary that's useful for texting and messaging.

Tagalog	English
Hello! / Hi!	Hello! / Hi!
Kamusta ka?	How are you?
Salamat!	Thank you!
Pasensya na.	Sorry.
Oo.	Yes.
Hindi.	No.
Pakiusap.	Please.
Kitakits mamaya!	See you later!

Basic Phrases for Texting and Messaging: Now, let's look at some common phrases used in texting.

Tagalog	English
Ano ang ginagawa mo?	What are you doing?
Hahaha!	LOL (Laughing Out Loud)
Okay ka lang ba?	Are you okay?
Miss na kita.	I miss you.
Papunta na ako.	I'm on my way.
I am late. I will arrive in 15 minutes.	Nahuhuli ako. Darating ako sa loob ng 15 minuto.

Breaking down the Tagalog phrase "Nahuhuli ako. Darating ako sa loob ng 15 minuto." into simple parts:

- Nahuhuli ako.
    - Nahuhuli = late (am being late)
    - ako = I
    - Meaning: I am late.
- Darating ako sa loob ng 15 minuto.
    - Darating = will arrive
    - ako = I
    - sa loob ng = within

- 15 = fifteen
- minuto = minutes
- Meaning: I will arrive in 15 minutes.

- Together, it communicates: "I am late. I will arrive in 15 minutes."

Common Text Abbreviations: Texting often involves using abbreviations. Here are a few.

Abbreviation	English	Tagalog Equivalent
G2G	Got to Go	Alis na ako
BRB	Be Right Back	Bbrb (or just BRB)
TY	Thank You	Slmt
NP	No Problem	Walang problema

Making Plans, Aligning, and Meeting Up: When making plans, aligning on details, or deciding where to meet, you might use phrases like:

Tagalog	English
Tuloy pa ba tayo ngayon?	Are we still on for today?
Anong oras?	What time?
Saan tayo magkikita?	Where shall we meet?

Breaking down the question "Tuloy pa ba tayo ngayon?":

- Tuloy: Continues or proceeds.
- pa ba: Still.
- tayo: We/us.
- ngayon: Today.

Sample Texting Dialogue

Tagalog	English
Person A: Hi! Kamusta ka?	Person A: Hi! How are you?
Person B: Okay lang, ikaw?	Person B: I'm okay, you?
Person A: Miss na kita. G2G, kitakits	Person A: I miss you. Got to go, see

mamaya!	you later!
Person B: Sige, ingat!	Person B: Okay, take care!

Exercise: Choose a phrase from the lesson, write it down, learn and practice it.

Tagalog	English

Lesson 119 - Lost & Found

This lesson will help you communicate in situations where you've lost something or found an item belonging to someone else.

Vocabulary

Tagalog	English
Nawala	Lost
Nakita	Found
Gamit	Item/Belonging
Hanapin	To look for/Search
Ibalik	To return
Tumingin	To look

Phrases

Tagalog	English
Nawala ang aking cellphone.	I lost my cellphone.
Nakakita ako ng nawawalang bag.	I found a lost bag.
Pwede mo ba akong tulungan hanapin ito?	Can you help me look for it?
Saan ko pwedeng ibalik ang nakitang gamit?	Where can I return the found item?

Saan ang Lost and Found dito?	Where is the Lost and Found here?

Conversation Example

Tagalog	**English**
A: Excuse me, nawala ang aking wallet. Nakita mo ba ito?	A: Excuse me, I lost my wallet. Have you seen it?
B: Hindi eh, pero subukan mong tanong sa Lost and Found.	B: No, but try asking at the Lost and Found.
A: Salamat! Saan po ba ang Lost and Found dito?	A: Thank you! Where is the Lost and Found here?
B: Doon sa may reception. Dapat may pangalan at numero doon.	B: It's near the reception. There should be a name and number there.

Lesson 120 - Inviting & Arranging

This lesson provides basic Tagalog vocabulary and phrases to help you extend invitations, make plans, and arrange meetings effectively.

Vocabulary for Inviting & Arranging

Tagalog	**English**
Imbita	Invite
Kita (verb)	To meet/see
Usapan	Agreement/Arrangement
Lugar	Place
Oras	Time
Petsa	Date
Pupunta	Will go
Sama	Join
Ayos	Okay/Fine
Tanggap	Accept

Sample Phrases for Inviting

Tagalog	English
Gusto mo bang sumama sa akin sa...?	Would you like to join me at...?
Iniimbita kita sa aking kaarawan.	I'm inviting you to my birthday.
Libre ka ba sa Sabado?	Are you free on Saturday?
Pwede ba tayong magkita sa...?	Can we meet at...?

Making Arrangements

Tagalog	English
Saang lugar tayo magkikita?	Where shall we meet?
Anong oras tayo magkikita?	What time shall we meet?
Puwede ba natin itong gawin sa...?	Can we do this on...?
Ayos ba sa iyo ang alas-siyete?	Is seven o'clock okay with you?

Declining and Accepting Invitations

Tagalog	English
Pasensya na, may iba akong lakad.	Sorry, I have another engagement.
Sige, pupunta ako.	Alright, I'll go.
Tanggap ko ang iyong imbita.	I accept your invitation.

Dialogue

Tagalog	English
Juan: Gusto mo bang sumama sa a-kin sa sinehan sa Biyernes?	Juan: Do you want to join me at the movies on Friday?
Mia: Libre ka ba sa alas-otso ng gabi?	Mia: Are you free at eight in the evening?
Juan: Oo, ayos lang sa akin. Anong pelikula ang panonoorin natin?	Juan: Yes, that's fine with me. What movie are we watching?
Mia: Ayos! Gusto kong manood ng bagong action film. Kitakits!	Mia: Great! I want to watch the new action film. See you then!

Inviting Someone to a Party

Tagalog	English
Gusto kitang imbitahan sa aking party sa Sabado. Pwede ka bang pu-munta?	I want to invite you to my party on Saturday. Can you come?
Feel free din na isama ang iyong mga kaibigan. Mas marami, mas masaya!	Feel free to bring your friends along. The more, the merrier!

Inviting Someone for Coffee and Dinner

Tagalog	English
Gusto mo bang magkape tayo min-san?	Would you like to have coffee with me sometime?
Pwede rin tayong mag-dinner pag-katapos. Saan mo gustong kumain?	We can also have dinner afterward. Where would you like to eat?

Asking Someone for a Date

Tagalog	English
May gusto sana akong itanong. Gusto mo ba akong samahan sa isang date?	I have something I'd like to ask. Would you like to go on a date with me?
Masaya ako kung maaari tayong lumabas at mag-spend ng oras magkasama.	I would be happy if we could go out and spend some time together.

Making Arrangements for a Weekend Trip

Tagalog	English
Plano ko sana ang isang weekend trip sa Tagaytay. Gusto mo bang sumama?	I'm planning a weekend trip to Ta-gaytay. Would you like to join?
Maganda doon at siguradong mag-eenjoy tayo. Sabihin mo lang kung okay sa iyo ang plano.	It's beautiful there, and I'm sure we'll enjoy it. Just let me know if the plan works for you.

Exercise: Choose a phrase from the lesson, write it down, learn and practice it.

Tagalog	English

Lesson 121 - Canceling & Declining

This lesson covers how to cancel and decline invitations or plans in Tagalog respectfully.

Vocabulary for Canceling & Declining

Tagalog	English
Kanselahin	To cancel
Hindi matutuloy	Will not proceed
Pasensya na	I'm sorry
Hindi ako makakapunta	I can't go
Ayaw ko	I don't want to
Salamat sa alok, pero...	Thank you for the offer, but...
Sa susunod na lang	Maybe next time

Sample Phrases for Canceling

Tagalog	English
Kailangan kong kanselahin ang ating usapan bukas. Pasensya na.	I need to cancel our meeting tomorrow. I'm sorry.
Hindi matutuloy ang party sa Biyernes, magkakaroon ng bagyo.	The party on Friday will not proceed, there will be a storm.

Declining Offers or Invitations

Tagalog	English
Hindi ako makakapunta sa iyong kaarawan, may prior commitment ako. Pa-sensya na.	I can't go to your birthday, I have a prior commitment. I'm sorry.
Salamat sa alok mo, pero hindi ako makakasama sa inyo ngayon.	Thank you for your invitation, but I can't join you now.

Responding to Cancellations

Tagalog	English
Naiintindihan ko. Sa susunod na lang tayo magkita.	I understand. Let's meet next time.
Walang problema.	No problem.

Sample Dialogue

Tagalog	English
Ana: Juan, pasensya na pero kailangan kong kanselahin ang ating lakad sa Sabado.	Juan, I'm sorry but I need to cancel our plan on Saturday.
Juan: Oh, bakit? May problema ba?	Oh, why? Is there a problem?
Ana: May biglaang pangyayari sa pamilya. Kailangan kong umuwi sa probinsya.	There's an unexpected family matter. I need to go back to the province.
Juan: Naiintindihan ko. Huwag kang mag-alala, magkikita na lang tayo sa ibang pagkakataon.	I understand. Don't worry, we'll just meet some other time.
Ana: Salamat sa pag-unawa, Juan. Babawi ako sa susunod.	Thank you for understanding, Juan. I'll make it up next time.

Break down of the phrase "Juan, pasensya na pero kailangan kong kanselahin ang ating lakad sa Sabado." word by word:

- Juan - Juan
- pasensya - sorry

- na - now/already
- pero - but
- kailangan - need
- kong - (short for "ko ng") I + ng-Linker
- kanselahin - to cancel
- ang - the (focus marker)
- ating - our
- lakad - plan/walk/trip
- sa - on
- Sabado - Saturday
- Meaning: "Juan, I'm sorry but I need to cancel our plan on Saturday."

Exercise: Choose a phrase from the lesson, write it down, learn and practice it.

Tagalog	**English**

Lesson 122 - Visiting

Whether visiting friends, family, or places of interest, understanding how to communicate your intentions and actions can make your experiences more fulfilling. This lesson will guide you through basic phrases and vocabulary for visiting.

Vocabulary for Visiting

Tagalog	**English**
Bisita	Visitor
Dalaw	To visit
Pasyal	To stroll/visit for leisure
Bahay	House
Museo	Museum
Simbahan	Church

Kaibigan	Friend
Kamag-anak	Relative
Magalang	Polite/Respectful
Regalo	Gift

Sample Phrases

Tagalog	**English**
Pwede ba akong bumisita sa inyo?	Can I visit you?
Gusto kong dalawin ang museo.	I want to visit the museum.
Magkano ang entrance fee sa simbahan?	How much is the entrance fee to the church?
Dadalaw ako sa bahay ng kaibigan ko.	I will visit my friend's house.
May dala akong regalo para sa iyo.	I brought a gift for you.

Expressing Intentions

Tagalog	**English**
Magpapasyal kami sa Baguio sa weekend.	We will go for a leisure visit to Baguio this weekend.
Gusto kong magpasalamat sa personal.	I want to say thank you in person.
Maaari ba tayong magkita?	Can we meet?

Being Polite

Tagalog	**English**
Pasensya na sa abala.	Sorry for the bother.
Maraming salamat sa pagtanggap sa akin.	Thank you very much for having me.
Nag-enjoy ako sa pagbisita.	I enjoyed my visit.

Dialogue

Tagalog	English
Ana: Hi, Juan! Pwede ba akong bumisita sa inyo bukas?	Ana: Hi, Juan! Can I visit you tomor-row?
Juan: Oo, siyempre! Anong oras ka darating?	Juan: Yes, of course! What time will you arrive?
Ana: Mga hapon, mga alas tres. May dala akong munting regalo para sa iyo.	Ana: In the afternoon, around three. I brought a small gift for you.
Juan: Salamat, Ana. Excited na akong makita ka.	Juan: Thank you, Ana. I'm excited to see you.

Exercise: Translate the phrases.

Tagalog	English
Gusto kong bumisita sa iyo.	
Pwede ba tayong magkita bukas?	
Gusto mo bang bumisita sa akin bu-kas?	

Solution

Tagalog	English
Gusto kong bumisita sa iyo.	I want to visit you.
Pwede ba tayong magkita bukas?	Can we meet tomorrow?
Gusto mo bang bumisita sa akin bu-kas?	Do you want to visit me tomorrow?

Lesson 123 - Romance & More

Basic Vocabulary

Tagalog	English
Pag-ibig	Love

Kasintahan	Boyfriend/Girlfriend
Asawa	Spouse
Pag-aasawa	Marriage
Anak	Child
Halok	Kiss
Tiwala	Trust
Bulaklak	Flowers
Puso	Heart
Maganda	Beautiful (for a woman)
Gwapo	Handsome or attractive (for a man)
Kasal	Wedding
Seks	Sex
Intimidad	Intimacy
Proteksyon	Protection
Pagbuntis	Pregnancy
Pag-iwas	Prevention

Making Compliments

Tagalog	**English**
Maganda ka.	You are beautiful.
Gwapo ka.	You are handsome.
Matalino ka.	You are smart.
Napakaganda ni Lisa.	Lisa is very beautiful.
Ang ganda mo ngayon.	You look very beautiful today.
Ang ganda ng iyong damit.	What a beautiful dress.
Gusto kita.	I like you.

Dating

Tagalog	**English**
Gusto mo bang lumabas kasama ako?	Would you like to go out with me?
Nais kong makilala ka pa lalo.	I would like to get to know you better.
Gusto ko ang iyong ngiti.	I like your smile.

Romance

Tagalog	English
Yakapin mo ako!	Give me a hug!
Gusto ko ang iyong malambot na balat.	I like your soft skin.
Maganda ka.	You are beautiful.
Gusto kong sumayaw kasama ka.	I want to dance with you.
Espesyal ka sa akin.	You are special to me.
Laging nasa isip kita.	You are always on my mind.

Relationship

Tagalog	English
Gusto kong maging tayo.	I want us to be together.
Gusto mo bang maging kasintahan kita?	Do you want to be my girlfriend?
Gusto kong maging tayo.	I want us to be boyfriend and girlfriend.
Gusto kong pag-usapan natin ang ating relasyon.	I want to talk about our relationship.
Mahal kita.	I love you.
Mahal mo ba ako?	Do you love me?
Masaya ako na nagkakilala tayo.	I am happy that we met.
Pwede ba kitang halikan?	Can I kiss you?
Pwede ba akong humingi ng halik?	Can I ask for a kiss?
Bigyan mo ako ng yakap.	Give me a hug.
Maglakad-lakad tayo.	Let's take a walk.
Mag-spend tayo ng oras nang magkasama.	Let's spend time together.
Gusto kong laging magkasama tayo.	I want to be together always.
Miss na miss kita.	I miss you.
Gusto kong pag-usapan natin ang tungkol sa ating relasyon.	I want to talk about our relationship.
Kailangan nating gumamit ng proteksyon.	We need to use protection.
May plano ka ba para sa hinaharap?	Do you have plans for the future?

Moving Together

Tagalog	English
Gusto mo bang tumira tayo nang magkasama?	Do you want us to live together?
Handa na ako sa bagong simula kasama ka.	I'm ready for a new beginning with you.

Proposing and Marriage

Tagalog	English
Gusto kong magpakasal sa iyo.	I want to marry you.
Handa na ba tayo para sa susunod na kabanata?	Are we ready for the next chapter?

Planning for a Family

Tagalog	English
Gusto mo bang magkaroon tayo ng anak?	Do you want us to have a child?
Handa na ba tayo maging magulang?	Are we ready to become parents?

Exercise: Choose a phrase from the lesson, write it down, learn and practice it.

Tagalog	English

Lesson 124 - Cursing & Swearing

One must be very careful with cursing or swear words, or better yet, not use them at all, to avoid escalation.

Feeling Annoyed or Frustrated

Tagalog	English
Naiinis ako.	I am annoyed.
Nabubuwisit ako.	I am frustrated.

Expressing Displeasure

Tagalog	English
Hindi ako masaya sa nangyari.	I am not happy with what happened.
Nakakadismaya talaga.	It's really disappointing.

When Something Goes Wrong

Tagalog	English
Palpak na naman!	It failed again!
Bakit ba palaging ganito?	Why is it always like this?
Grabe! / Sobrang grabe!	Unbelievable! / Totally unbelievable!
Ikaw ba ay sira-ulo?	Are you out of your mind?
Hangal.	Fool.
Gago ka.	You fool.
Kalokohan!	Nonsense!
Ang kulit mo.	You're such a nuisance.
Ang tanga tanga mo.	You are so foolish.
Sinungaling!	Liar!

Summary & Outlook

Tapos na! Congratulations you've made it this far! You've probably gone through various phases of motivation and frustration in learning the language, just like I did. Learning a language is like running a marathon. The beginning was a lot of fun for me; I learned simple things like greetings, "How are you?" etc. The reactions were positive and motivating.

When I wanted to delve deeper into the language, I had to "fight" through concepts and structures of the language that were different for me, understand the different sentence structure and the concept of focus, etc. This was indeed also a phase of frustration, and it took a while before I had success experiences that motivated me again.

In the "frustration phase," it helped me to set fixed dates to develop a routine and regularity. I dealt with how I can learn effectively and also looked for a Tagalog teacher, made sure I was having fun, etc. This helped me to overcome the first "frustration phase" after the initial success.

Once you have the basic foundations and understand the concepts of the language, it's certainly good to start making small forays into the "real world" to train all senses, such as writing, reading, listening, and understanding. For example, you can find children's stories in Tagalog on YouTube to get used to the sound of the language, you can search the internet for newspaper articles and begin to decode individual sentences to develop access to the language, and finally, you can start to think in Tagalog as an exercise. I believe it's also important to have a partner or teacher to practice speaking. And finally, you should reward yourself with a trip to the Philippines and simply try out your knowledge in the motherland of the language.

I wish you continued fun, and I hope this Tagalog crash course & language guide has helped you find access to the language.

Thank You

Thank you for choosing this book. I hope it serves you well. If you like it, I would appreciate it if you recommend it. I also look forward to a review on Amazon. And above all, I wish you all the best in learning this interesting language.

No matter how you have fared in learning Tagalog, if something is on your mind, you have questions, etc., let me know! Whether it's praise, criticism, or your personal tip – I look forward to your message, questions, or feedback.
I decided to write this book because I could not find another book in English that provides an easy introduction to daily situations and grammar in a simple way, and thus I hope to make it easier for other people to start learning the language. I tried my best to provide you with accurate information in a compact form to the best of my knowledge. Nevertheless, errors sometimes creep in. If you find any, please let me know so I can correct them in the next edition.

Feel free to visit the website:

www.cebuano.site

You can write via email to: mail(at)cebuano.site

Dictionary Tagalog - English

Notes: Verbs are shown in their root form. You need to strip the prefixes and look for the root form of the verb.

Tagalog	English
aalis	leave
abala	busy, occu-pied
abo	ash; gray
abot	reach
abril	april
abugado	lawyer
adiyos	goodbye!
adobo	chicken or pork cooked in vinegar and spices
agosto	august
ahas	snake
akin	mine
aklat	book
aklatan	library
aksidente	accident
aktor	actor
akyat	climb
ala	una- one o'clock
alaala	memory; gift
alahas	jewelry
alak	wine
alala	remember
alam	know
alas-diyes	ten o'clock
alas-dos	two o'clock
alas-dose	twelve o'clock
alas-kuwatro	four o'clock
alas-nuwebe	nine o'clock
alas-onse	eleven o'clock
alas-otso	eight o'clock
alas-sais	six o'clock
alas-singko	five o'clock
alas-siyete	seven o'clock
alas-tres	three o'clock
alat	salty salty
alikabok	dust
alimango	crab
alis	leave, depart
alisin	to remove
aliwan	entertain-ment, pas-time
almusal	breakfast
alon	wave
ama	father
amin	ours (plural exclusive pro-noun)
amo	master, boss, employer
amoy	smell, odor
anak na babae	daughter
anak na lalaki	son
anak sa labas (used for step-son but can have a different con-notation, often used for a child	stepson

born out of wed-lock)	
ani	harvest
anibersaryo	anniversary
anim	six
animnapu	sixty
anino	shadow
ano	what
año	year
anti-bata	against child-ren
anunsiyo	advertise-ment, an-nouncement
anyaya (syn. paanyaya)	invitation
apat	four
apatnapu	forty
apelyido	last name
aplaya	beach, se-ashore
aplikante	applicant
aplikasyon	application
apo	grandchild
aral	study, learn
araw	sun; day
arkila	rent
arte (syn. sining)	art
artista	performer, a person skilled in an art
asawa	wife
asim	sour taste; maasim (adj.) sour
asin	salt
aso (1)	dog
aso (2)	smoke

aspile	pin
asukal	sugar
at	and
atay	liver
ate	elder sister
awa	pity
awit	song
ay!	exclamation of despair, sadness
ayaw	dislike; don't/doesn't want
ayos	being ok, good
ayusin	fix
aywan	to not know. aywan ko (i don't know).
ba	questionmar-ker (yes/no)
baba	chin
bababa	get off
babae	woman
baboy	pig
baga	live charcoal
baga (contextual meaning)	lungs
bago	new
bagong pasok	new entry, newcomer
bagoong	fermented shrimp or an-chovies
bagsak-presyo	slashed or discounted price
bagyo	storm

baha	flood
bahagi	a part, portion
bahala na!	common expression meaning “come what may.”
bahay	house
baitang	grade; steps (of stairs)
baka	beef
baka, karne ng baka	cow, beef
bakasyunan	a resort
bakod	fence; yard
bakuran	yard
bakya	wooden shoes
balak	plan, aim, purpose
balakang	hips
balat	outer covering; shell; skin
balik	return
balikat	shoulder
balikbayan	a person who returns to his/her homeland for a visit
balita	news
balot	wrapped (Duck embryo)
balutin	wrap
bangka	boat, small boat

bangka (Note: The word "boat" is repeated.)	boat
banig	buri mat
bansa	country
bantay	watchman, guard
banyo	bathroom
banyo	bathroom, toilet
bapor	ship
barangay	smallest political unit
barbero	barber, barbershop
baril	gun
barko	large boat
baro’t saya	traditional blouse and skirt
basa (1)	wet, moist
basa (2)	read
basag	break
basag-ulo	fight; troublemaker
baso	glass
bata	child; -ng babae girl, -ng lalaki boy
batas	law
bataw	hyacinth bean
baul	chest
bawat isa	each
bayad	pay
baywang	waist
benta	sell
berde	green

bigas	rice (un-cooked)
bigay	give
bigla	suddenly
bili	buy
bilibid	prison
bilugan	round
binuhos	throw (usually used for liquids)
binyag	baptism
biro	joke
bisig	arms
bisikleta	bicycle
bisita	visitor
bitamina	vitamins
bituin	star
biyahe	travel, trip
biyulin	violin
blusa	blouse
bombilya	electric bulb
boses (syn. tinig)	voice
bote	bottle
botika	pharmacy
braso	arm
bubong	ceiling; roof
bughaw	blue
bughaw, asul	blue
buhangin	sand
buhay	life, alive
buhok	hair
bukana	front
bukas	tomorrow
buko	young coconut
bukod sa	except, aside from, besides
bulsa	pocket

bumaba	went down
bumaha	got flooded
bumalik	go back
bumbero	firefighter
bumibili	buy
bundok	mountain
buntis	pregnant
burol	hill
bus	bus
buwan	month, moon
buwan-buwan	monthly
daan	road
daan (syn. kalye, kalsada)	road, street; hundred
dadaan	will pass by (subject focus)
dadaanan	will pass by (indirect object focus)
dagat	ocean
dahan-dahan	slowly
dahon	leaf
daigdig	world
dakila	great; foremost
dala	bring
dalampasigan	seashore
dalaw	visit
dalawa	two
dalawahan	doubles
dalawampu	twenty
daliri	finger
daliri sa paa	toes
dalo	to attend an event
daloy	flow
damdamin	feeling,

	emotion
damit	dress / clothes
dapat	should
dati	former; formerly
dating	come, arrive
daungan	pier
daw	it is said
deboto	devotee
delikado	dangerous
dentista	dentist
deposito	deposit
di-awtorisado	unauthorized
dibdib	chest, breast
dilim (syn. karimlan)	darkness
din	also, too
din/rin	also
dingding	walls
dinig	listen
dinismiss	got dismissed
disenyo	design
disgrasya (syn. aksidente)	accident
Disyembre	December
dito	here (near the speaker)
dito/rito	here
diyan	there (near the person spoken to)
diyan/riyan	there
diyaryo (syn. pahayagan)	newspaper
diyos (syn. bathala, maykapal)	god, supreme being
diyosa	goddess
doktor	doctor
doktor (syn. manggagamot)	doctor of medicine
doon	there (far from the person talking)
doon/roon	over there
dormitoryo	dormitory
drayber	driver
dugo	blood
dulo	end
dumalaw	visited
dumaranas	experiencing
dumating	to arrive; arrival
dumi	dirt, waste, excrement
dunong (syn. karunungan)	knowledge, ability
durian	durian
duwag	coward
duyan	hammock, cradle
edad	age
eksamen	examination; to examine
electrika	electric, electrical
elegante	elegant, classy
elementarya	elementary school
Enero	January
ensalada	salad
ensayo	rehearsals
ermitanyo	hermit
eroplano	airplane

erya	area
eskinita	alley
eskuwela	school
eskuwelahan	school
espanya	spain
espesyal	special
estasyon	station, waiting shed
estudyante	student
estudyante, mag-aaral	student, pupil
gabi	evening
gabi	yam
galing	from
galing sa	come from
galit	anger; angry (when used as an adjective)
gamit	use
gamot	medicine
ganda	beauty
ganito	like this
ganoon ba?	is that so?
ganyan	like that
garahe	garage
gastos	expenses, spend
gatas	milk
gawa	make, do
gilid	side
ginang	mrs.
ginisa	sauteed
ginoong	mister
ginto	gold
gising	wake up
gitna	center; middle

goma	rubber
grado	grade, class
gradwadong pag-aaral	graduate study
gripo	faucet
groseri	grocery
grupo	group
gubat	forest
guhit	line
gulay	vegetable
gumagala	roaming around
gumaling	got well
gumigising	wake up
gunting	scissors
gupit	haircut
gupitin	to cut (with a scissor)
guro	teacher
gusali	building
gusto	like; want
gutom	hungry; hunger
gwapo	handsome
haba	elongated
haba (as a noun)	length
habang	while, so long as
hagdan	stairs, ladder
hagurin	massage
halaan	clams
halaga	cost, importance
halalan	election
halaman	plant
halamang gamot	herbal plant
halik	kiss
halimbawa	example

haluin	mix
hanap	search
handaan	celebration, party
hangal	ignorant, stupid
hanggang	to; until
hangin	air, wind
hapag-kainan	dining table
hapon	afternoon
hapón	japan
hapunan	dinner
harap	front
hardin	garden
hardin (syn. halamanan)	garden, lawn
hari	king
hatid	take someone to a place
hatinggabi	midnight
hatol	judgment, decision
hawak	hold
hawakan	to hold
hayop	animal
heto	here, here it is
higa	lie (as in lying down)
hilaga	north
hilaw	raw, unrip
hindi	no
hindi kailanman	never
hininga	breath
hinlalaki	thumb
hinog	ripe
hintay	wait

hintayan	a waiting place
hinto	stop
hinuli	caught
hipo	touch
hipon	shrimp
hiramin	borrow
hitsura	looks like
hiwa	cut
hiwain	cut
hiwalay	separate
hiya	shame
hugas	wash
hugis-puso	heart-shaped
hukbo	army
hukom	judge
huli	last
hulog	fall
hulyo	july
humiga	to lie down
huminga	to breathe
humingi	asked
huminto	stop
humiram	borrowed
Hunyo	June
husto	exact, fit, enough
huwag	don't
Huwebes	Thursday
iba	different
ibaba	lower part
ibabaw	above
ibasura	throw out/put in a garbage bin
ibig	love; like
ibig sabihin	meaning
ibigay	to give

ibon	bird
ihawan	griller, roaster
ihawin	broil
ikalawa	second
ikatlo	third
ikaw	you
ikinalulungkot ko.	i am sad about this.
ikinasal	got married
ikinukuwento	telling a story
ilagay	to put, to place
ilalagay	put
ilalim	under
ilan	how many
ilaw	light, light fixtures
ilista	to list down
ilog	river
ilong	nose
imbestigasyon	investigation
imbis	instead
ina	mother
ina, nanay	mother
inaahon	brought to the surface
inalagaan	took care of
inalok	offered
inani	harvested
inapalutang	floating
inay	mother
inempake	pack (a suitcase)
ingay	noise
inggit	envy
inhinyero	engineer
inihanda	prepared

inihaw	broiled
iniipon	gathered
iniresta	prescribed
init	heat, warmth
inom	drink
insidente	incident
intindi	understand
inum	to drink
inumin	drink
inuubo	coughing
ipagulong	roll
ipinagtataka	suprised
ipinakita	showed
ipinanganak	born
iprito	fry
isa	one
isahan	single, singular
isama	to take along; include
isara	to close something
isasauli	will return
isauli	to return something
isda	fish
isdaan	place where fish is sold
isinasaad	implied; said
isinuot	wore (completed aspect of wear)
isip	think, mind, thought
iskedyul	schedule
isla	island
istasyon	station (e.g., bus station)

istasyon ng pulis	police station
istasyon ng tren	train station
isuot	to wear, to put on
itaas	on top
itapon	to throw a-way
itay	father
itim	black
itinanim	planted
itinatag	established
itlog	egg
ito	this
ituro	to teach something, to show or point
iwan	to leave be-hind
iyak	cry
iyan	that (far from the speaker)
iyon	that (far from speaker and listener)
jeepney / dyip	jeep (for transporta-tion)
ka	you
kaagad	immediately
kaakibat	together
kaarawan	birthday
kaaway	enemy
kababata	childhood friend
kababayan	fellow citizen
kabayo	horse
kabibi	empty clam shell

kabihasnan	civilization
kabisado	memorized
kabuhayan	livelihood
kabundukan	mountain
kabutihan	goodness, virtue
kadueto	duet partner
kagabi	last night
kagalang-galang	honorable, respectable
kagalit	enemy
kagatin	to bite
kaginhawahan	relief from pain, consola-tion; luxury
kagubatan	forest
kahapon	yesterday
kahel	orange
kahon	box
kahoy	wood
kaibigan	friend
kailangan	need
kain	eat
kainan	eatery
kakanin	rice delicacies
kakilala	acquaintance
kaklase	classmate
kalaban	adversary
kalabasa	pumpkin
kalabaw	carabao
kalagayan	condition
kalahati	half
kalakal	merchandise, goods
kalakip	included, en-closed
kalamansi	philippine le-mon

kalan	stove
kalaro	playmate
kalawang	rust
kalayaan	indepen-dence, li-berty; free
kaldero	cauldron, pot
kalesa	two-wheeled vehicle pulled by a horse
kaligayahan	happiness, contentment
kalihim	secretary
kaliligo	just finished bathing
kaliwa	left
kalsada	road
kalusugan	health, well-being
kalye	street
kama	bed
kamag-anak	relative
kamatayan	death
kamatis	tomato
kamay	hand
kambal	twin
kami	we (exclu-sive)
kamias	tropical sour fruit
kamisadentro	man's shirt
kamiseta	undershirt
kampana	church bell
kamukha	looks like
kanan	right
kandila	candle
kanila	theirs
kanin	rice (cooked)

kanina	earlier
kanluran	west
kanser	cancer
kanta	sing
kantina	canteen
kanto	corner
kanya	hers
kapalaran	fate
kapatid	sibling
kape	coffee
kapitbahay	neighbor
karagatan	ocean
karamdaman	illness
karangalan	award
karapatan	right
karatula	sign
karayom	needle
karne	meat
karnihan	place where meat is sold
kasal	wedding
kasama	companion, companion; comrade
kasapi	member of an organiza-tion
kasayaw	dance part-ner
kaserola	casserole, cooking uten-sils
kasi	because
kasintahan	boyfriend / girlfriend
kasya	fits
katamtaman	medium
katao	number of

	people
katas	juice
katawagan	name
katawan	body
katimugan	south
katotohanan	truth
katrabaho	coworker
katulong	helper, servant
kaunti	a few; a little
kawad	wire; electric wire
kawalan-kumpiyansa	lack of confidence
kawali	pan
kawani	employee
kawawa	pitiful
kawayan	bamboo
kay	marker to indicate ownership
kaya	so, can, be able to
kayá	that is why
káya	can
kayo	you (plural)
kaysa	than
kayumanggi	brown
keso	cheese
kilay	eyebrow
kilikili	armpit
kina	plural marker to indicate ownership
kinapanayam	interviewed
kinatawan	representative
kinuha ang	took a picture

larawan	
kita	see
klase	kind of; class
klinika	clinic tuhod
klub	club
ko	my, i
kolehiyo	college
komedor	dining room
komunidad	community
konduktor	conductor
konsiyerto	concert
konsulta	consult; consultation
kontinente	continent
korona	crown
kotse	car
kubeta	toilet
kuha	take
kuko	fingernail
kulambo	mosquito net
kulang	lacking
kulay	color
kulay kape	brown
kulay mais	the color of corn; blonde
kulog	thunder
kumain	to eat
kumakain	eat
kumakanta	sing
kumakaway	waving
kumaliwa	turn left
kumanan	turn right
kumatok	knocked
kumot	blanket
kumpuni	to repair
kumuha	to get
kumuha ng larawan	took pictures

kumusta	how are you?
kundiman	native love song
kundol	wax gourd
kung	if, when, as to
kurbata	tie
kurtina	curtain
kuru-kuro	opinion
kusina	kitchen
kusinera/o	cook
kutsara	spoon
kutsarita	teaspoon
kutsero	calesa driver
kutsilyo	knife
kuwaderno	notebook
kuwadrado	square
kuwadro	picture frame
kuwarto	room/be-droom
kuweba	cave
kuwenta	bill, account
kuwento	story, fiction
kuwero	leather
kuwintas	necklace
kuya	elder brother
kwarto	room
laba	wash clothes
laban	fight, contest
labanan	to fight someone or something
labanos	radish
labas	outside
labi	lips
labimpito	seventeen
labindalawa	twelve
labing-anim	sixteen

labing-apat	fourteen
labing-isa	eleven
labingwalo	eighteen
labinlima	fifteen
labinsiyam	nineteen
labintatlo	thirteen
labis	surplus; more than enough
lagay	condition, state, situa-tion
lagda	signature
lagdaan	sign your name
lagi	always
lagnat	fever
lagyan	put
lahat	all, everyth-ing, every-body
lahi	race of pe-ople, nationa-lity
lakad	walk, stroll
lakas	strength, force
lakbay	travel
laki	size
lalagyan	container
lalaki	man
lalamunan	throat
lalo na	especially
lamang	only
lambat	fishing net
lamig	coldness
lamok	mosquito
lang	only
langaw	housefly

langgam	ants
langis	oil
langka	jackfruit
langoy	swim
lansangan	street
lansones	lanzones (type of fruit)
lapis	pencil
larawan	picture
laro	play, game
laruan	toy
lasa	taste
lasing	drunkard
lasingan	a noisy drin-king party
lason	poison
lata	tin can
laway	saliva
laya	freedom
layo	distance
layon	aim, purpose
leche flan	custard
leeg	neck
libang	entertain
libangan	recreation, entertain-ment
libre	free
libro	book
ligaya	happiness
ligo	bathe, shower
liham	letter
lihim	secret
likas	native of, na-tural
likha	creation, pro-duct

likod	back
lila	violet/purple
lilipat	move
lima	five
limampu	fifty
limot	forget
lindol	earthquake
linga	sesame seed
linggo	week
linggo-linggo	weekly
linis	clean
linisin	to clean
lipat	move
lipon	group
lipunan	socicty
listahan	list
litrato	photograph
litson	roasted pig
litsunin	to roast
lola	grandma
lolo	grandpa, grandfather
longganisa	native sau-sage
loob	in/inside
lubid	rope
luha	tears
luma	old
lumaban	fought
lumakad	to walk
lumalaki	growing, in-creasing in size
lumalangoy	swimming
lumampas	go past
lumangoy	swam
lumapag	landed
lumapit	to come near,

	to approach
lumilipad	fly
lumipad	to fly
lumipat	transfer
lumpia	spring roll
lumubog	to sink
Lunes	Monday
lungsod	city
lungsod, siyudad	city
luntian	green
lupa	land, earth
luto	cook
luya	ginger
maaari	may
maaayos	will be fixed
maaga	early
maalat	salty
maanghang	spicy
maaraw	sunny
maasim	sour
mababang paar-alan	elementary school
mababaw ang luha	cries easily
mabagal	slow
mabaho	bad-smelling
mabait	kind/nice
mabangga	to bump against, to collide with
mabango	fragrant
mabigat	heavy
mabuhay	long live!; to live
mabuti	good
mabuti-buti	better
madalang	rare, infre-quent

madalas	often
madaldal	talkative
madali	easy; fast
madaling-araw	dawn
madilim	dark
madumi/marumi	dirty
magaan	light (weight)
magalang	courteous
magaling	good, excel-lent; free from sickness
mag-anak	family
maganda	beautiful
mag-aral	to study
mag-asawa	husband and wife; to marry
magasin	magazine
magbasa	to read
mag-check in	to check in
magdasal	to pray
maghain	to set the table
maghanda	prepare
maghapon	all day long
maghugas	to wash
mag-ingat	to be careful
mag-isip	to think
magkahawak-kamay	holding hands
magkaiba	different
magkakakilala	know each other
magkano	how much?
magkapareho	same
magkapatid	a set of brothers or sisters

magkasakit	get sick
magkatulad	similar, same
magkita	to meet
magkwento, sabihin	tell
maglaba	to wash clothes
maglalaro	will play (a game)
maglaro	to play; player
magluluto	will cook
magluto	cook
mag-order	to order
magpaalam	to bid goodbye
magpahinga	to rest
magpapadala	send
magpapalit	exchange
magpareserba	to have something reserved for someone
magpasyal	to take a walk
magreserba	to reserve
magsalita	speak
magsasaka	farmer
magsimba	to hear mass, go to church
magsugat	be wounded
magtanim	to plant
magtayo	build
magulang	parents
magulat	to be surpri-sed
magustuhan	will like
magutom	to be hungry
mahaba	long

mahal (1)	expensive
mahal (2)	love
mahangin	windy
mahihirap	poor
mahina	weak
mahiya	ashamed
mahúhuli	will be late
mahusay	efficient, exceptional
maingay	noisy
mainggitin	envious
mainit	hot
maitim	black
maitim ang budhi	bad person
makabago	modern, in-telligent, wise
makabayan	patriotic, na-tionalistic
makaligtaan	forget
makalipas	after
makapal	thick
makina	machine; se-wing machine
makinis	smooth
makita	to see
makiusap	to plead, to make a re-quest
makulit	annoying; wearisome
malabnaw	dilute
malakas	strong
malaki	big
malaman	to know
malambot	soft
malamig	cold
malapit	near

malawak	wide
malaya	free, inde-pendent
malayo	far, distant
maligaya	happy
maligo	to take a bath
maliit	small
malinis	clean
maliwanag	bright, clear
malungkot	sad
malungkutin	always sad
malusog	healthy
maluwang	too wide
mamamayan	citizen
mamatay	die
mamaya	later
mamulot	to pick some-thing up
manalangin	to pray
mananayaw	dancer
manang	elder sister
mang-aawit	singer
mangga	mango
manggagawa	worker
mangingibig	one who lo-ves
mangyari	happen
mani	peanut
manibalang	between un-ripe and ripe
manigo	prosperous
maniwala	to believe
manok	chicken
manong	older person
mansanas	apple
mantika	oil
mantikilya	butter
manunulat	writer

mapait	bitter
mapakla	acrid; tangy
maputi	white
marami	many, a lot
marka	grade; trade-mark
Marso	March
Martes	Tuesday
marumi	dirty
marunong	intelligent, wise
mas gusto	like better
mas maaga	earlier
mas malaki	bigger
masahe	massage
masakit	hurt
masakitin	sickly
masama	evil, bad, wi-cked
masarap	delicious
masaya	joyful, happy
masayahin	always happy
masayang-masaya	very happy
masikip	tight
masipag	industrious
masungit	grouchy
masunurin	obedient
masyado	excessive
masyadong maalat	too salty
mata	mata
mataas na paar-alan	high school
mataba	fat
matalik na kaibigan	close friend
matalino	intelligent

matamis	sweet
matamisin	to make into sweet
matanda	old person; aged, elderly, old
matangkad	tall
materyales	materials
matigas	hard
matigas ang mukha	looks stern
matutuklaw	will be bitten; refers only to snake bites
matuwa	to be glad
mauhaw	to be thirsty
maulan	rainy
maulap	cloudy
maupo	please sit
may	have
mayaman	rich, wealthy
may-ari	owner
Mayo	May
maysakit	patient, sick person
medyas	socks, sto-ckings
melon	melon
menos... para	before (used for indicating minutes)
meryenda	snack
mesa	table
metal	metal
mga	used for the plural form
militante	militant
milyon	million

minsan	once; some-times
minuto	minute
misa	religious mass
misang pasasala-mant	thanksgiving mass
miting	meeting
miyerkoles	wednesday
Miyerkules	Wednesday
mo	your
mukha	face
mula	from
mula noong	since
mula sa	from
mundo	world
munti	small
mura	cheap
musika	music
mustasa	mustard
na	already
na naman	again
naaalala	remember
na-aksidente	met an acci-dent
nabali	broken (for example, arm or leg)
nabuhay	lived
nabuntis	got pregnant
nag-aalala	worried
nag-aaral	study
nagagalit	angry
nag-alok	offered
nagbabakasyon	go on vaca-tion
nagbabasa	read
nagba-brush	brush (hair)

nagbakasyon	took a vacation
nagbibihis	dress up
nagbibisikleta	ride a bicycle
nagdalang-tao	got pregnant
nag-diyeta	dieted
nag-eehersisyo	exercise
nag-eensayo	rehearse
naghahanap	looks for
naghihilamos	wash (face)
nag-iimbita	invites
nag-i-scuba-diving	went scuba diving
nag-i-snorkeling	went snorkeling
nagkasakit	got sick
naglalakad	walk
naglalaro	play (game)
naglalaro ng soccer	play soccer
nagluluto	cook
nagmamahal	love
nagmamaneho	drive
nagpagamot	got treatment
nagpagupit	have someone cut your hair
nagpahinga	rest
nagpaluto	have someone cook for you
nagpamasahe	have someone give you a massage
nagpapaypay	fanning
nagpa-photocopy	have someone make copies for you
nagpapraktis	practice (for example, martial arts)
nagpatingin sa doktor	visited a doctor
nagpatuwid	had (hair) straightened
nagpipinta	paint
nagpopolitisa	politicizing
nagsa-skydiving	go skydiving
nagsa-soccer	play soccer
nagsauli	returned
nagsisimula	starts
nagsisipilyo	brush (teeth)
nagso-snowboarding	go snowboarding
nagsunog ng kilay	studied hard
nagsusuklay	comb
nagsusulat	write
nagtapos	graduated
nagtatrabaho	work
nagtitinda	selling
nahahati	divide; split
nahawa	got infected
nahiwa	got cut
nahulog	fell; dropped
nais	would like
naisip	thought
nakaaalala	can remember
nakabatay	based on
nakakahiya	shameful
nakakainis	irritating
nakakatanda	makes one look old

nakalimutan	forgot
nakangiti	smiling
naka-salamin	wears glasses
nakatali	tied
nakatayo	standing
nakatipid	saved money
nakatira	live
naka-upo	sitting
nakikinig	listens to (music, songs, radio)
nakikiraramay ako.	my condo-lences.
nakita	saw
naku	an expression of surprise
naliligo	take a bath/take a shower
nalilito	confused
naman	also (used as an expres-sion)
namasyal	went sight-seeing
namatay	passed on; died
nambubugbog	person who beats up an-other
namili	went shop-ping
namimitas	picking (for example, picking ap-ples)
namin	ours (exclu-sive)
nanalo	won

nananawagan	calling to
nanay	mother
nandito/narito	here
nandiyan/nariya n	there
nandoon/naroo n	over there
nang	when; used as a relative pronoun
nangangamba	afraid
nanlalata	feeling weak
nanonood	watches (te-levision, mo-vie, game)
napagod	became tired
napaka-alat	too salty
napakahaba	too long
napakaiksi	too short
napakalaki	too big
napakaliit	too small
napakaluwang	too loose
napakasikip	too tight
napapalibutan	surrounded
naparito	came
naparoon	went
napaso	got slightly burned
napatay	was killed
naplano	planned
naputol ang paa	foot got cut
narito	here
naroon	there
nars	nurse
nasa	preposition indicating lo-cation
nasaan	where

nasawi	died
nasugatan	got injured
nasunog	got burned
natalo	lost
natanggal	got removed; got fired
natanggap	got accepted
natatakot	afraid
natatapos	ends
natayo	was built
natin	ours (inclu-sive)
natutulog	sleep
naulanan	got rained on
nauuhaw	thirsty
nawala	lost
negosyante	business per-son
negosyo	business, in-dustry
nerbiyos	nervousness
ng sipag	of diligence
nga	please, really, truly
ngayon	today
ngipin	teeth
ngiti	smile
ngumiti	smiled
ngunit	but
nguso	upper lip
nila	their
nilaga	boiled
nilagang baka	boiled beef
ninang	godmother
ningas	flame
ninong	godfather
ninuno	ancestor
niya	his/her

niyayakap	hug
niyebe	snow
niyog	old coconut
nobela	novel
Nobyembre	November
noo	forehead
nood	watch, look at
noon	at that time
noong	when (for continuing actions)
noong isang bu-wan	last month
noong isang linggo	last week
noong unang pa-nahon	once upon a time
nota	musical note
nuno	grandparent
o	or
oho (or opo)	yes sir/ma-dam
oktobre	october
Oktubre	October
oo	yes
opisina	office
oras	time, hour
orasan	clock
orasyon	angelus
orihinal	original
ospital	hospital
oyayi	lullaby
paa	feet
paalam	farewell; goodbye
paano	how
paaralan	school

paborito	favorite
pabuya	tip, gratuity
padala	send
pader	wall
pag-angkat	export
pag-asa	hope
pagbibiyahe	travelling
pagdadalamhati	grief, extreme sorrow
pagdalaw	visit
pagdikitin	seal
pagdiriwang	celebration
pagdiriwang, pista	celebration, festival
pag-ibig	love
pagitan	between
pagkain	food
pagkamatay	death
pagkatapos	after; afterwards
pagkilos	to act
paglabag	violation
paglalakbay	journey
paglalayag	sail
paglubog ng araw	sunset
pagod	tired
pagseselos	jealousy
pagsinta	love
pagtigil	to stay
pahaba	lengthwise
pahayag	statement
pahinga	rest
pakibigyan	please give
pakilala	introduce
pakinabang	profit, gain
pakirehistro	please register

pako	nail
pakpak	wing
paksa	subject, theme
pakuluin	boil
pakwan	watermelon
palabas	presentation, show
palad	palm of hand; fate
palagay	guess, opinion
palagi/lagi	always
palamigan	refrigerator
palapag	floors/stories
palaruan	playground
palasyo	palace
palay	rice plant
palayan	ricefield
palayaw	nickname
palayok	clay pot
palda	skirt
palengke	market
paligid	surroundings
paligid-ligid	around
palikuran	toilet
paliparan	airport
palitan	exchange rate
pamahalaan	government
pamangkin	niece/nephew
pamantasan	university
pamasahe	fare
pamaypay	fan
pambura	eraser
pamilya	family
paminsan-	sometimes

minsan	
pampalamig	refreshment
pampito	seventh
pamumuno	led by
panaderya	bakery
panahon	weather
pananalig	faith
pandak, maikli	short
pandalawahan	for two
pangalan	name
pangalawa	second
pangalawang pangulo	vice-president
pang-anim	sixth
pang-apat	fourth
pangatlo	third
panghimagas	dessert
panghuli	last
panginoon	master; lord
pangit	ugly
pangkalahatan	general
pangkat	group
panglima	fifth
pangsampu	tenth
pangsiyam	ninth
pangulo	president
pangwalo	eighth
panis	rotten/bad
pantalon	pants
panyo	handkerchief
papasok sa klase	will go to class
papaya	papaya
papel	paper
papuntang	going to
paraan	way
paradahan	parking lot
pareho	the same,

	similar
paroroonan	destination
parusa	punishment
pasahero	passenger
pasalubong	a present from a trip
pasaporte	passport
pasaway	unconventional, stubborn
pasensiya ka na.	sorry. (literally, sorry you.)
pasinaya	inauguration
pasko	christmas
paslit	child
paso	burn
pasok	enter
pasukan	entrance
pasyente	patient
patani	lima bean
patay	dead
patayin	kill
patingin	to take a look
patis	fish sauce
patnugot	director, editor
patola	luffa
patong	layer
paunang bayad	advanced payment
pauwi	on the way home
pawis	perspiration; laborer
payak	simple
payapa	peaceful
payat	thin, slim
payong	umbrella

Pebrero	February
pelikula	film
pera	money
permiso	permission
pero	but
pihado	surely, certainly
pilak	silver
pili	choose, sel-ect
pilipinas	philippines
pinabalik	asked to re-turn
pinadala	sent
pinahirapan	tortured; lite-rally, given hardship
pinaiimbis-tigahan	having inves-tigated
pinaka-ayaw	like least
pinakagusto	like best
pinakamalaki	biggest
pinakatuktok	highest point
pinalitan	changed
pinaputok	fired
pinasingaw	steamed
pinggan	plate
pinisil	squeeze
pinsan	cousin
pinta	to paint
pinto	door
pintor	painter
pintuan	door
pintura	paint
pinuno	leader
pinya	pineapple
pipa	pipe
piraso	piece

pirma	signature
pirmahan	sign your name
pirmi	always, fixed
pisara	blackboard
pisngi	cheek
piso	peso
pista	feast; town fiesta
pito	seven
pitumpu	seventy
piyano	piano
plantsa	flat iron
platito	small plate; saucer
plato	plate
pluma	fountain pen
pno	tree
po	honorific
polo	shirt
posporo	match
pransiya	france
premyo	prize, reward
pribado	private
prito	fry
probinsiya	province
programa	program
proseso	process
proyekto	project
prutas	fruit
publiko	public
pugon	stove, oven
pula	red
pulang asukal	brown sugar (literally, red sugar)
pulbos	powder
pulis	policeman,

	police officer
pulitika	politics
pulong	meeting
pulubi	beggar
pumanaw	passed on; died
pumapasok sa klase	go to class
pumasok sa klase	attended class
pumunta	went
pumupunta	go/come
pumutok	fired
punó	full
puno (adj.)	full
puno (n.)	tree; leader, chief, source
punong-lungsod	capital city
punta	go
pupunta	will go
pusa	cat
pusit	squid
puso	heart
putahe	a dish or vi-and
puti	white
puto	rice cake
putok	blast
putol	cut
puwede	can
puwersang mili-tar	military forces
puwesto	location, a stall or stand in a market
puwet	buttocks
radyo	radio
rain	ulan

rambutan	rambutan (fruit)
raw (or daw)	it is said
rebelde	rebel
rebolusyon	revolution
regalo	gift
rekado	condiments for cooking
reklamo	complaint
relihiyon	religion
relo	watch
reseta	prescription
resibo	receipt
restawran	restaurant
riles	railroad, spe-cifically for trains
rin	also
rinig	hear
rosas	pink
sa	in; on; at; marker to in-dicate owner-ship
sa ilalim	under
sa kasamaang palad	unfortunately
sa labas	outside
sa loob	inside
sa pamamagitan	using
saan	where
sabado	saturday
sabado de gloria	holy saturday
sabaw	broth
sabay	at the same time
sabi	say, tell
sabon	soap

sagana	abundant, plenty
saging	banana
sagot	answer
sagrado	sacred
sahig	floor
sahod	salary, wage
sakay	ride, drive (as a passenger)
sakim	selfish
sakit	sickness; pain
saksi	witness
sala	living room
salamat	thank you
salamin	glass; eyeglasses; mirror
salapi	money
salarin	murderer
salawal	trousers
saligang-batas	constitution
salita	word, langu-age
salitang-	root word
salu-salo	party, banquet
sama	accompany
samahan (n.)	club, society
samahan (v.)	to accom-pany
sama-sama	altogether
samba	worship
sampaguita	national flower of the philippines
sampu	ten
sana	hope
sandaan	a hundred

sandali	a moment
sandalyas	sandals
sanga	branch
sanlibo	a thousand
sapatos	shoes
sara	close
sarado	closed
sarili	self
sari-sari	various
sariwa	fresh
sarsa	sauce
sasakay	get on; ride
sasakyan	vehicle
sawsawan	dipping sauce
sayang	it's a pity
sayaw	dance
seda	silk
segundo	second
seksyon	section (in class)
selyo	stamp; dry seal
sementeryo	cemetery
sentimos	centavos
sepilyo	toothbrush
serbesa	beer
serbidor	server: waiter
serbisyo	service
sero	zero
Setyembre	September
sibuyas	onion
sigarilyas	winged bean
sigarilyo	cigarette
sigaw	shout, scream
sige	okay/sure
sige na	please
siko	elbow

sikreto	secret
sila	they
silangan	east
silid	room
silid-kainan	dining room
silid-tulugan	bedroom
silya	chair
simbahan	church
simbolo	symbol
simula	start, begin
sina	plural marker for names
sinabi	said
sinakop	occupied; colonized
sinangag	fried rice
sinasaad	implied; said
sine	film
sinehan	cinema, movie theater
sinelas	slippers
singil	amount charged for services or sold goods
singkamas	turnip
singsing	ring
sinisisi	blaming
sino	who
sinulat	wrote
sinulid	thread
sipon	cold
sira	broken
sisidlan	container
sitaw	string bean
siya	he/she
siyam	nine
siyamnapu	ninety

siyempre.	of course
siyensiya	science
siyudad	city
soberanya	sovereignty
sobre	envelope
sopas	soup
subdibisyon	subdivision
sugat	wound
suka	vinegar
sukat	try on; size
suki	steady client
suklay	comb
sukli	change (money)
sulat	write, letter
sulok	corner
sumakit	became painful
sumali	join
sumama	to go with
sumasakay	ride
sumasayaw	dance
sumbrero	hat
sumisid	dived
sumisigaw	shout
sumunod	to follow
sundalo	soldier
sundo	pick up
sunog	fire
susi	key
suskrisyon	subscription
susunod	next
taas	height;
taba	fat
tabak	a native sword
tabako	cigar; tobacco

tabi	beside
tabing-dagat	seashore
tabla	board
tabletas	tablets
tagapagsilbi	server
tagapangasiwa	manager
tagapangulo	president
tag-araw	summer
taga-saan	from where
taggutom	famine
tag-init	hot season/summer season
taglagas	autumn/fall
taglamig	winter
tago	hide
tagsibol	spring
tag-ulan	rainy season
tagumpay	victory
tahanan	home
tahi	to sew; sewing
tainga	ears
takbo	run
takip	cover
takot	afraid
taksi	taxi
taksil	traitor
tala	star
talaan	list, record
talaga?	really?
talambuhay	biography
tali	string
talon	jump, waterfall
talong	eggplant
tama	right
tamaan	hit

tamad	lazy
tambol	drum
tanawin	view
tandaan	remember
tanga	stupid, irresponsible
tanggalin	remove
tanggap	receive
tanghali	noon
tanghalian	lunch
tanghaling tapat	exactly at noon
tanim	plant
taniman	plantation
tanong	ask, question
tanyag	well-known; popular
tao	person
tao po!	literally, person here!
taon	year
taon, edad	years, age
taon-taon	annually
tapak	step on
tapat	across
tapos	finish, complete something
tarangkahan	gate
tasa	cup
tatapusin	will finish
tatay	father
tatlo	three
tatlumpu	thirty
tauhan	personnel
tawa	laugh
tawad	discount
tawag	call

tawagan	to call
tayo (1)	stand
tayo (2)	we (inclusive)
tela	cloth
telebisyon	television
telepono	telephone
temperatura	temperature
tenga	ear
tiisin	sufferings
tiket	ticket
tila	it seems
timbangan	scale, balance
timog	south
tinapay	bread
tinda	goods
tindahan	store
tindahan ng bulaklak	flower shop
tindahan ng laruan	toy store
tindahan ng prutas	fruit store
tingin	look
tingnan	look
tinidor	fork
tinta	ink
tinutusok	pierce
tira	live, reside
tisa	chalk
tita	aunt
tito	uncle
titser	teacher
tiwala	believe
tiya	aunt
tiyan	stomach
tiyo	uncle
tokador	dresser
totoo	true, real

toyo	soy sauce
trabaho	work, job
trak	truck
trangkaso	flu
transportasyon	transportation
traysikel	tricycle (motorcycle or bicycle with a sidecar)
tren	train
tsaa	tea
tse!	expression of disgust
tsina	china
tsuper	driver
tubig	water
tubo	pipe
tuhod	knee
tula	poem
tulay	bridge
tulog	sleep
tulong	help
tuloy	come in; to go ahead
tuloy ka	come in
tumanggap	received
tumawa	laughed
tumayo	stand
tumutugtog	play (an instrument)
tunay	real
tungkol sa	about; referring to
tunog	sound
tuntunin	rule
turo	teach
tutugtog	will play

tuwa	happiness
tuwalya	towel
tuwid	straight
tuya	sarcasm, irony
tuyo	dry
tuyong isda	dried fish
tuyong-tuyo	very dry
uban	gray/white hair
ubo	cough
ubod	core
ugali	custom; habit
ugat	human vein, root of a plant
uhaw	thirst
ulam	anything eaten with rice
ulan	rain
ulap	cloud
ulat	report
uli	once again
uling	charcoal
ulit	again
ulo	head
umaawit	sing
umaga	morning
umako	to assume responsibility
umakyat	climb
umalis	to go away
umano	alleged
umawit	to sing
umibig	to love
umikot	go round; go around
uminom	to drink

umisip	to think
umiyak	cried
umpisa	beginning, start
umupo	sit
umuwi	to go home
una	first
unan	pillow
uniporme	uniform
uod	worm
upa	pay; rent
upang	so, so that
upo	sit
upuan	chair
uri	kind
usapan	conversation
utak	brain; mautak adj. intelligent
utang	debt
utos	command, order
uulitin	repeat
uwi	go home
wakas	end; at sa wakas finally
wala	don't have
walang anuman	welcome
walang lasa	bland
walang pagsidlan ng galak	very happy
walang-hiya	shameless
walang-pagod	tireless
walis	broom
walo	eight
walumpu	eighty
wasak, sira	destroyed
wasto	correct,

	appropriate
watawat	flag, banner
welga	labor strike
wika	language
y medya	half (used in telling time; thirty minutes)
yabag	footstep
yakap	hug, embrace
yaman	wealth

yari	ready, finis-hed
yari sa	made of
yata	perhaps
yelo	ice
yumao	died

Dictionary English - Tagalog

English	Tagalog
about; referring to	tungkol sa
above	ibabaw
abundant, plenty	sagana
accident	aksidente
accompany	samahan
acquaintance	kakilala
acrid; tangy	mapakla
across	tapat
actor	aktor
advanced payment	paunang bayad
adversary	kalaban
advertisement, announcement	anunsiyo
afraid	takot
after	makalipas
after; afterwards	pagkatapos
afternoon	hapon
again	muli
against children	anti-bata
age	edad
aim, purpose	layon
air, wind	hangin
airplane	eroplano
airport	paliparan
all day long	maghapon
all, everything, everybody	lahat
alleged	umano
alley	eskinita
already	na
also	din/rin
also (used as an expression)	naman
also, too	din
altogether	sama-sama
always	lagi
always happy	masayahin
always sad	malungkutin
always, fixed	pirmi
charge	singil
an expression of surprise	naku
ancestor	ninuno
and	at
angelus	orasyon
anger; angry	galit
angry	nagagalit
animal	hayop
anniversary	anibersaryo
annoying; wearisome	makulit
annually	taon-taon
answer	sagot
ants	langgam
anything eaten with rice	ulam
apple	mansanas
applicant	aplikante
application	aplikasyon
april	abril
area	erya

arm	braso
armpit	kilikili
arms	bisig
army	hukbo
around	paligid-ligid
art	arte (syn. sining)
ash; gray	abo
ashamed	mahiya
ask, question	tanong
asked	humingi
asked to re-turn	pinabalik
at that time	noon
at the same time	sabay
attended class	pumasok sa klase
august	agosto
aunt	tiya, tita
autumn/fall	taglagas
award	karangalan
back	likod
bad person	maitim ang budhi
bad-smelling	mabaho
bakery	panaderya
bamboo	kawayan
banana	saging
baptism	binyag
barber, bar-bershop	barbero
based on	nakabatay
bathe, shower	ligo
bathroom	banyo
bathroom, toilet	banyo
be wounded	magsugat

beach, se-ashore	aplaya
beautiful	maganda
beauty	ganda
became pain-ful	sumakit
became tired	napagod
because	kasi
bed	kama
bedroom	silid-tulugan
beef	baka
beer	serbesa
before (used for indicating minutes)	menos... para
beggar	pulubi
beginning, start	umpisa
being ok, good	ayos
believe	tiwala
beside	tabi
better	mabuti-buti
between	pagitan
between un-ripe and ripe	manibalang
bicycle	bisikleta
big	malaki
bigger	mas malaki
biggest	pinakamalaki
bill, account	kuwenta
biography	talambuhay
bird	ibon
birthday	kaarawan
bitter	mapait
black	itim
blackboard	pisara
blaming	sinisisi

bland	walang lasa
blanket	kumot
blast	putok
blood	dugo
blouse	blusa
blue	asul
boat	bangka (Note: The word "boat" is repeated.)
boat, small boat	bangka
body	katawan
boil	pakuluin
boiled	nilaga
boiled beef	nilagang baka
book	libro
born	ipinanganak
borrow	hiramin
borrowed	humiram
bottle	bote
box	kahon
boyfriend / girlfriend	kasintahan
brain; mautak adj. intelli-gent	utak
branch	sanga
bread	tinapay
break	basag
breakfast	almusal
breath	hininga
bridge	tulay
bright, clear	maliwanag
bring	dala
broil	ihawin
broiled	inihaw
broken	sira
broken (for	nabali

example, arm or leg)	
broom	walis
broth	sabaw
brought to the surface	inaahon
brown	kulay kape, kayumanggi
brown sugar (literally, red sugar)	pulang asukal
brush (hair)	nagba-brush
brush (teeth)	nagsisipilyo
build	magtayo
building	gusali
buri mat	banig
burn	paso
bus	bus
business per-son	negosyante
business, in-dustry	negosyo
busy, occu-pied	abala
but	pero, ngunit
butter	mantikilya
buttocks	puwet
buy	bili
calesa driver	kutsero
call	tawag
calling to	nananawagan
came	naparito
can	puwede, kaya
can remem-ber	nakaaalala
cancer	kanser
candle	kandila
canteen	kantina

capital city	punong-lungsod
car	kotse
carabao	kalabaw
casserole, cooking utensils	kaserola
cat	pusa
caught	hinuli
cauldron, pot	kaldero
cave	kuweba
ceiling; roof	bubong
celebration	pagdiriwang
celebration, festival	pagdiriwang, pista
celebration, party	handaan
cemetery	sementeryo
centavos	sentimos
center; middle	gitna
chair	upuan, silya
chalk	tisa
change	sukli
changed	pinalitan
charcoal	uling
cheap	mura
cheek	pisngi
cheese	keso
chest	baul
chest, breast	dibdib
chicken	manok
chicken or pork cooked in vinegar and spices	adobo
child	paslit
child; -ng babae girl, -ng	bata

lalaki boy	
childhood friend	kababata
chin	baba
china	tsina
choose, select	pili
christmas	pasko
church	simbahan
church bell	kampana
cigar; tobacco	tabako
cigarette	sigarilyo
cinema, movie theater	sinehan
citizen	mamamayan
city	lungsod, siyudad
civilization	kabihasnan
clams	halaan
classmate	kaklase
clay pot	palayok
clean	linis
climb	akyat
clinic tuhod	klinika
clock	orasan
close	sara
close friend	matalik na kaibigan
closed	sarado
cloth	tela
cloud	ulap
cloudy	maulap
club	klub
club, society	samahan (n.)
coffee	kape
cold	sipon, malamig
coldness	lamig
college	kolehiyo
color	kulay
comb	suklay

come from	galing sa
come in	tuloy ka
come in; to go ahead	tuloy
come, arrive	dating
command, order	utos
common expression meaning "come what may."	bahala na!
community	komunidad
companion, companion; comrade	kasama
complaint	reklamo
concert	konsiyerto
condiments for cooking	rekado
condition	kalagayan
condition, state, situation	lagay
conductor	konduktor
confused	nalilito
constitution	saligang-batas
consult; consultation	konsulta
container	lalagyan, sisidlan
continent	kontinente
conversation	usapan
cook (1)	kusinera/o
cook (2)- to cook	luto
core	ubod
corner	kanto, sulok
correct,	wasto

appropriate	
cost, importance	halaga
cough	ubo
coughing	inuubo
country	bansa
courteous	magalang
cousin	pinsan
cover	takip
cow, beef	baka, karne ng baka
coward	duwag
coworker	katrabaho
crab	alimango
creation, product	likha
cried	umiyak
cries easily	mababaw ang luha
crown	korona
cry	iyak
cup	tasa
curtain	kurtina
custard	leche flan
custom; habit	ugali
cut	hiwa, putol
dance	sayaw
dance partner	kasayaw
dancer	mananayaw
dangerous	delikado
dark	madilim
darkness	dilim (syn. karimlan)
daughter	anak na babae
dawn	madaling-araw
dead	patay
death	kamatayan
debt	utang

December	Disyembre
delicious	masarap
dentist	dentista
deposit	deposito
design	disenyo
dessert	panghimagas
destination	paroroonan
destroyed	wasak, sira
devotee	deboto
die	mamatay
died	nasawi
died	namatay
dieted	nag-diyeta
different	iba
dilute	malabnaw
dining table, dining room	hapag-kainan
dinner	hapunan
dipping sauce	sawsawan
director, editor	patnugot
dirt, waste, excrement	dumi
dirty	madumi/marumi
discount	tawad
dish or viand	putahe
dislike; don’t/doesn’t want	ayaw
distance	layo
dived	sumisid
divide; split	nahahati
doctor	doktor
doctor of medicine	doktor (syn. manggagamot)
dog	aso
don’t	huwag

don’t have	wala
door	pintuan
dormitory	dormitoryo
doubles	dalawahan
dress / clothes	damit
dress up	nagbibihis
dresser	tokador
dried fish	tuyong isda
drink	inom
drive	nagmamaneho
driver	drayber
drum	tambol
drunkard	lasing
dry	tuyo
duet partner	kadueto
durian	durian
dust	alikabok
each	bawat isa
ear	tenga
earlier	kanina, maaga
ears	tainga
earthquake	lindol
east	silangan
easy; fast	madali
eat	kain
eatery	kainan
efficient, exceptional	mahusay
egg	itlog
eggplant	talong
eight	walo
eight o’clock	alas-otso
eighteen	labingwalo
eighth	pangwalo
eighty	walumpu
elbow	siko
elder brother	kuya

elder sister	ate
election	halalan
electric bulb	bombilya
electric, electrical	electrika
elegant, classy	elegante
elementary school	elementarya
eleven	labing-isa
eleven o'clock	alas-onse
elongated	haba
employee	kawani
empty clam shell	kabibi
end	dulo
end; at sa wakas finally	wakas
ends	natatapos
enemy	kaaway
enemy	kagalit
engineer	inhinyero
enter	pasok
entertain	libang
entertain-ment, pas-time	aliwan
entrance	pasukan
envelope	sobre
envious	mainggitin
envy	inggit
eraser	pambura
especially	lalo na
established	itinatag
evening	gabi
evil, bad, wi-cked	masama
exact, fit,	husto

enough	
exactly at noon	tanghaling tapat
examination; to examine	eksamen
example	halimbawa
except, aside from, besides	bukod sa
excessive	masyado
exchange	magpapalit
exchange rate	palitan
exclamation of despair, sa-dness	ay!
exercise	nag-eehersisyo
expenses, spend	gastos
expensive	mahal (1)
experiencing	dumaranas
export	pag-angkat
expression of disgust	tse!
eyebrow	kilay
face	mukha
faith	pananalig
fall	hulog
family	pamilya
famine	taggutom
fan	pamaypay
fanning	nagpapaypay
far, distant	malayo
fare	pamasahe
farewell; goodbye	paalam
farmer	magsasaka
fat	mataba
fat	taba
fate	kapalaran

father	tatay, itay, ama
faucet	gripo
favorite	paborito
feast; town fiesta	pista
February	Pebrero
feeling weak	nanlalata
feeling, emotion	damdamin
feet	paa
fell; dropped	nahulog
fellow citizen	kababayan
fence; yard	bakod
fermented shrimp or anchovies	bagoong
fever	lagnat
few; a little	kaunti
fifteen	labinlima
fifth	panglima
fifty	limampu
fight, contest	laban
film	sine
finger	daliri
fingernail	kuko
finish, complete something	tapos
fire	sunog
fired	pinaputok
firefighter	bumbero
first	una
fish	isda
fish sauce	patis
fishing net	lambat
fits	kasya
five	lima
five o'clock	alas-singko

fix	ayusin
flag, banner	watawat
flame	ningas
flat iron	plantsa
floating	inapalutang
flood	baha
floor	sahig
floors/stories	palapag
flow	daloy
flower shop	tindahan ng bulaklak
flu	trangkaso
fly	lumilipad
food	pagkain
foot got cut	naputol ang paa
footstep	yabag
for two	pandalawahan
forehead	noo
forest	kagubatan
forget	limot
fork	tinidor
former; formerly	dati
forty	apatnapu
fought	lumaban
fountain pen	pluma
four	apat
four o'clock	alas-kuwatro
fourteen	labing-apat
fourth	pang-apat
fragrant	mabango
france	pransiya
free	libre
free, independent	malaya
freedom	laya
fresh	sariwa
fried rice	sinangag

friend	kaibigan
from	galing, muka, taga
from where	taga-saan
front	bukana, harap
fruit	prutas
fruit store	tindahan ng prutas
fry	prito
full	puno
garage	garahe
garden	hardin
garden, lawn	hardin (syn. halamanan)
gate	tarangkahan
gathered	iniipon
general	pangkalahatan
get off	bababa
get on; ride	sasakay
get sick	magkasakit
gift	regalo
ginger	luya
give	bigay
glass	baso
glass; eyeglasses; mirror	salamin
go	punta
go back	bumalik
go home	uwi
go on vacation	nagbabakasyon
go past	lumampas
go round; go around	umikot
go skydiving	nagsa-skydiving
go snowboarding	nagso-snowboarding

go to class	pumapasok sa klase
go/come	pumupunta
god, supreme being	diyos (syn. bathala, maykapal)
goddess	diyosa
godfather	ninong
godmother	ninang
going to	papuntang
gold	ginto
good	mabuti
good, excellent; free from sickness	magaling
goodbye!	adiyos
goodness, virtue	kabutihan
goods	tinda
got accepted	natanggap
got burned	nasunog
got cut	nahiwa
got dismissed	dinismiss
got flooded	bumaha
got infected	nahawa
got injured	nasugatan
got married	ikinasal
got pregnant	nabuntis
got rained on	naulanan
got removed; got fired	natanggal
got sick	nagkasakit
got slightly burned	napaso
got treatment	nagpagamot
got well	gumaling
government	pamahalaan
grade, class	grado

grade; steps (of stairs)	baitang
grade; trade-mark	marka
graduate study	gradwadong pag-aaral
graduated	nagtapos
grandchild	apo
grandma	lola
grandpa, grandfather	lolo
grandparent	nuno
gray/white hair	uban
great; fore-most	dakila
green	berde
grief, extreme sorrow	pagdadalamhati
griller, roaster	ihawan
grocery	groseri
grouchy	masungit
group	grupo
growing, in-creasing in size	lumalaki
guess, o-pinion	palagay
gun	baril
had (hair) straightened	nagpatuwid
hair	buhok
haircut	gupit
half	kalahati
half (used in telling time; thirty minutes)	y medya

hammock, cradle	duyan
hand	kamay
handkerchief	panyo
handsome	gwapo
happen	mangyari
happiness	ligaya
happiness, contentment	kaligayahan
happy	maligaya
hard	matigas
harvest	ani
harvested	inani
hat	sumbrero
have	may
have some-one cook for you	nagpaluto
have some-one cut your hair	nagpagupit
have some-one give you a massage	nagpamasahe
have some-one make copies for you	nagpa-photo-copy
having inves-tigated	pinaiimbis-tigahan
he/she	siya
head	ulo
health, well-being	kalusugan
healthy	malusog
hear	rinig
heart	puso
heart-shaped	hugis-puso
heat, warmth	init

heavy	mabigat
height	taas
help	tulong
helper, servant	katulong
herbal plant	halamang gamot
here	dito/rito, nandito/narito
hermit	ermitanyo
hers	kanya
hide	tago
high school	mataas na paaralan
highest point	pinakatuktok
hill	burol
hips	balakang
his/her	niya
hit	tamaan
hold	hawak
holding hands	magkahawak-kamay
holy saturday	sabado de gloria
home	tahanan
honorable, respectable	kagalang-galang
honorific	po
hope	pag-asa
horse	kabayo
hospital	ospital
hot	mainit
hot season/summer season	tag-init
house	bahay
housefly	langaw
how	paano
how are you?	kumusta
how many	ilan

how much?	magkano
hug	niyayakap
hug, embrace	yakap
human vein, root of a plant	ugat
hundred	sandaan
hungry; hunger	gutom
hurt	masakit
husband and wife; to marry	mag-asawa
hyacinth bean	bataw
i am sad about this.	ikinalulungkot ko.
ice	yelo
if, when, as to	kung
ignorant, stupid	hangal
illness	karamdaman
immediately	kaagad
implied; said	sinasaad
in/inside	loob
in; on; at; marker to indicate ownership	sa
inauguration	pasinaya
incident	insidente
included, enclosed	kalakip
independence, liberty; free	kalayaan
industrious	masipag
ink	tinta
inside	sa loob
instead	imbis

intelligent	matalino
intelligent, wise	marunong
interviewed	kinapanayam
introduce	pakilala
investigation	imbestigasyon
invitation	anyaya (syn. paanyaya)
invites	nag-iimbita
irritating	nakakainis
is that so?	ganoon ba?
island	isla
it is said	daw
it seems	tila
it's a pity	sayang
jackfruit	langka
January	Enero
japan	hapón
jealousy	pagseselos
jeep (for transportation)	jeepney / dyip
jewelry	alahas
join	sumali
joke; jester	biro
journey	paglalakbay
joyful, happy	masaya
judge	hukom
judgment, decision	hatol
juice	katas
july	hulyo
jump, waterfall	talon
June	Hunyo
just finished bathing	kaliligo
key	susi

kill	patayin
kind	uri
kind of; class	klase
kind/nice	mabait
king	hari
kiss	halik
kitchen	kusina
knee	tuhod
knife	kutsilyo
knocked	kumatok
know	alam
know each other	magkakakilala
knowledge, ability	dunong (syn. karunungan)
labor strike	welga
lack of confidence	kawalan-kumpiyansa
lacking	kulang
land, earth	lupa
landed	lumapag
language	wika
lanzones (type of fruit)	lansones
large boat	barko
last	huli
last month	noong isang buwan
last name	apelyido
last night	kagabi
last week	noong isang linggo
later	mamaya
laugh	tawa
laughed	tumawa
law	batas
lawyer	abugado
layer	patong

lazy	tamad
leader	pinuno
leaf	dahon
leather	kuwero
leave	aalis
leave, depart	alis
led by	pamumuno
left	kaliwa
length	haba (as a noun)
lengthwise	pahaba
letter	liham
library	aklatan
lie (as in lying down)	higa
life, alive	buhay
light (weight)	magaan
light, light fixtures	ilaw
like best	pinakagusto
like better	mas gusto
like least	pinaka-ayaw
like that	ganyan
like this	ganito
like; want	gusto
lima bean	patani
line	guhit
lips	labi
list	listahan
list, record	talaan
listen	dinig
listens to (music, songs, radio)	nakikinig
literally, person here!	tao po!
live	nakatira
live charcoal	baga
live, reside	tira

lived	nabuhay
livelihood	kabuhayan
liver	atay
living room	sala
location, a stall or stand in a market	puwesto
long	mahaba
long live!; to live	mabuhay
look	tingin
looks for	naghahanap
lost	nawala
love	mahal
lower part	ibaba
luffa	patola
lullaby	oyayi
lunch	tanghalian
lungs	baga (contextual meaning)
machine; sewing machine	makina
made of	yari sa
magazine	magasin
make, do	gawa
makes one look old	nakakatanda
man	lalaki
man's shirt	kamisadentro
manager	tagapangasiwa
mango	mangga
many, a lot	marami
March	Marso
marker to indicate ownership	kay
market	palengke
massage	masahe

master, boss, employer	amo
master; lord	panginoon
mata	mata
match	posporo
materials	materyales
May	Mayo
meaning	ibig sabihin
meat	karne
medicine	gamot
medium	katamtaman
meeting	miting, pulong
melon	melon
member of an organization	kasapi
memorized	kabisado
memory; gift	alaala
merchandise, goods	kalakal
met an acci-dent	na-aksidente
metal	metal
midnight	hatinggabi
militant	militante
military forces	puwersang mili-tar
milk	gatas
million	milyon
mine	akin
minute	minuto
mister	ginoong
mix	haluin
modern, in-telligent, wise	makabago
moment	sandali
Monday	Lunes
money	pera
month, moon	buwan

monthly	buwan-buwan
morning	umaga
mosquito	lamok
mosquito net	kulambo
mother	ina, inay, nanay
mountain	bundok
move	lipat
mrs.	ginang
murderer	salarin
music	musika
musical note	nota
mustard	mustasa
my condo-lences.	nakikiraramay ako.
my, i	ko
nail	pako
name	pangalan, kata-wagan
national flower of the philippines	sampaguita
native love song	kundiman
native of, na-tural	likas
native sau-sage	longganisa
near	malapit
neck	leeg
necklace	kuwintas
need	kailangan
needle	karayom
neighbor	kapitbahay
nervousness	nerbiyos
never	hindi kailanman
new	bago
new entry, newcomer	bagong pasok

news	balita
newspaper	diyaryo (syn. pahayagan)
next	susunod
nickname	palayaw
niece/nephe w	pamangkin
nine	siyam
nine o'clock	alas-nuwebe
nineteen	labinsiyam
ninety	siyamnapu
ninth	pangsiyam
no	hindi
noise	ingay
noisy	maingay
noisy drinking party	lasingan
noon	tanghali
north	hilaga
nose	ilong
notebook	kuwaderno
novel	nobela
November	Nobyembre
number of people	katao
nurse	nars
obedient	masunurin
occupied; co-lonized	sinakop
ocean	dagat
October	Oktubre
of course	siyempre.
of diligence	ng sipag
offer	alok
office	opisina
often	madalas
oil	langis
okay/sure	sige

old	luma
old coconut	niyog
old person; aged, elderly, old	matanda
older person	manong
on the way home	pauwi
on top	itaas
once again	uli
once upon a time	noong unang panahon
once; some-times	minsan
one	isa
one who lo-ves	mangingibig
onion	sibuyas
only	lamang
opinion	kuru-kuro
or	o
orange	kahel
original	orihinal
ours (exclu-sive)	namin
ours (inclu-sive)	natin
ours (plural exclusive pro-noun)	amin
outer covering; shell; skin	balat
outside	labas
over there	doon/roon, nandoon/naroo n
owner	may-ari

pack (a suit-case)	inempake
paint	pintura, nagpi-pinta
painter	pintor
palace	palasyo
palm of hand; fate	palad
pan	kawali
pants	pantalon
papaya	papaya
paper	papel
parents	magulang
parking lot	paradahan
part, portion	bahagi
party, banquet	salu-salo
passenger	pasahero
passport	pasaporte
patient	pasyente
patient, sick person	maysakit
patriotic, na-tionalistic	makabayan
pay	bayad
pay; rent	upa
peaceful	payapa
peanut	mani
pencil	lapis
performer, a person skilled in an art	artista
perhaps	yata
permission	permiso
person	tao
person who beats up an-other	nambubugbog

personnel	tauhan
perspiration; laborer	pawis
peso	piso
pharmacy	botika
philippine le-mon	kalamansi
philippines	pilipinas
photograph	litrato
piano	piyano
pick up	sundo
picking (for example, picking ap-ples)	namimitas
picture	larawan
picture frame	kuwadro
piece	piraso
pier	daungan
pierce	tinutusok
pig	baboy
pillow	unan
pin	aspile
pineapple	pinya
pink	rosas
pipe	pipa, tubo
pitiful	kawawa
pity	awa
place where fish is sold	isdaan
place where meat is sold	karnihan
plan, aim, purpose	balak
planned	naplano
plant	halaman, tanim
plantation	taniman
planted	itinanim

plate	plato
play (an instrument)	tumutugtog
play (game)	naglalaro
play, game	laro
playground	palaruan
playmate	kalaro
please	sige na
please give	pakibigyan
please register	pakirehistro
please sit	maupo
please, really, truly	nga
plural marker for names	sina
plural marker to indicate ownership	kina
pocket	bulsa
poem	tula
poison	lason
police station	istasyon ng pulis
policeman, police officer	pulis
politicizing	nagpopolitisa
politics	pulitika
poor	mahihirap
powder	pulbos
practice (for example, martial arts)	nagpapraktis
pregnant	buntis
prepare	maghanda
prepared	inihanda
preposition indicating location	nasa

prescribed	iniresta
prescription	reseta
present from a trip	pasalubong
presentation, show	palabas
president	pangulo
prison	bilibid
private	pribado
prize, reward	premyo
process	proseso
profit, gain	pakinabang
program	programa
project	proyekto
prosperous	manigo
province	probinsiya
public	publiko
pumpkin	kalabasa
punishment	parusa
put	lagyan
questionmarker (yes/no)	ba
race of people, nationality	lahi
radio	radyo
radish	labanos
railroad, specifically for trains	riles
rain	ulan
rainy	maulan
rainy season	tag-ulan
rambutan (fruit)	rambutan
rare, infrequent	madalang
raw, unrip	hilaw

reach	abot
read	basa
ready, finis-hed	yari
real	tunay
really?	talaga?
rebel	rebelde
receipt	resibo
receive	tanggap
received	tumanggap
recreation, entertain-ment	libangan
red	pula
refreshment	pampalamig
refrigerator	palamigan
rehearsals	ensayo
rehearse	nag-eensayo
relative	kamag-anak
relief from pain, consola-tion; luxury	kaginhawahan
religion	relihiyon
religious mass	misa
remember	tandaan
remove	tanggalin
rent	arkila
repeat	uulitin
report	ulat
representa-tive	kinatawan
resort	bakasyunan
rest	pahinga
restaurant	restawran
return	balik
returned	nagsauli
revolution	rebolusyon
rice (cooked)	kanin

rice (un-cooked)	bigas
rice cake	puto
rice delicacies	kakanin
rice plant	palay
ricefield	palayan
rich, wealthy	mayaman
ride	sumasakay
ride a bicycle	nagbibisikleta
ride, drive (as a passenger)	sakay
right	tama
right (as in right side)	kanan (as in turn right)
ring	singsing
ripe	hinog
river	ilog
road	daan, kalsada, kalya
roaming around	gumagala
roasted pig	litson
roll	ipagulong
room	kwarto, kuwarto
root word	salitang-
rope	lubid
rotten/bad	panis
round	bilugan
rubber	goma
rule	tuntunin
run	takbo
rust	kalawang
sacred	sagrado
sad	malungkot
said	sinabi
sail	paglalayag
salad	ensalada
salary, wage	sahod

saliva	laway
salt	asin
salty	maalat, alat
same	magkapareho
sand	buhangin
sandals	sandalyas
sarcasm, irony	tuya
saturday	sabado
sauce	sarsa
sauteed	ginisa
saved money	nakatipid
saw	nakita
say, tell	sabi
scale, balance	timbangan
schedule	iskedyul
school	eskuwela, eskuwelahan
science	siyensiya
scissors	gunting
seal	pagdikitin
search	hanap
seashore	tabing-dagat
second	pangalawa, segundo
secret	sikreto, lihim
secretary	kalihim
section (in class)	seksyon
see, (to see)	kita
self	sarili
selfish	sakim
sell	benta
selling	nagtitinda
send	dala
sent	pinadala
separate	hiwalay
September	Setyembre

server	tagapagsilbi
server: waiter	serbidor
service	serbisyo
sesame seed	linga
set of brothers or sisters	magkapatid
seven	pito
seven o'clock	alas-siyete
seventeen	labimpito
seventh	pampito
seventy	pitumpu
shadow	anino
shame	hiya
shameful	nakakahiya
shameless	walang-hiya
ship	bapor
shirt	polo
shoes	sapatos
short	pandak, maikli
should	dapat
shoulder	balikat
shout	sumisigaw
shout, scream	sigaw
showed	ipinakita
shrimp	hipon
sibling	kapatid
sickly	masakitin
sickness; pain	sakit
side	gilid
sign	karatula
sign your name	lagdaan, pirmahan
signature	lagda, pirma
silk	seda
silver	pilak
similar, same	magkatulad
simple	payak
since	mula noong

sing	kanta, aawit
singer	mang-aawit
single, singu-lar	isahan
sit	upo
sitting	naka-upo
six	anim
six o'clock	alas-sais
sixteen	labing-anim
sixth	pang-anim
sixty	animnapu
size	laki
skirt	palda
slashed or discounted price	bagsak-presyo
sleep	tulog
slippers	sinelas
slow	mabagal
slowly	dahan-dahan
small	maliit
small plate; saucer	platito
smallest poli-tical unit	barangay
smell, odor	amoy
smile	ngiti
smiled	ngumiti
smiling	nakangiti
smoke	aso (2)
smooth	makinis
snack	meryenda
snake	ahas
snow	niyebe
so, can, be able to	kaya
so, so that	upang
soap	sabon

soccer	soccer
society	lipunan
socks, sto-ckings	medyas
soft	malambot
soldier	sundalo
sometimes	paminsan-minsan
son	anak na lalaki
song	awit
sorry. (lite-rally, sorry you.)	pasensiya ka na.
sound	tunog
soup	sopas
sour	maasim
sour taste; maasim (adj.) sour	asim
south	timog
sovereignty	soberanya
soy sauce	toyo
spain	espanya
speak	magsalita
special	espesyal
spicy	maanghang
spoon	kutsara
spring	tagsibol
spring roll	lumpia
square	kuwadrado
squeeze	pinisil
squid	pusit
stairs, ladder	hagdan
stamp; dry seal	selyo
stand	tayo
star	bituin
start, begin	simula

starts	nagsisimula
statement	pahayag
station (e.g., bus station)	istasyon
station, waiting shed	estasyon
steady client	suki
steamed	pinasingaw
step on	tapak
stepson	anak sa labas (used for stepson but can have a different connotation, often used for a child born out of wedlock)
stomach	tiyan
stop	hinto
store	tindahan
storm	bagyo
story, fiction	kuwento
stove	kalan
stove, oven	pugon
straight	tuwid
street	daan (syn. kalye, kalsada)
strength, force	lakas
string	tali
string bean	sitaw
strong	malakas
student	estudyante
student, pupil	estudyante, mag-aaral
studied hard	nagsunog ng kilay
study	nag-aaral

study, learn	aral
stupid, irresponsible	tanga
subdivision	subdibisyon
subject, theme	paksa
subscription	suskrisyon
suddenly	bigla
sufferings	tiisin
sugar	asukal
summer	tag-araw
sun; day	araw
sunny	maaraw
sunset	paglubog ng araw
suprised	ipinagtataka
surely, certainly	pihado
surplus; more than enough	labis
surrounded	napapalibutan
surroundings	paligid
swam	lumangoy
sweet	matamis
swim	langoy
swimming	lumalangoy
symbol	simbolo
table	mesa
tablets	tabletas
take	kuha
take a bath/take a shower	naliligo
take someone to a place	hatid
talkative	madaldal
tall	matangkad
taste	lasa

taxi	taksi
tea	tsaa
teach	turo
teacher	guro, titser
tears	luha
teaspoon	kutsarita
teeth	ngipin
telephone	telepono
television	telebisyon
tell	magkwento, sabihin
telling a story	ikinukuwento
temperature	temperatura
ten	sampu
ten o'clock	alas-diyes
tenth	pangsampu
than	kaysa
thank you	salamat
thanksgiving mass	misang pasasa-lamant
that (far from speaker and listener)	iyon
that (far from the speaker)	iyan
that is why	kayá
the color of corn; blonde	kulay mais
the same, si-milar	pareho
their	nila
theirs	kanila
there (far from the per-son talking)	doon
there (near the person spoken to)	diyan

they	sila
thick	makapal
thin, slim	payat
think, mind, thought	isip
third	ikatlo
thirst	uhaw
thirsty	nauuhaw
thirteen	labintatlo
thirty	tatlumpu
this	ito
thought	naisip
thousand	sanlibo
thread	sinulid
three	tatlo
three o'clock	alas-tres
throat	lalamunan
throw (usu-ally used for liquids)	binuhos
throw out/put in a garbage bin	ibasura
thumb	hinlalaki
thunder	kulog
Thursday	Huwebes
ticket	tiket
tie	kurbata
tied	nakatali
tight	masikip
time, hour	oras
tin can	lata
tip, gratuity	pabuya
tired	pagod
tireless	walang-pagod
to accompany	samahan (v.)
to act	pagkilos
to arrive;	dumating

arrival	
to assume responsibility	umako
to attend an event	dalo
to be careful	mag-ingat
to be glad	matuwa
to be hungry	magutom
to be surpri-sed	magulat
to be thirsty	mauhaw
to believe	maniwala
to bid goodbye	magpaalam
to bite	kagatin
to breathe	huminga
to bump against, to collide with	mabangga
to call	tawagan
to check in	mag-check in
to clean	linisin
to close so-mething	isara
to come near, to approach	lumapit
to cut (with a scissor)	gupitin
to drink	inum
to eat	kumain
to fight some-one or some-thing	labanan
to fly	lumipad
to follow	sumunod
to get	kumuha
to give	ibigay
to go away	umalis

to go home	umuwi
to go with	sumama
to have something re-served for someone	magpareserba
to hear mass, go to church	magsimba
to hold	hawakan
to know	malaman
to leave be-hind	iwan
to lie down	humiga
to list down	ilista
to love	umibig
to make into sweet	matamisin
to meet	magkita
to not know. aywan ko (i don't know).	aywan
to order	mag-order
to paint	pinta
to pick some-thing up	mamulot
to plant	magtanim
to play; player	maglaro
to plead, to make a re-quest	makiusap
to pray	manalangin
to put, to place	ilagay
to read	magbasa
to remove	alisin
to repair	kumpuni
to reserve	magreserba

to rest	magpahinga
to return so-mething	isauli
to roast	litsunin
to see	makita
to set the table	maghain
to sew; sew-ing	tahi
to sing	umawit
to sink	lumubog
to stay	pagtigil
to study	mag-aral
to take a bath	maligo
to take a look	patingin
to take a walk	magpasyal
to take along; include	isama
to teach something, to show or point	ituro
to think	mag-isip, umisip
to throw a-way	itapon
to walk	lumakad
to wash	maghugas
to wash clothes	maglaba
to wear, to put on	isuot
to; until	hanggang
today	ngayon
toes	daliri sa paa
together	kaakibat
toilet	kubeta, paliku-ran
tomato	kamatis
tomorrow	bukas

too big	napakalaki
too long	napakahaba
too loose	napakaluwang
too salty	masyadong maalat, napaka-alat
too short	napakaiksi
too small	napakaliit
too tight	napakasikip
too wide	maluwang
took a picture	kinuha ang lara-wan
took a vaca-tion	nagbakasyon
took care of	inalagaan
took pictures	kumuha ng lara-wan
toothbrush	sepilyo
tortured; lite-rally, given hardship	pinahirapan
touch	hipo
towel	tuwalya
toy	laruan
toy store	tindahan ng la-ruan
traditional blouse and skirt	baro't saya
train	tren
train station	istasyon ng tren
traitor	taksil
transfer	lumipat
transporta-tion	transportasyon
travel	lakbay
travel, trip	biyahe
travelling	pagbibiyahe

tree	pno
tree; leader, chief, source	puno (n.)
tricycle (motorcycle or bicycle with a sidecar)	traysikel
tropical sour fruit	kamias
trousers	salawal
truck	trak
true, real	totoo
truth	katotohanan
try on; size	sukat
Tuesday	Martes
turn left	kumaliwa
turn right	kumanan
turnip	singkamas
twelve	labindalawa
twelve o'clock	alas-dose
twenty	dalawampu
twin	kambal
two	dalawa
two o'clock	alas-dos
two-wheeled vehicle pulled by a horse	kalesa
ugly	pangit
ulan	rain
umbrella	payong
una- one o'clock	ala
unauthorized	di-awtorisado
uncle	tiyo, tito
unconventional, stubborn	pasaway
under	ilalim

undershirt	kamiseta
understand	intindi
unfortunately	sa kasamaang palad
uniform	uniporme
university	pamantasan
upper lip	nguso
use	gamit
used for the plural form	mga
using	sa pamamagitan
various	sari-sari
vegetable	gulay
vehicle	sasakyan
very dry	tuyong-tuyo
vice-president	pangalawang pangulo
victory	tagumpay
view	tanawin
vinegar	suka
violation	paglabag
violet/purple	lila
violin	biyulin
visit	bisitahin, dalaw
visited	dumalaw
visited a doctor	nagpatingin sa doktor
visitor	bisita
vitamins	bitamina
voice	boses (syn. tinig)
waist	baywang
wait	hintay
waiting place	hintayan
wake up	gising
walk	naglalakad
walk, stroll	lakad
wall	pader
walls	dingding

was built	natayo
was killed	napatay
wash	hugas
wash (face)	naghihilamos
wash clothes	laba
watch	relo
watch, look at	nood
watches (television, movie, game)	nanonood
watchman, guard	bantay
water	tubig
watermelon	pakwan
wave	alon
waving	kumakaway
wax gourd	kundol
way	paraan
we (exclusive)	kami
we (inclusive)	tayo (2)
weak	mahina
wealth	yaman
wears glasses	naka-salamin
weather	panahon
wedding	kasal
Wednesday	Miyerkules
week	linggo
weekly	linggo-linggo
welcome	walang anuman
well-known; popular	tanyag
went	pumunta, naparoon
went down	bumaba
went scuba diving	nag-i-scuba-diving
went shopping	namili

went sightseeing	namasyal
went snorkeling	nag-i-snorkeling
west	kanluran
wet, moist	basa
what	ano
when (for continuing actions)	noong
when	nang
where	saan
while, so long as	habang
white	puti
who	sino
wide	malawak
wife	asawa
will be bitten; refers only to snake bites	matutuklaw
will be fixed	maaayos
will be late	mahúhuli
will cook	magluluto
will finish	tatapusin
will go	pupunta
will go to class	papasok sa klase
will like	magustuhan
will pass by	dadaanan
will pass by	dadaan
will play	tutugtog
will play (a game)	maglalaro
will return	isasauli
windy	mahangin
wine	alak
wing	pakpak

winged bean	sigarilyas
winter	taglamig
wire; electric wire	kawad
witness	saksi
woman	babae
won	nanalo
wood	kahoy
wooden board	tabla
wooden shoes	bakya
word, langu-age	salita
wore (com-pleted aspect of wear)	isinuot
work	nagtatrabaho
work, job	trabaho
worker	manggagawa
world	mundo
worm	uod
worried	nag-aalala
worship; to worship	samba
would like	nais
wound	sugat

wrap	balutin
wrapped (Duck emb-ryo)	balot
write	nagsusulat
write, letter	sulat
writer	manunulat
wrote	sinulat
yam	gábi
yard	bakuran
year	ano, taon
years, age	taon, edad
yes	oo
yes sir/ma-dam	oho (or opo)
yesterday	kahapon
you	ikaw, ka
you (plural)	kayo
young coconut	buko
your	mo
zero	sero

Verb Conjugation Table

Tagalog verbs are conjugated based on three key elements: Focus, Aspect (or tense), and Verb Group (like "mag-" or "in-"). These elements determine how a verb changes to convey different meanings.

- Focus determines whether the action is centered on the doer (Actor Focus) or the object/receiver (Object Focus).
- Aspect indicates the time of the action: completed, ongoing, or future.
- Verb Group guides the prefix or infix used in the conjugation.

Here's how to use the conjugation table:

English Verb Reference Table: This table lists English verbs with a reference number to find the corresponding Tagalog verb in the conjugation table.

Tagalog Verb Conjugation Table: This table shows the root of the Tagalog verb, its English meaning, and its conjugations in both Actor Focus and Object Focus for all three aspects.

These tables will help you find and conjugate Tagalog verbs based on the English verbs.

Note: In Tagalog, you can transform adjectives into verbs, a process called "pagpapandiwa" or verbification. This feature allows the language to turn static descriptions into dynamic actions or states. For instance, the adjective "liban", meaning "absent," can be conjugated with verb affixes to express different tenses:

- Lumiban - This past tense, actor-focused verb form means "was absent" or "had been absent."
- Lumiliban - In the present progressive tense, this actor-focused form means "is being absent" or "habitually absent."

This way of using verbs is similar to the English expression "to be absent," where absence is treated as an action that the subject performs. By adding verb affixes to adjectives or nouns, Tagalog speakers can vividly describe actions and states, showing how static qualities can influence subjects dynamically.

English	Verb Root	Line #
absent	liban	208
abuse	abuso	2
accept	tanggap	359
accuse	akusa	5
acquire	kuha	177
act	arte	19
add (forward)	dagdag	69
agitate (someone)	galit	90
angry (to be angry)	galit	91
annoy	inis	147
answer	sagot	281
approach	lapit	204
arrive	dating	80
ask about	tanong	364
ask for (something)	hingi	126
assume	akala	3
attack	lusob	224
attain	kamit	162
attend	dalo	75
attention (give)	pansin	246
attract	akit	4
avoid	layo	207
bad (to become)	sama	290
ban	bawal	43
bark	tahol	349
begin	umpisa	395
believe	niwala	235
big (make it)	laki	201
big (to become)	laki	200
birth (to give birth, to be born)	anak	16
bite	kagat	156
boil	laga	191
borrow (money)	hiram	129
borrow (utang)	utang	402
brag (or boast)	yabang	412
break	sira	313
break (glassware)	basag	41
break (irreparable)	wasak	411

introduce (something)	kita	173
invent	imbento	142
invite	imbita	143
involve	sali	286
join (game)	sali	287
join (someone)	sama	292
joke	loko	220
jump	talon	356
keep (put aside)	tabi	342
keep (save)	tago	345
kill	patay (as nag verb)	256
kill	patay (as um verb)	257
kill (slaughter)	katay	166
kiss	halik	110
knock (door)	katok	167
knock down	giba	101
know (someone)	kilala	169
know (something)	alam	11
laugh	tawa	370
laundry	laba	184
lay	lagay	193
lie (tell a lie)	sinungaling	310
lie down	higa	119
light up	ilaw	141
like (something)	gusto	106
listen (something)	kinig	171
loan (money)	utang	403
look (something)	tingin	380
lose	wala	408
love (someone romantically)	ibig	140
love (someone)	mahal	226
make	gawa	99
market (go to)	palengke	241
marry	kasal	164
measure (dimension)	sukat	321
measure (weight)	timbang	377
meet (someone)	kita	174
move (something)	lipat	218

present (something)	kilala	170
press (iron)	plantsa	265
pretty (become)	ganda	94
pretty (make one's self)	ganda	95
prevent (oneself)	pigil	258
prevent (something)	pigil	259
promise	pangako	245
promote (someone/job)	promote	266
promote (something)	taguyod	346
pull	hila	122
push	tulak	384
put	lagay	195
put down	baba	27
put in (the mouth)	subo	318
put in (through a hole)	pasok	252
put on (clothes)	suot	336
put on (turn on)	bukas	62
question	tanong	365
quick (to make it)	bilis	53
quiet	tahimik	348
raise (animals)	aruga	20
raise (children)	laki	203
raise (hand)	taas	341
reach	abot	1
reach (destination)	dating	81
read (something)	basa	39
read (to someone)	basa	40
receive	tanggap	360
refuse, decilne	ayaw	23
reject	tanggi	361
remember	alala	9
remove (clothes)	hubad	134
remove (someone)	alis	14
remove (something)	alis	13
rent (car)	arkila	18
rent (general)	renta	278
rent (house)	upa	397
repeat (behavior)	ulit	392
repeat (work)	ulit	393
report (complain)	sumbong	327

swallow	lunok	223
sweep (clean)	walis	410
take	kuha (mag verb)	180
take	kuha (um verb)	181
take care (of one's self)	ingat	144
take care (of someone)	alaga	8
take care (something)	ingat	145
talk	salita	288
teach	turo	390
tease	biro	54
tell	sabi	280
test (examine)	suri	338
test (try out)	subok	319
think	isip	154
throw	tapon	366
tighten	higpit	120
travel (by plane), fly	lipad	216
travel (vacation)	bakasyon	30
travel (visit)	pasyal	253
travel (voyage)	lakbay	199
turn off	patay	255
turn off	sara	297
turn on	bukas	63
type (type)	makinilya	227
understand (someone)	intindi	151
understand (something)	intindi	150
use	gamit	92
vanish	wala	409
violate (a law)	labag	185
violate (an order)	suway	339
visit	bisita	55
visit	dalaw	73
vote	boto	57
wait	hintay	127
walk	lakad	198
want	gusto	107
warn	babala	28
wash	hugas	135
watch (movie/TV)	nood	236
watch (someone)	bantay	38

The Tagalog conjugation table starts at the next page.

			Actor Focus			Object Focus		
#	Root	English	Completed	Ongoing	Future	Completed	Ongoing	Future
1	abot	reach	umabot	umaabot	aabot	inabot	inaabot	aabutin
2	abuso	abuse	umabuso	umaabuso	aabuso	inabuso	inaabuso	aabusuhin
3	akala	assume	nag-akala	nag-aakala	mag-aakala	inakala	inaakala	aakalain
4	akit	attract	naakit	naaakit	maaakit	inakit	inaakit	aakitin
5	akusa	accuse	nag-akusa	nang-aakusa	mang-aakusa	inakusahan	in-aakusahan	aakusahan
6	akyat	bring up	nag-akyat	nag-aakyat	mag-aakyat	inakyat	inaakyat	iaakyat
7	akyat	go up, climb	umakyat	umaakyat	aakyat	inakyat	inaakyat	aakyatin
8	alaga	take care (of some-one)	nag-alaga	nag-aalaga	mag-aalaga	inalagaan	inaalagaan	aalagaan
9	alala	remember	naalala	naaalala	maaalala	inalala	inaalala	aalalahanin
10	alala	worry	nag-alala	nag-aalala	mag-aalala	inalala	inaalala	aalahanin
11	alam	know (so-mething)		inalam	inaalam			aalamin
12	alis	depart	umalis	umaalis	aalis			
13	alis	remove (some-thing)	nag-alis	nag-aalis	mag-aalis	inalis	inaalis	aalisin
14	alis	remove (someone)	nagpaalis	nagpapaalis	magpapaalis	pinaalis	pinapaalis	papaalisin

15	alis	withdraw (from acti-vity)	umalis	umaalis	aalis			
16	anak	birth (to give birth/to be born)	nanganak	nangang-anak	mangang-anak	ipinanganak	pinapan-ganak	ipapanganak
17	aral	study	nag-aral	nag-aaral	mag-aaral	pinag-aralan	pinag-aar-alan	pag-aaralan
18	arkila	rent (car)	umarkila	umaarkila	aarkila	inarkila	inaarkila	aarkilahin
19	arte	act	umarte	umaarte	aarte	inartehan	inaartehan	aartehan
20	aruga	raise (ani-mals)	nag-aruga	nag-aaruga	mag-aaruga	inarugaan	inaarugaan	aaraguan
21	asa	expect	umasa	umaasa	aasa	inasahan	inaasahan	aasahan
22	awit	sing	umawit	umaawit	aawit	inawit	inaawit	aawitin
23	ayaw	refuse, de-cilne	umayaw	umaayaw	aayaw	inayawan	inaayawan	aayawan
24	ayos	sort	nag-ayos	nag-aayos	mag-aayos	inayos	inaayos	aayusin
25	baba	drop off (someone)	nagbaba	nagbababa	magbababa	ibinaba	ibinababa	ibababa
26	baba	go down	bumaba	bumababa	bababa	binaba	binababa	ibababa
27	baba	put down	nagbaba	nagbababa	magbababa	ibinaba	ibinababa	ibababa
28	babala	warn	nagbabala	nagbababala	magbaba-bala	binalaan	binabalaan	babalaan
29	bagsak	drop down	nagbagsak	nag-babagsak	mag-babagsak	binagsak	binabagsak	ibabagsak

30	bakasyon	travel (vacation)	nag-bakasyon	nag-babakasyon	mag-babakasyon	bi-nakasyunan	bi-nabakasyunan	babakasyunan
31	bali	break (long objects)	bumali	bumabali	babali	binali	binabali	babaliin
32	balik	bring back	nagbalik	nagbabalik	magbabalik	ibinalik	ibinabalik	ibabalik
33	balik	come back	bumalik	bunabalik	babalik	binalikan	binabalikan	babalikan
34	balita	report (news)	nagbalita	nagbabalita	magbabalita	binalita	binabalita	ibabalita
35	balot	wrap	nagbalot	nagbabalot	magbabalot	binalot	binabalot	babalutin
36	bangon	rise up (from lying)	bumangon	bumab-angon	babangon	binangon	bi-nabangon	ibabangon
37	bantay	guard (look after)	nagbantay	nagbabantay	mag-babantay	binantayan	bi-nabantayan	babantayan
38	bantay	watch (so-meone)		pinanood	pinapanood	papanoorin		
39	basa	read (so-mething)	nagbasa	nagbabasa	magbabasa	binasa	binabasa	babasahin
40	basa	read (to someone)	bumasa	bumabasa	babasa			
41	basag	break (glass-ware)	nagbasag	nagbabasag	magbabasag	binasag	binabasag	babasagin
42	bati	greet (so-meone)	bumati	bumabati	babati	binati	binabati	babatiin
43	bawal	ban	nagbawal	nagbababawal	magbababawal	ibinawal	ibinababawal	ibababawal

44	bayad	pay	nagbayad	nagbabayad	magbabayad	binayaran	bi-nabayaran	babayaran
45	benta	sell	nagbenta	nagbebenta	magbebenta	ibinenta	ibinebenta	ibebenta
46	bigay	give	nagbigay	nagbibigay	magbibigay	binigay	binibigay	ibibigay
47	bigay	grant (mo-ney/chance)	nabigay	nagbibigay	magbibigay	binigyan	binibigyan	bibigyan
48	bigay	hand over (some-thing)		ibinigay	ibinibigay			ibibigay
49	bihis	change (clothes)	nagbihis	nagbibihis	magbibihis	binihisan	binibihisan	bibihisan
50	bihis	dress (put on)	nagbihis	nagbibihis	magbibihis	binihisan	binibihisan	bibihisan
51	bilang	count	bumilang	bumibilang	bibilang	binilang	binibilang	bibilangin
52	bili	buy	bumili	bumibili	bibili	binili	binibili	bibilhin
53	bilis	quick (to make it)	bumilis	bumibilis	bibilis	bilisan	binibilisan	bibilisan
54	biro	tease	nagbiro	nagbibiro	magbibiro	biniro	binibiro	bibiruin
55	bisita	visit	bumisita	bumibista	bibisita	binisita	binibisita	bibisitahin
56	bitbit	carry (with arm)	nagbitbit	nagbibitbit	magbibitbit	binitbit	binibitbit	bibitbitin
57	boto	vote	bumoto	bumoboto	boboto	ibinoto	ibinoboto	iboboto
58	buhay	bring to life	bumuhay	bumubuhay	bubuhay	binuhay	binubuhay	bubuhayin
59	buhos	pour	nagbuhos	nagbubuhos	magbubuhos	binuhos	binubuhos	ibubuhos
60	bukas	open (so-mething)	nagbukas	nagbubukas	magbubukas	binuksan	binubuksan	bubuksan

61	bukas	open (by it-self)	bumukas	bumubukas	bubukas			
62	bukas	put on (turn on)	nagbukas	nagbubukas	magbubukas	binuksan	binubuksan	bubuksan
63	bukas	turn on	nagbukas	nagbubukas	magbubukas	binuksan	binubuksan	bubuksan
64	bulong	whisper	bumulong	bumubulong	bubulong	ibinulong	ibinubulong	ibubulong
65	bura	erase	nagbura	nagbubura	magbubura	binura	binubura	buburahin
66	busog	full (with food)	nabusog	nabubusog	mabubusog			
67	buti	improve	bumuti	bumubuti	bubuti	binuti	binubuti	ibubuti
68	daan	pass by	dumaan	dumadaan	dadaan	dinaanan	di-nadaanan	dadaanan
69	dagdag	add (for-ward)	nagdagdag	nagdaragdag	magdaragdag	dinagdagan	di-naragdagan	dadagdagan
70	dala	bring (so-mething)	nagdala	nagdadala	magdadala	dinala	dinadala	dadalhin
71	dala	carry (with arm)	nagdala	nagdadala	magdadala	dinala	dinadala	dadalhin
72	dala	deliver	nagdala	nagdadala	magdadala	dinala	dinadala	dadalhin
73	dalaw	visit	dumalaw	dumadalaw	dadalaw	dinalaw	dinadalaw	dadalawin
74	dali	hurry (to be)	nagmadali	nagmama-dali	magmama-dali	minadali	minamadali	mamadaliin
75	dalo	attend	dumalo	dumadalo	dadalo	dinaluhan	dinadal-uhan	dadaluhan
76	dama	feel (some-thing)	dumama	dumarama	dadama	dinama	dinadama	dadamhin

77	damdam	feel (bad)	nagdamdam	nagdaramdam	magdaramdam	dinamdam	dinaramdam	daramdamin
78	dampot	pick up (something)	dumampot	dumadampot	dadampot	dinampot	dinadampot	dadamputin
79	dasal	pray	nagdasal	nagdadasal	magdadasal	dinasal	dinadasal	idadasal
80	dating	arrive	dumating	dumarating	darating	dinatnan	dinaratnan	daratnan
81	dating	reach (destination)	dumating	dumarating	darating			
82	daya	cheat	nandaya	nandadaya	mandadaya	dinaya	dinadaya	dadayain
83	dighay	burp	dumighay	dumidighay	didighay			
84	dilig	water (plants)	nagdidilig	nagdidilig	magdidilig	diniligan	dinidiligan	didiligan
85	dinig	hear (something)	nadinig	nadidinig	madidinig	dininig	dinidinig	didinggin
86	dusa	suffer	nagdusa	nagdudusa	magdusa	ipinagdusa	ipinagdudusa	pagdudusahan
87	galing	come from	nanggaling	nanggagaling	manggagaling			
88	galing	feel (better)	gumaling	gumagaling	gagaling			
89	galing	heal	gumaling	gumagaling	gagaling	iginaling	iginagaling	igagaling
90	galit	agitate (someone)	sumulong	sumusulong	susulong	sinulong	sinusulong	susulungin
91	galit	angry (to be angry)	nanggalit	nanggagalit	manggagalit	ginalit	ginagalit	gagalitin
92	gamit	use	gumamit	gumagamit	gagamit	ginamit	ginagamit	gagamitin

93	gamot	cure (ga-mot)	gumamot	gumagamot	gagamot	ginamot	ginagamot	gagamutin
94	ganda	pretty (become)	gumanda	gumaganda	gaganda	ginanda	ginaganda	igaganda
95	ganda	pretty (make one's self)	nagpaganda	nagpapa-ganda	magpapa-ganda	pinaganda	pinapa-ganda	pagaganda-hin
96	garahe	park (in the garage)	naggarahe	naggaga-rahe	maggaga-rahe	iginarahe	iginaga-rahe	igagarahe
97	gawa	create	gumawa	gumagawa	gagawa	ginawa	ginagawa	gagawin
98	gawa	do	gumawa	gumagawa	gagawa	ginawa	ginagawa	gagawin
99	gawa	make	gumawa	gumagawa	gagawa	ginawa	ginagawa	gagawain
100	gayat	cut (vege-tables)	naggayat	naggagayat	maggagayat	ginayat	ginagayat	gagayatin
101	giba	knock down	naggiba	naggigiba	maggigiba	giniba	ginigiba	gigibain
102	guhit	draw (pic-ture)	nagguhit	nagguguhit	magguguhit	ginuhit	ginuguhit	guguhitin
103	gulong	roll	gumulong	gumugulong	gugulong	ginulong	ginugulong	igugulong
104	gupit	cut (with scissors)	naggupit	naggugupit	maggugupit	ginupit	ginugupit	gugupitin
105	gupit	haircut (to have)	nagpagupit	nagpapagu-pit	magpapagu-pit	ginupitan	ginugupi-tan	gugupitan
106	gusto	like (some-thing)		nagustuhan	nagugustuha n			magugustuh an
107	gusto	want		ginusto	ginugusto	gugustuhin		
108	habla	sue	naghabla	naghahabla	maghahabla	hinabla	hinahabla	ihahabla

109	hagod	rub (skin)	naghagod	naghahagod	maghaha-god	hinagod	hinahagod	hahagurin
110	halik	kiss	humalik	humahalik	hahalik	hinalikan	hinahalikan	hahalikan
111	hanap	find	humanap	humahanap	hahanap	hinanap	hinahanap	hahanapin
112	handa	prepare (food)	naghandá	naghahandá	magha-handá	hinandá	hinahandá	ihahandá
113	handa	prepare (get ready)	humandá	humahandá	hahandá			
114	harap	face (so-meone / something)	humarap	humaharap	haharap	hinarap	hinaharap	haharapin
115	hati	divide	naghati	naghahati	maghahati	hinati	hinahati	hahatiin
116	hatid	drop off (someone)	naghatid	naghahatid	maghahatid	hinatid	hinahatid	ihahatid
117	hawak	carry (with hand)				hinawakan	hinaha-wakan	hahakawan
118	hawak	hold	humawak	humahawak	hahawak	hinawakan	hinaha-wakan	hahawakan
119	higa	lie down	humiga	humihiga	hihiga	hinigaan	hinihigaan	hihigaan
120	higpit	tighten	naghigpit	naghihigpit	maghihigpit	hinigpitan	hinihigpitan	hihigpitan
121	hikab	yawn	naghikab	naghihikab	maghihikab	hinikaban	hinihikaban	hihikaban
122	hila	pull	naghila	naghihila	maghihila	hinila	hinihila	hihilahin
123	hindi	no (to say no)	humindi	humihindi	hihindi	hinihindi'an	hinihindi'an	hihindi'an
124	hinga	breathe	huminga	humihinga	hihinga			
125	hinga	rest	nagpahinga	nagpapa-hinga	magpapa-hinga			

126	hingi	ask for (so-mething)	humingi	humihingi	hihingi	hiningi	hinihingi	hihingi
127	hintay	wait	naghintay	naghihintay	maghihintay	hinintay	hinihintay	hihintayin
128	hinto	stop	huminto	humihinto	hihinto	hinintuan	hinihintuan	hihintuan
129	hiram	borrow (money)	humiram	humihiram	hihiram	hiniram	hinihiram	hihiramin
130	hirap	suffer (hardship)	naghirap	naghihirap	maghihirap	hinirap	hinihirap	ihihirap
131	hiwa	cut (slice)	naghiwa	naghihiwa	maghihiwa	hiniwa	hinihiwa	hihiwain
132	hiwa	slice	naghiwa	naghihiwa	maghihiwa	hiniwa	hinihiwa	hihiwain
133	hubad	dress (re-move)	naghubad	nahuhubad	maghuhu-bad	hinubad	hinuhubad	huhubarin
134	hubad	remove (clothes)	naghubad	naghuhubad	maghuhu-bad	hinubad	hinuhubad	huhubarin
135	hugas	wash	naghugas	naghuhugas	maghuhugas	hinugasan	hinu-hugasan	huhugasan
136	huli	catch (so-meone)	humuli	humuhuli	huhuli	hinuli	hinuhuli	huhulihin
137	hulog	drop	naghulog	naghuhulog	maghuhulog	hinulog	hinuhulog	ihuhulog
138	hulog	fall	nahulog	nahuhulog	mahuhulog	hinulog	hinuhulog	ihuhulog
139	huni	whistle	humuni	humuhuni	huhuni	hinunihan	hinuhuni-han	huhunihan
140	ibig	love (so-meone ro-mantically)	umibig	umiibig	iibig	inibig	iniibig	iibigin
141	ilaw	light up	umilaw	umiilaw	iilaw	inilawan	iniilawan	iilawan
142	imbento	invent	nag-imbento	nag-iimbento	mag-im-bento	inimbento	iniimbento	iimbentuhin

143	imbita	invite	nag-imbita	nag-iimbita	mag-iimbita	inimbita	iniimbita	iimbitahin
144	ingat	take care (of one's self)	nag-ingat	nag-iingat	mag-iingat	iningatan	iniingatan	iingatan
145	ingat	take care (some-thing)	nag-ingat	nag-iingat	mag-iingat	iningatan	iniingatan	iingatan
146	ingay	noise	nag-ingay	nag-iingay	mag-iingay	iningayan	iniingayan	iingayan
147	inis	annoy	nang-inis	nang-iinis	mang-iinis	ininis	iniinis	iinisin
148	init	heat up (some-thing)	nag-init	nag-iinit	mag-iinit	ininit	iniinit	iinitin
149	inom	drink	uminom	umiinom	iinom	ininom	iniinom	iinumin
150	intindi	understand (some-thing)	umintindi	umiintindi	iintindi	inintindi	iniintindi	iintindihin
151	intindi	understand (someone)		naintindihan	naiintindihan	maiintin-dihan		
152	ipon	collect	nag-ipon	nag-iipon	mag-iipon	inipon	iniipon	iipunin
153	isda	fish	nangisda	nangingisda	mangisda			
154	isip	think	nag-isip	nag-iisip	mag-iisip	inisip	iniisip	iisip
155	iyak	cry	umiyak	umiiyak	iiyak	iniyakan	iniiyakan	iiyakan
156	kagat	bite	kumagat	kumakagat	kakagat	kinagat	kinakagat	kakagatin
157	kailangan	need	nangailan-gan	nangang-ailangan	mangang-ailangan	kinailangan	kinakailan-gan	kakailanga-nin
158	kain	eat	kumain	kumakain	kakain	kinain	kinakain	kakainin

159	kain	feed	nagpakain	nagpapakain	magpapa-kain	pinakain	pinapakain	papakainin
160	kamay	hand (to use it)	nagkamay	nagkakamay	mag-kakamay	kinamay	kinakamay	kakamayin
161	kamay	handshake (to give)	nagkamayan	nagkakama-yan	magkakama-yan	kinamayan	kinakama-yan	kakamayan
162	kamit	attain	nakamit	nakakamit	makakamit	nakamtan	nakakamta n	makakamtan
163	kante	sing	kumanta	kumakanta	kakanta	kinanta	kinakanta	kakantahin
164	kasal	marry	nagpakasal	nagpapaka-sal	magpapaka-sal	kinasal	kinakasal	ikakasal
165	kasal	wed	nagpakasal	nagpapaka-sal	magpapaka-sal	pinakasalan	pinapaka-salan	papakasalan
166	katay	kill (slaug-hter)	nagkatay	nagkakatay	magkakatay	kinatay	kinakatay	kakatayin
167	katok	knock (door)	kumatok	kumakatok	kakatok	kinatok	kinakatok	kakatukin
168	kilala	introduce (someone)	nagpakilala	nagpapa-kilala	magpapa-kilala	pinakilala	pinapa-kilala	ipapakilala
169	kilala	know (so-meone)	nakipagkilala	nakikipag-kilala	makikipag-kilala	kinilala	kinikilala	kikilalanin
170	kilala	present (some-thing)		ipinakilala	ipinakikilala	ipapakilala		
171	kinig	listen (so-mething)	nakinig	nakikinig	makikinig	pinakinggan	pinapa-kinggan	papakinggan
172	kipkip	carry (un-derarm)	nagkipkip	nagkikipkip	magkikipkip	kinipkip	kinikipkip	kikipkipin

173	kita	introduce (something)	nagpakita	nagpapakita	magpapakita	pinakita	pinapakita	ipapakita
174	kita	meet (someone)	nagkita	nagkikita	magkikita	nakipagkita	nakikipagkita	makikipagkita
175	kita	see	nakakita	nakakakita	makakakita	nakita	nakikita	makikita
176	kopya	copy	kumopya	kumokopya	kokopya	kinopya	kinokopya	kokopyahin
177	kuha	acquire	kumuha	kumukuha	kukuha	kinuha	kinukuha	kukuhain
178	kuha	get	kumuha	kumukuha	kukuha	kinuha	kinukuha	kukunin
179	kuha	withdraw (money)	kumuha	kumukuha	kukuha	kinuha	kinukuha	kukuha
180	kuha (nag verb)	take	nanguha	nangunguha	mangunguha	kinunan	kinukunan	kukunan
181	kuha (um verb)	take	kumuha	kumukuha	kukuha	kinuha	kinukuha	kukuhanin
182	kumusta	hello (to say)	nangumusta	nangungumusta	mangungumusta	kinumusta	kinukumusta	kukumustahin
183	kusot	rub (wash)	nagkusot	nagkukusot	magkukusot	kinusot	kinukusot	kukusutin
184	laba	laundry	naglaba	naglalaba	maglalaba	nilabhan	nilalabhan	lalabhan
185	labag	violate (a law)	lumabag	lumalabag	lalabag	nilabag	nilalabag	lalabagin
186	laban	fight	lumaban	lumalaban	lalaban	nilabanan	nilalabanan	lalabanan
187	labas	bring out	naglabas	naglalabas	maglalabas	nilabas	nilalabas	ilalabas
188	labas	exit	lumabas	lumalabas	lalabas	nilabasan	nilalabasan	lalabasan
189	labas	go out	lumabas	lumalabas	lalabas	nilabas	nilalabas	lalabasin

190	labas	over	nagbantay	nagbabantay	mag-babantay	binantayan	bi-nabantayan	babantayan
191	laga	boil	naglaga	naglalaga	maglalaga	nilaga	nilalaga	ilalaga
192	lagay	install	naglagay	naglalagay	maglalagay	nilagay	nilalagay	ilalagay
193	lagay	lay	naglagay	naglalagay	maglalagay	nilagay	nilalagay	ilalagay
194	lagay	place	naglagay	naglalagay	maglalagay	nilagay	nilalagay	ilalagay
195	lagay	put	naglagay	naglalagay	maglalagay	nilagay	nilalagay	ilalagay
196	lagnat	fever (to have)		nilagnat	nilalagnat			lalagnatin
197	lakad	hike	naglakad	naglalakad	maglalakad	nilakad	nilalakad	lalakarin
198	lakad	walk	naglakad	naglalakad	maglalakad	nilakad	nilalakad	lalakarin
199	lakbay	travel (vo-yage)	naglakbay	naglalakbay	maglalakbay	nilakbay	nilalakbay	lalakbayin
200	laki	big (to become)	lumaki	lumalaki	lalaki			
201	laki	big (make it)				nilakihan	nilalakihan	lalakihan
202	laki	grow (become big)	lumaki	lumalaki	lalaki	inilaki	inilalaki	ilalaki
203	laki	raise (children)	nagpalaki	nagpapalaki	magpapalaki	pinalaki	pinapalaki	papalakihin
204	lapit	approach	lumapit	lumalapit	lalapit	nilapitan	nilalapitan	lalapitan
205	laro	play (game)	naglaro	naglalaro	maglalaro	nilaro	nilalaro	lalaruin
206	layas	go away	lumayas	lumalayas	lalayas			

207	layo	avoid	lumayo	lumalayo	lalayo	nilayuan	nilalayuan	lalayuan
208	liban	absent	lumiban	lumiliban	liliban	nilibanan	nililibanan	lilibanan
209	libang	entertain	naglibang	naglilibang	manlilibang	nilibang	nililibang	lilibangin
210	ligaw	court (ro-mance)	lumigaw	lumiligaw	liligaw	niligawan	nililigawan	liligawan
211	limot	forget (so-meone)	lumimot	lumilimot	lilimot	nilimot	nililimot	lilimutin
212	linis	clean (become)	naglinis	naglilinis	maglilinis	nilinis	nililinis	lilinisin
213	linis	clean (clean)	luminis	lumilinis	lilinis			
214	linlang	deceive	nanglinlang	nanlilinlang	manlilinlang	nilinlang	nililinlang	lilinlangin
215	lipad	fly	lumipad	lumilipad	lilipad	nilipad	nililipad	liliparin
216	lipad	travel (by plane)	lumipad	lumilipad	lilipad	nilipad	nililipad	liliparin
217	lipat	move (transfer)	lumipat	lumilipat	lilipat	nilipatan	nililipatan	lilipatan
218	lipat	move (so-mething)	naglipat	naglilipat	maglilipat	nilipat	nililipat	ililipat
219	lito	confuse	nalito	nalilito	malilito	nalito	nililito	lilituhin
220	loko	joke	nangloko	nanglololoko	manglololoko	niloko	nilololoko	lolokohin
221	lubog	sink	lumubog	lumulubog	lulubog	nilubog	nilulubog	ilulubog
222	lungkot	sad	nalungkot	nalulungkot	malulungkot	ikinalungkot	ikinalulung-kot	ikalulungkot
223	lunok	swallow	lumunok	lumulunok	lulunok	nilunok	nilulunok	lulunukin
224	lusob	attack	lumusob	lumulusob	lulusob	niluson	nilulusob	lulusubin
225	luto	cook	nagluto	nagluluto	magluluto	niluto	nililuto	lulutuin

226	mahal	love (someone)	nagmahal	nagmamahal	magmamahal	minahal	minamahal	mamahalin
227	makinilya	type (type)	nagmakinilya	nagmamakinilya	magmamakinilya	minakinilya	minamakinilya	mamakinilyahin
228	maneho	drive	nagmaneho	nagmamaneho	magmamaneho	minaneho	minamaneho	mamanehuin
229	mangha	wonder (be amazed)	namangha	namamangha	mamamangha	namanghaan	namamanghaan	mamamanghaan
230	masahe	rub (massage)	nagmasahe	nagmamasahe	magmamasahe	minasahe	minamasahe	mamasahiin
231	masid	observe	nagmasid	nagmamasid	magmamasid	minasdan	minamasdan	mamasdan
232	muhi	hate (suklam)	namuhi	namumuhi	mamumuhi	kinamuhi'an	kinakamuhi'an	kamumuhi'an
233	nakaw	rob	nagnakaw	nagnanakaw	magnanakaw	ninakaw	ninanakaw	nanakawin
234	ngiti	smile	ngumiti	nguningiti	ngingiti	nginitian	nginingitian	ngingitian
235	niwala	believe	naniwala	naniniwala	maniniwala	pinaniwalaan	pinaniniwalaan	paniniwalaan
236	nood	watch (movie/TV)	nanood	nanonood	manonood	pinanood	pinapanood	papanoorin
237	okupa	occupy	nag-okupa	nag-ookupa	mag-ookupa	inokupa	inookupa	ookupahin
238	order	order (something)	nag-order	nag-oorder	mag-oorder	inorder	inoorder	oorderin
239	paalam	goodbye (to say)	nagpaalam	nagpapaalam	magpapaalam			
240	palakpak	clap	pumalakpak	pumapalakpak	papalakpak	pinalakpakan	pinapalakpakan	papalakpakan

241	palengke	market (go to)	nagpalengke	nagpapalengke	magpapalengke	pinapalengke	pinapalengke	papalengkeh
242	palit	change	nagpalit	nagpapalit	magpapalit	pinalitan	pinapalitan	papalitan
243	palit	revise (change)	nagpalit	nagpapalit	magpapalit	pinalitan	pinapalitan	papalitan
244	panalo	win	nanalo	nananalo	mananalo	napanalunan	napapanalunan	papanalunan
245	pangako	promise	nangako	nangangako	mangangako	ipinangako	ipinapangako	ipapangako
246	pansin	attention (give)	napansin	napapansin	mapapansin	pinansin	pinapansin	papansinin
247	parada	park (parking lot)	pumarada	pumaparada	paparada	ipinarada	ipinaparada	ipaparada
248	pasa	pass (exam)	pumasa	pumapasa	papasa	pinasa	pinapasa	papasa
249	pasa	pass on	nagpasa	nagpapasa	magpapasa	ipinasa	ipinapasa	ipapasa
250	pasan	carry (on the back)	nagpasan	nagpapasan	magpapasan	pinasan	pinapasan	papasanin
251	pasok	enter (a place)	pumasok	pumapasok	papasok	pinasok	pinapasok	papasukin
252	pasok	put in (through a hole)	nagpasok	nagpapasok	magpapasok	ipinasok	ipinapasok	ipapasok
253	pasyal	travel (visit)	namasyal	namamasyal	mamamasyal	pinasyalan	pinapasyalan	papasyalan
254	patay	die	namatay	namamatay	mamamatay	pinatay	pinapatay	papatayin
255	patay	turn off	nagpatay	nagpapatay	magpapatay	pinatay	pinapatay	papatayin

256	patay (as nag verb)	kill	nagpatay	nagpapatay	magpapatay	pinatay	pinapatay	papatayin
257	patay (as um verb)	kill	pumatay	pumapatay	papatay	pinatay	pinapatay	papatayin
258	pigil	prevent (oneself)	nagpigil	nagpipigil	magpipigil	pinigilan	pinipigilan	pipigilan
259	pigil	prevent (some-thing)		pinigil	pinipigil	pipigilin		
260	pili	choose	pumili	pumipili	pipili	pinili	pinipili	pipiliin
261	pili	pick (choose)	pumili	pumipili	pipili	pinili	pinipili	pipiliin
262	pinta	paint (art)	nagpinta	nagpipinta	magpipinta	ipininta	ipinipinta	pipintahin
263	pinta	paint (on an object)	nagpinta	nagpipinta	magpipinta	pinintahan	pini-pintahan	pipintahan
264	pirma	sign (sig-nature)	pumirma	pumipirma	pipirma	pinirmahan	pinipirma-han	pipirmahan
265	plantsa	press (iron)	nagplantsa	nagpa-plantsa	magpla-plantsa	pinaltsa	pinaplantsa	paplantsahin
266	promote	promote (some-one/job)	na-promote	napo-pro-mote	mapo-pro-mote	pinromote	pinopro-mote	ipopromote
267	pugot	cut (behead)	nagpugot	nagpupugot	magpupugot	pinugot	pinupugot	pupugutan
268	pukpok	hit (instru-ment)	namukpok	namu-mukpok	mamu-mukpok	pinukpok	pinupukpok	pupukpukin
269	punas	wipe	nagpunas	nagpupunas	magpupunas	pinunasan	pinupuna-san	pupunasan

270	punit	break (tear)	nagpunit	nagpupunit	magpupunit	napunit	napupunit	mapupunit
271	punit	cut (tear off)	pumunit	pumupunit	pupunit	pinunit	pinupunit	pupunitin
272	puno	fill up (container)	nagpuno	nagpupuno	magpupuno	pinuno	pinupuno	pupunuin
273	puno	full (become)	napuno	napupuno	mapupuno			
274	punta	come	pumunta	pumupunta	pupunta	pinuntahan	pinupuntahan	pupuntahan
275	punta	go	pumunta	pumupunta	pupuntahan	pinuntahan	pinupuntahan	pupuntahan
276	putol	cut (break)	pumutol	pumuputol	puputol	pinutol	pinuputol	puputulin
277	regalo	gift (to give)	nagregalo	nagreregalo	magreregalo	niregaluhan	nireregaluhan	reregaluhan
278	renta	rent (general)	nagrenta	nagrerenta	magrerenta	nirenta	nirerenta	rerentahin
279	sabi	say	nagsabi	nagsasabi	magsasabi	sinabi	sinasabi	sasabihin
280	sabi	tell	nagsabi	nagsasabi	magsasabi	sinabi	sinasabi	sasabihin
281	sagot	answer	sumagot	sumasagot	sasagot	sinagot	sinasagot	sasagutin
282	saka	farm	nagsaka	nagsasaka	magsasaka	sinaka	sinasaka	sasakahan
283	sakay	ride	sumakay	sumasakay	sasakay	sinakyan	sinasakyan	sasakyan
284	sakit	hurt (transitive)	nasaktan	nasasaktan	masasaktan	sinaktan	sinasaktan	sasaktan
285	sakit	hurt (intransitive)	sumakit	sumasakit	sasakit			
286	sali	involve	sumali	sumasali	sasali	sinali	sinasali	isasali
287	sali	join (game)	sumali	sumasali	sasali	sinalihan	sinasalihan	sasalihan

288	salita	talk	nagsalita	nagsasalita	magsasalita	sinalita	sinasalita	sasalitain
289	salo	catch (so-mething)	sumalo	sumasalo	sasalo	sinalo	sinasalo	sasaluin
290	sama	bad (to become)	sumama	sumasama	sasama			
291	sama	bring along	nagsama	nagsasama	magsasama	isinama	isinasama	isasama
292	sama	join (some-one)	sumama	sumasama	sasama	sinamahan	sinasama-han	sasamahan
293	samba	worship	nagsamba	nagsasamba	magsa-samba	sinamba	sinasamba	sasambahin
294	sampay	hang (clothes)	nagsampay	nagsasam-pay	magsasam-pay	sinampay	sinasam-pay	isasampay
295	sanla	pawn	nagsanla	nagsasanla	magsasanla	sinanla	sinasanla	isasanla
296	sara	close	nagsara	nagsasara	magsasara	sinara	sinasara	isasara
297	sara	turn off	nagsara	nagsasara	magsasara	sinara	sinasara	isasara
298	sauli	return	nagsauli	nagsasauli	magsasauli	isinauli	isinasauli	isasauli
299	saya	enjoy	nagsaya	nagsasaya	magsasaya	pinagsayaan	pinagsa-sayaan	pagsa-sayaan
300	saya	happy (become)	sumaya	sumasaya	sasaya	ikinasaya	ikinasa-saya	ikakasaya
301	saya	happy (to enjoy)	nagsaya	nagsasaya	magsasaya	pinagsaya	pinagsa-saya	ipapagsaya
302	sayaw	dance	sumayaw	sumasayaw	sasayaw	sinayaw	sinasayaw	sasayawin
303	senyas	sign (to give a sign)	sumenyas	sumesenyas	sesenyas	sinenyasan	sinesenya-san	sesenyasan
304	sibak	cut (w. ax)	nagsibak	nagsisibak	magsisibak	sinibak	sinisibak	sisibakin

305	siesta	nap	nagsiesta	nagsisiesta	magsisiesta			
306	sigaw	shout	sumigaw	sumisigaw	sisigaw	sinigaw	sinisigaw	isisigaw
307	sigaw	shout (at each other)	nagsigawan	nagsisiga-wan	magsisiga-wan	sinigawan	sinisiga-wan	sisigawan
308	silip	peek	sumilip	sumisilip	sisilip	sinilip	sinisilip	sisilipin
309	simangot	pout	sumimangot	sumisiman-got	sisimangot	siniman-gutan	sinisiman-gutan	sisiman-gutan
310	sinunga-ling	lie (tell a lie)	nagsinunga-ling	nagsisinun-galing	magsisinun-galing	sinusunga-ling	sinisinun-galing	sisinungaling
311	sipilyo	brush (teeth)	nagsipilyo	nagsisipilyo	magsisipilyo	sinipilyo	sinisipilyo	sisipilyuhin
312	sipol	whistle	sumipol	sumisipol	sisipol	sinipulan	sinisipulan	sisipulan
313	sira	break	sumira	sumisira	sisira	sinira	sinisira	sisirain
314	sira	break (out of order)	nagsira	nagsisira	magsisira	nasira	nasisira	masisira
315	sira	damage	sumira	sumisira	sisira	sinira	sinisira	sisirain
316	sira	destroy	nanira	naninira	maninira	sinira	sininira	sisirain
317	sira	destroy (character)	nanira	naninira	maninira	siniraan	sinisiraan	sisiraan
318	subo	put in (the mouth)	nagsubo	nagsusubo	magsusubo	sinubo	sinusubo	isusubo
319	subok	test (try out)	sumubok	sumusubok	susubok	sinubok	sinusubok	susubukin
320	sugal	gamble	nagsugal	nagsusugal	magsusugal	sinugal	sinusugal	isusugal

321	sukat	measure (dimension)	nagsukat	nagsusukat	magsusukat	sinukat	sinusukat	susukatin
322	suklay	brush (hair)	nagsuklay	nagsusuklay	magsusuklay	sinuklay	sinusuklay	susuklayin
323	suko	give up (surrender)	sumuko	sumusuko	susuko	isinuko	isinusuko	isusuko
324	sulat	write (something)	nagsulat	nagsusulat	magsusulat	sinulat	sinusulat	isusulat
325	sulat	write (someone)	sumulat	sumusulat	susulat	sinulatan	sinusulatan	susulatan
326	sulit	examine (test)	nagsulit	nagsusulit	magsusulit	sinulit	sinusulit	susulitin
327	sumbong	report (complain)	nagsumbong	nagsusumbong	magsusumbong	isinumbong	isinusumbong	isusumbong
328	sundo	pick up (someone)	nagsundo	nagsusundo	magsusundo	sinundo	sinusundo	susunduin
329	sunod	follow after	sumunod	sumusunod	susunod	sinundan	sinusundan	susundan
330	sunod	obey	sumunod	sumusunod	susunod	sinunod	sinusunod	susunurin
331	sunog	burn	nagsunog	nagsusunog	magsusunog	sinunog	sinusunog	susunugin
332	sunong	carry (on the head)	nagsunong	nagsusunong	magsusunong	sinunong	sinusunong	susunungin
333	suntok	hit (fist)	nanuntok	nanununtok	manununtok	sinuntok	sinusuntok	susuntukin
334	suot	enter into	sumuot	sumusuot	susuot	sinuotan	sinusuotan	susuotan
335	suot	insert	nagsuot	nagsusuot	magsusuot	sinuot	sinusuot	susuutin
336	suot	put on (clothes)	nagsuot	nagsusuot	magsusuot	sinuot	sinusuot	susuutin

337	suri	examine (analyze)	nagsiri	nagsusiri	magsusiri	siniri	sinusiri	susiriin
338	suri	test (examine)	nagsuri	nagsusuri	magsusuri	sinuri	sinusuri	susuriin
339	suway	violate (an order)	sumuway	sumusuway	susuway	sinuway	sinusuway	susuwayin
340	taas	elevate	nagtaas	nagtataas	magtataas	tinaas	tinataas	tataasin
341	taas	raise (hand)	nagtaas	nagtataas	magtataas	itinaas	itinataas	itataas
342	tabi	keep (put aside)	nagtabi	nagtatabi	magtatabi	itinabi	itinatabi	itatabi
343	tago	hide (something)	nagtago	nagtatago	magtatago	tinago	tinatago	itatago
344	tago	hide (one's self or someone)	nagtago	nagtatago	magtatago	tinaguan	tinataguan	tataguan
345	tago	keep (save)	nagtago	nagtatago	magtatago	itinago	itinatago	itatago
346	taguyod	promote (something)	nagtaguyod	nag-tataguyod	mag-tataguyod	tinaguyod	tinataguyod	itataguyod
347	tahi	sew	nagtahi	nagtatahi	magtatahi	tinahi	tinatahi	tatahiin
348	tahimik	quiet	tumahimik	tumatahimik	tatahimik	tinahimik	tinatahimik	itatahimik
349	tahol	bark	tumahol	tumatahol	tatahol	tinahulan	tinatahulan	tatahulan
350	taka	wonder (be puzzled)	nagtaka	nagtataka	magtataka	ipinagtaka	ipinag-tataka	ipagtataka
351	takbo	run	tumakbo	tumatakbo	tatakbo	tinakbo	tinatakbo	tatakbuhin
352	takip	cover	nagtakip	nagtatakip	magtatakip	tinakpan	tinatakpan	tatakpan

353	takip	cover up	nagtakip	nagtatakip	magtatakip	pinagtapan	pinapag-takpan	papagtakpan
354	takot	frighten (someone)	nanakot	nananakot	mananakot	tinakot	tinatakot	tatakutin
355	takot	scare	natakot	natatakot	matatakot	tinakot	tinatakot	tatakutin
356	talon	jump	tumalon	tumatalon	tatalon	tinalon	tinatalon	tatalunin
357	tanan	elope	nagtanan	nagtatanan	magtatanan	tinanan	tinatanan	itatanan
358	tanggal	cut (re-move)	nagtanggal	nagtatanggal	magtatang-gal	tinanggal	tinatanggal	tatanggalin
359	tanggap	accept	tumanggap	tumatang-gap	tatanggap	tinanggap	tinatang-gap	tatanggapin
360	tanggap	receive	tumanggap	tumatang-gap	tatanggap	tinanggap	tinatang-gap	tatanggapin
361	tanggi	reject	tumanggi	tamatanggi	tatanggi	tinanggihan	tinatang-gihan	tatanggihan
362	tango	nod	tumango	tumatango	tatango	tinangu'an	tinatangu'a n	tatangu'an
363	tanim	plant	nagtanim	nagtatanim	magtatanim	tinanim	tinatanim	itatanim
364	tanong	ask about	nagtanong	nagtatanong	mag-tatanong	tinanong	tinatanong	tatanungin
365	tanong	question	nagtanong	nagtatanong	mag-tatanong	tinanong	tinatanong	tatanungin
366	tapon	throw	nagtapon	nagtatapon	magtatapon	tinapon	tinatapon	itatapon
367	tapos	finish (so-mething)		tinapos	tinatapos			tatapusin
368	tapos	graduate (from school)	nagtapos	nagtatapos	magtatapos			

369	tatad	cut (chop)	nagtadtad	nagtatadtad	magtatadtad	tinadtad	tinatadtad	tatadtarin
370	tawa	laugh	tumawa	tumatawa	tatawa	tinawanan	tinata-wanan	tatawanan
371	tawag	call (phone)	tumawag	tumatawag	tatawag	tinawag	tinatawag	tatawagin
372	tawag	call up (phone)	tumawag	tumatawag	tatawag	tinawagan	tinata-wagan	tatawagan
373	tawid	cross	tumawid	tumatawid	tatawid	tinawid	tinatawid	tatawirin
374	tayo	build	nagtayo	nagtatayo	magtatayo	itinayo	itinatayo	itatayo
375	tayo	rise (stand up)	tumayo	tumatayo	tatayo			
376	tayo	stand	tumayo	tumatayo	tatayo	tinayuan	tinatayuan	tatayuan
377	timbang	measure (weight)	nagtimbang	nagtitimbang	magtitim-bang	tinimbang	tinitimbang	titimbangin
378	tinda	sell (tinda)	nagtinda	nagtitinda	magtitinda	itininda	itinitinda	ititinda
379	tingin	examine (medical)	nagpatingin	nagpapa-tingin	magpapa-tingin	tiningnan	tinatingnan	titingnan
380	tingin	look (so-mething)	tumingin	tumitingin	titingin	tiningnan	tinitingnan	titingnan
381	tira	hit on/at (someone)	tumira	tumitira	titira	tinira	tinitira	titirahin
382	trabaho	work	nagtrabaho	nagtat-rabaho	magtat-rabaho	tinrabaho	tinatrabaho	tatrabahuin
383	tugtog	play (in-strument)	tumugtog	tumutugtog	tutugtog	tinugtog	tinutugtog	tutugtugin
384	tulak	push	nagtulak	nagtutulak	magtutulak	tinulak	tinutulak	itutulak
385	tulog	sleep	natulog	natutulog	matutulog	tinulugan	tinutulugan	tutulugan

386	tulong	help	tumulong	tumutulong	tutulong	tinulungan	tinutu-lungan	tutulungan
387	tuloy	continue (patuloy)	nagpatuloy	nagpapa-tuloy	magpapa-tuloy			
388	tuloy	go on	tumuloy	tumutuloy	tutuloy	tinuluyan	tinutuluyan	tutuluyan
389	turo	point	nagturo	nagtuturo	magtuturo	tinuro	tinuturo	ituturo
390	turo	teach	nagturo	nagtuturo	magtuturo	tinuro	tinuturo	ituturo
391	ulat	report (so-mething)	nag-ulat	nag-uulat	mag-uulat	inulat	inuulat	iuulat
392	ulit	repeat (be-havior)	umulit	umuulit	uulit	inulit	inuulit	uulitin
393	ulit	repeat (work)	nag-ulit	nag-uulit	mag-uulit	inulit	inuulit	uulitin
394	ulit	revise (re-work)	nag-ulit	nag-uulit	mag-uulit	inulit	inuulit	uulitin
395	umpisa	begin	nag-umpisa	nag-uumpisa	mag-uum-pisa	inumpisahan	inuum-pisahan	uumpisahan
396	unlad	develop	umunlad	umuunlad	uunlad	inunlad	inuunlad	uunlarin
397	upa	rent (house)	umupa	umuupa	uupa	inupahan	inuupahan	uupahan
398	upo	sit	umupo	umuupo	uupo	inupuan	inuupuan	uupuan
399	usap	converse	nag-usap	nag-uusap	mag-uusap	pinag-usapan	pinapag-usapan	papag-usapan
400	usog	move over (someone)	umusog	umuusog	uusog			
401	usog	move over (s.t.)	nag-usog	nag-uusog	mag-uusog	inusog	inuusog	iuusog

402	utang	borrow (utang)	umutang	umuutang	uutang	inutang	inuutang	uutangin
403	utang	loan (mo-ney)	umutang	umuutang	uutang	inutangan	inuutangan	uutangan
404	utos	order (so-meone)	nag-utos	nag-uutos	mag-uutos	inutusan	inuutusan	uutusan
405	utot	fart	umutot	umuutot	uutot	inutot	inuutot	uututin
406	uwi	bring home	nag-uwi	nag-uuwi	mag-uuwi	inuwi	inuuwi	uuwian
407	wagi	win	nagwagi	nagwawagi	magwawagi	ipinagwagi	ipinapag-wagi	ipapagwagi
408	wala	lose	nawala	nawawala	mawawala	winawala	winawala	iwawala
409	wala	vanish	nawala	nawawala	mawawala	winala	winawala	wawalain
410	walis	sweep (clean)	nagwalis	nagwawalis	magwawalis	winalis	winawalis	wawalisin
411	wasak	break (irre-parable)	nagwasak	nagwawasak	magwa-wasak	nawasak	nawa-wasak	mawawasak
412	yabang	brag (or boast)	nagyabang	nagya-yabang	magya-yabang	ipinag-	ipinapag-	ipag-
413	yakap	embrace	yumakap	yumayakap	yayakap	niyakap	niyayakap	yayakapin
414	yakap	hug	yumakap	yumayakap	yayakap	niyakap	niyayakap	yayakapin
415	yari	occur	nangyari	nangyayari	mangyayari			

Disclaimer

The information contained in this book has been created by the author to the best of their knowledge. Since content errors cannot be completely excluded, these details are provided without any warranty, guarantee, or obligation on the part of the publisher or the author. Therefore, they assume no liability for any inaccuracies. Liability of the author or the publisher is thus excluded.
The names of persons or places used in the examples are fictitious. Any resemblance to living or real persons would be purely coincidental.
The reproduction of trademarks, trade names, product names, etc., in this work, does not imply, even without specific labeling, that such names are to be considered free in terms of trademark and brand protection legislation and therefore may be used by anyone.
For better readability of the texts, the simultaneous use of male, female, and diverse (m/f/d) language forms has been partially omitted. In this work, only the male or female form of person-related nouns may be chosen occasionally. This in no way implies discrimination against the other gender. Women, men, and all genders should feel equally addressed by the content of this book.

The online materials are a voluntary offer and do not represent a claim associated with the purchase of the book. Changes are reserved, and the materials might not be offered in the future.

Copyright

Developing a book like this requires considerable effort and is associated with various costs. With respect to copyright, it is hoped that further books like this can be developed.

Made in the USA
Middletown, DE
26 September 2024